The Wyoming Lynching of Cattle Kate, 1889

It's not that we're so dumb,
it's just that what we know ain't so.

— attributed to Will Rogers

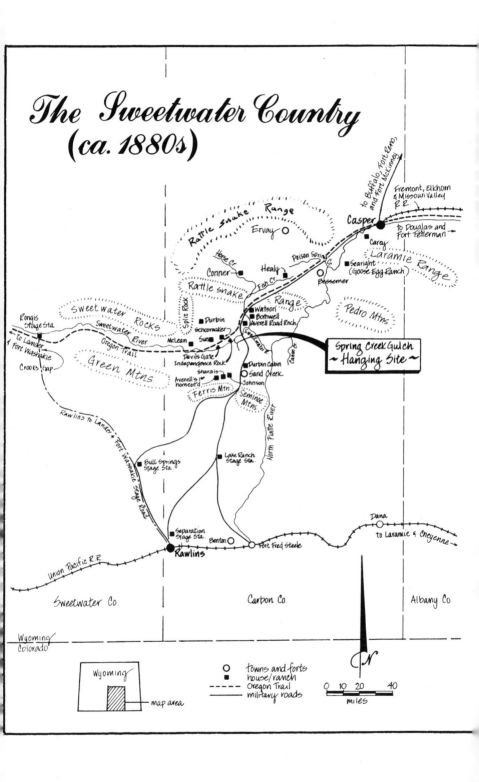

THE WYOMING LYNCHING OF CATTLE KATE, 1889

BY

GEORGE W. HUFSMITH

HIGH PLAINS PRESS
GLENDO, WYOMING

Those with additional information
are invited to write the author at
P.O. Box 3949
Jackson, Wyoming 83001

Library of Congress Cataloging-in-Publication Data

Hufsmith, George W.
The Wyoming lynching of Cattle Kate, 1889
by George W. Hufsmith.
p. cm.
Includes bibliographical references and index.
ISBN 0-931271-14-2 (hardcover)
ISBN 0-931271-16-9 (softcover)
1. Cattle Kate, d. 1889.
2. Lynching—Wyoming—History—19th century.
3. Ranch life—Wyoming—History—19th century.
4. Wyoming—History.
I. Title.
F761.C39H84 1993   92-35361
978.7'02'092—dc20   CIP

HIGH PLAINS PRESS
539 CASSA ROAD
GLENDO, WYOMING 82213

PREFACE

This writer is aware that a crazed male, in a fit of passion and anger, often under the influence of liquor or drugs, can resort to mindless violence resulting in the death of a helpless woman. Unhappily, it seems to happen regularly in today's loosely disciplined society. But for *six* men, in a Victorian era that placed women on alabaster pedestals, to jointly agree to garrote a helpless young woman *and* an innocent man on the flimsiest of evidence, and to arrogantly carry out the awful sentence of death in the face of millenniums of law to the contrary, is altogether beyond the comprehension of this author. And yet that is exactly what happened in the Territory of Wyoming on the sunny afternoon of July 20, 1889.

My roots proudly auger deep into Wyoming. My great grandparents immigrated from Prussia and then settled in Cheyenne in the fledgling Territory of Wyoming in 1874, two years before Custer's Last Stand. Because of my personal background I am fascinated by the early history of Wyoming, much of which is still buried in colorful myths.

As a youngster I remember being hypnotized by the story of "Cattle Kate," who was murdered not even a year before Wyoming's admission to the Union. I became increasingly obsessed by this puzzling event in which none of the pieces seemed to fit together quite right. Later, as an adult, I was driven to dig deeper into this incident, and before long, I began to uncover a Pandora's box chock-full of incredible little-known facts I hadn't dreamed would still be in existence after the passage of a whole century.

The more I learned the greater became my curiosity, and soon I was caught up and sucked down into a maelstrom of research which seems never to end. It has become an obsession, a sickness. But I must confess to having had a wonderfully exciting time groping back through a whole century of obfuscation in search of the truth.

Ever since the lynching, Wyomingites have treated the subject as a hands-off, hush-hush matter, which was never discussed in polite society. If the subject were inadvertently broached, it was greeted with utter silence. The person who had introduced the matter was immediately made to understand that he had somehow made a gross breach of etiquette.

As it turns out, the truth has been hidden under multi-layers of false and misleading information in order to protect six influential men who were so rich and politically powerful that they were never punished or even reprimanded. A gruesome and brutal story has emerged which now cries out to be told.

My search has taken me over strange and beautiful country. This and the wonderful people I have met, interviewed, and sought help from in the pursuit of the truth, have made this journey back into the distant past one of the most unforgettable experiences of my life.

CONTENTS

PART ONE: THE SETTING

1. The Myth

When I first began probing into the so-called "Cattle Kate" affair, I had no idea that the whole story was pure fabrication. Most of the story of the 1889 lynching of Ellen Watson and James Averell was invented by Edward Towse, in the employ of the Wyoming Stock Growers Association. He was a reporter for the powerful *Cheyenne Daily Leader,* a newspaper controlled by the opulent cattle interests in the Territory of Wyoming. Along with the other Cheyenne papers, the *Leader* was a mouthpiece for the Wyoming Stock Growers Association. That exclusive brotherhood wielded more political power than anybody or anything in the territory, and it controlled not only the *Leader,* but every other Cheyenne newspaper lock, stock and barrel.

It now seems certain that the Association gave instructions to the *Leader's* reporter Edward Towse to lay down an editorial smoke screen to accomplish the impossible—to justify the shocking and unprovoked lynchings of two innocent young homesteaders, a man and a woman. Over the next several days and months, Towse, and subsequently the editors of the other Cheyenne papers, composed many fictitious articles to obscure the truth of that lynching.

The first article was the most damaging and sets the tone for everything to follow. Towse wrote the article after George

Henderson, a cattle detective for John Clay's famous two-and-one-half-million acre Quarter Circle 71 Ranch, received a telegram in Cheyenne. The contents of the telegram are still unknown and the sender is still unidentified, but newspapers reported it contained just ten words. The sender had ridden hard for fifty miles south from the Sweetwater country to the town of Rawlins on the Union Pacific Railroad in south-central Wyoming to alert the Wyoming Stock Growers Association of the twin murders committed by prominent Association members. As soon as Henderson received the telegram, he rushed over to the offices of the *Leader,* and Edward Towse's imaginative wheels were promptly set in motion—all this while the bodies of the victims were still slowly revolving and baking in the hot July sun at the end of ordinary lariats.

This first article was successful beyond Towse's wildest dreams, and it has seared its way into the history of the West like a white-hot branding iron. It has been quoted and requoted until nearly everyone has come to believe the absurd fabrications that Towse invented, and these fabrications have supplanted the facts for a hundred years. Unfortunately, his inventions probably will never be completely expunged from history.

Not too long after the garroting, it was reported that one of the lynchers bitterly declared, "If one of them had not been a woman, the whole matter would have been forgotten long ago!"[1] But one of them was a woman, and the matter is now history and will not be forgotten.

But let's take a look at Towse's first article in the *Cheyenne Daily Leader* from which nearly every other writer has taken his cue to this day. [The original spelling that appeared in the article is used in this reprint and in all subsequently reprinted newspaper articles. The spelling of "Averell" particularly evaded many newspapermen.]

CHEYENNE DAILY LEADER
Tuesday Morning, July 23, 1889

A DOUBLE LYNCHING
Postmaster Averill and his Wife Hung for Cattle Stealing
They were tireless Maverickers who defied the law.
The man weakened but the woman cursed to the last.

A man and a woman were lynched near historic Independence Rock on the Sweetwater River in Carbon County Sunday night. They were Postmaster James Averill and a virago who had been living with him as his wife for some months. Their offense was cattle stealing, and they operated on a large scale, recruiting quite a bunch of young steers from the range of that section.

News of the double hanging was brought to Rawlins by a special courier and telegraphed to foreman Geo. B. Henderson of the 76 outfit [actually the Quarter Circle 71 outfit], who happened to be in the capital. Mr. Henderson's firm has its home ranch in that country and has been systematically robbed by rustlers for years. Averill and the woman were fearless maverickers. The female was the equal of any man on the range. Of robust physique she was a daredevil in the saddle, handy with a six-shooter and adept with the lariat and branding iron. Where she came from no one seems to know, but that she was a holy terror all agreed. She rode straddle,[2] always had a vicious broncho for a mount and seemed never to tire of dashing across the range.

The thieving pair were ordered to leave the country several times,[3] but paid no attention to the warnings, sending the message that they could take care of themselves, that mavericks were common property and that they would continue to appropriate unmarked cattle.

Lately it has been rumored that the woman and Averill were engaged in a regular round up of mavericks and would gather several hundred for shipment this fall. The ugly story was partially verified by the stealthy visit of a cowboy to their place Saturday. He reported that their corral held no less than fifty head of newly branded steers, mostly yearlings, with a few nearly grown.

The statement of the spy circulated rapidly, and thoroughly incensed the ranchmen, who resolved to abate the menace to the herds. Word was passed along the river and early in the night from ten to twenty men,[4] made desperate by steady loss, gathered at a designated rendezvous and quietly galloped to the Averill ranch. A few hundred yards from the cabin they dismounted and approached cautiously. This movement was well advised for Averill had murdered two men[5] and would not hesitate to shoot, while the woman was always full of fight.

Within the little habitation sat the thieving pair before a rude fireplace. The room was clouded with cigarette smoke. A whiskey bottle with two glasses was on the deal table, and firearms were scattered around the interior so as to be within easy reach.

The leader of the regulators stationed a man with a Winchester at each window and led a rush into the door. The sound of "Hands up!" sounded above the crash of glass as the rifles were leveled at the strangely assorted pair of thieves. There was a

One of only three known photographs of Ellen Watson shows her astride a very old horse in front of her stock shed in her "Sunday-go-to-meeting" dress. The photo seems hastily posed, probably to send home to her folks in Kansas. Notice the throat latch on the bridle is left unbuckled, and the horse is bareback, as if no time was taken to saddle the mount. (Wyoming State Museum.)

struggle, but the lawless partners were quickly overpowered and their hands bound.

Averill, always feared because he was a murderous coward, showed himself a cur. He begged and whined, and protested innocence, even saying the woman did all the stealing. The female was made of sterner stuff. She exhausted a blasphemous vocabulary upon the visitors, who essayed to stop the vile flow by gagging her, but found the task too great. After applying every imaginable opprobrious epithet to the lynchers, she cursed everything and everybody, challenging the Deity to cheat her enemies by striking her dead if he dared. When preparations for the short trip to the scaffold were made she called for her own horse and vaulted to its back from the ground.

Ropes were hung from the limb of a big cottonwood tree[6] on the south bank of the Sweetwater.[7] Nooses were adjusted to the necks of Averill and his wife and their horses led from under them. The woman died with curses on her foul lips.

A point overlooked by the amateur executioners was tying the limbs of the victims, and the kicking and writhing of these members was something awful.

Yesterday morning the bodies were swayed to and fro by a gentle breeze which wafted the sweet odor of modest prairie flowers across the plain. The faces were discolored and shrunken tongues hung from between the swollen lips, while a film had gathered over the bulging eyes and unnatural position of the limbs completed the frightful picture.

An inquest may be held over the remains of the thieves, but it is doubtful if any attempt will be made to punish the lynchers. They acted in self protection, feeling that the time to resort to violent measures had arrived.

This is the first hanging of a woman in Wyoming.

Many readers found the story just piquantly lurid enough and quickly decided that it must be true. It just *had* to be true. Responsible men could not have committed such an unthinkable crime without extraordinary provocation. It simply had to be true that Ellen Watson was beneath contempt, a depraved prostitute, and her paramour, Jim Averell, must have been a murdering, drunken pimp. Both deserved to die or the gibbeting of two young, married homesteaders would have precipitated such a violent explosion of public outrage that a backlash against the lynchers would have been inevitable.

However, in Wyoming at least, not all concerned citizens were persuaded that the *Cheyenne Daily Leader* was telling the truth, the whole truth, and nothing but the truth. Any member of a small community understands that absolutely everybody knows absolutely everything about everybody else, and they are right ninety-nine percent of the time. Wyoming was, and still is, a sparsely populated community, so nearly everybody knew, or knew about, or could gossip about, everybody else. So many citizens in the territory, barring most of the members of the Association and their fellow travelers, were convinced that the Cheyenne newspapers were probably covering up for the high-handed cattle kings. People took sides and a sizzling newspaper debate exploded across the Territory.

2. CATTLE BARONS' DILEMMA

The cattle barons (Owen Wister, author of *The Virginian,* called them "the better classes") hoped the poorer classes wouldn't find out about new federal homestead legislation called the "Desert Land Act," and an assortment of other homestead acts, which encouraged the have-nothing citizens back East to migrate to the West and stake out 160 parched acres of the public domain for their own. Then, if a homesteader could somehow get water onto the land, irrigate it, build a house and live in it continuously for five years without starving (three years with military service), the federal government would grant him fee simple to the land.

This would accomplish the government's primary purpose, which was to settle the West with Americans as quickly as possible, thereby strengthening its claim to the Louisiana Purchase—which the United States had fairly recently bought from France, who never really owned it in the first place because they stole it from the Spanish who never really owned it either, insofar as they stole it from the Indians who had possession of it even earlier, but who didn't really own it either.

However, the masses back East did find out about these homestead acts, and right pronto, too. But, unfortunately, they erroneously believed (as apparently Congress did too, ignorantly) that 160 acres on the Potomac River was the same as

160 acres on Horse Creek out in Carbon County, Wyoming. Countless poor Easterners, who had nothing to lose, pulled up stakes and began moving West with everything they could drag along, to do whatever was required of them so they could own a piece of "milk and honey America."

There were several hitches in this whole opportunity. One was the attitude of the already entrenched stockmen. Congress forgot, or didn't know, or didn't really give a damn, that hundreds of cattlemen were already living on this public land. They grazed many millions of head of cattle and horses on it, built ranches on it, sometimes even irrigated and improved it, and oftentimes even fenced it in (which was illegal). They acted as if it really were theirs, which it wasn't.

Now to be fair to the cattle barons, we must admit that the cattlemen were there first—except for the earlier fur trappers and some earlier explorers and the still earlier Indians. The cattlemen had been using this public land just as if they had title to it, but ironically they had begun to damage it by overgrazing, which didn't make sense because they really did eventually want to get ownership of it. So along came Congress and offered to give away all this land to virtually anyone and in ridiculously small, 160-acre parcels. The stage was set for some very nasty business and with quite predictable results.

To throw some historical perspective on this matter, let's look at how the cattleman got himself into this in the first place. But, this time we're going to put the blame where it really belongs, not on the cattleman (surprise?) but squarely in the lap of the pioneer. The immigrants who came across on the Oregon Trail, more often than not, brought along cattle and chickens and other farm animals. Often the animals that pulled the settlers' wagons were big, robust, and tough-hided oxen, who could pull those heavily-loaded covered wagons much better than horses or mules.

By using draft oxen, the immigrants could bring their live-stock along and use the critters to pull the wagons, too. But, since these creatures were expected to pull the wagon a distance only somewhat less than two thousand miles, the oxen often suffered from the bovine equivalent of backpacker's shoulder-strap rash, athlete's foot, malnutrition and fallen arches. As a result, it was often necessary for the pioneer to abandon precious possessions and sometimes even the wagons and the trail-weary animals, and proceed ahead on foot.

One alternative was to delay the balance of that laborious trek until the animals could regain some weight and until their hooves, legs and shoulder-gall could heal up. This often resulted in a serious, sometimes fatal, loss of time. It could mean death to be caught crossing the Rockies in winter, even if an immigrant wasn't burdened with a heavily-loaded wagon. On the other hand, there was one other alternative.

It was feasible to buy, borrow, or steal someone else's hitherto unemployed oxen, and continue on with fresh, pulling animals. The worn out animals could shift for themselves on the prairie in the improbable eventuality that they might survive the winter. But, to everyone's astonishment, the animals not only survived the winter, they showed up in the spring healthier and heartier than before. Now, anyone with a grain of savvy can put two and two together. And that's how the pioneers created a problem for the cattle barons.

Cattlemen in the southwest, where water was scarce and the grass was overgrazed, moved their livestock away from stub-grass, cactus, ticks, heal-flies, scorching heat, and south-land cattle diseases, up to the cool, north-country. There the cattle fattened on nutritious mountain grass on government land at little expense. The owners sold the resulting grass-fat beef to Eastern consumers at a high profit. Initially titanic herds of underweight, skittish, long-horned cattle were driven from the southwestern ranges up into the northern grasslands where fabulous fortunes were made almost overnight.

However, those cattlemen made one serious mistake. They blabbed about this profitable scheme to everyone who matched their own economic and social prestige. In 1881, James S. Brisbin even wrote a book detailing how to make big money with livestock, entitled *The Beef Bonanza; or, How to Get Rich on the Plains.* So nearly every enterprising cattleman with a large herd, or with enough money to purchase a herd, climbed onto the bandwagon. Everyone made just oodles of money and socialized happily with one another.

Cheyenne, Wyoming, became the headquarters for those livestock fortunes. The "Magic City of the Plains" arrogantly boasted the first municipal electric and telephone systems in North America, if not the world. It flaunted one of the most sumptuous and snobbish societies. In such an affluent environment, the cattle emperors decided they needed a men's club to match their social stature, so they built one. It was first called the "Cactus Club," but the name didn't stick, because it didn't reflect the aristocratic preeminence they were anxious to exhibit, so the name was altered to the more sedate "Cheyenne Club."[1]

It was furnished in the style of an exclusive English men's club and sported the first newly-fashionable Mansard roof in the city. The main floor included a high, wide veranda on three sides from which to look down on the surrounding manicured lawns and grounds. An elegant dining room, a billiard room, a card room, a reading lounge, and a plush-carpeted sitting room with red velvet floor-to-ceiling drapes completed the plan of the main floor.

Full-length, diamond-shaped mirrors reflected potted palm trees, and overstuffed velour upholstery and beautifully tooled leather furniture decorated the rooms. The basement

The Cheyenne Club, the headquarters of the cattle industry in Wyoming, resembled an exclusive English men's club. Note the men on the porch. (Wyoming State Museum.)

housed an elaborate kitchen with dumb waiters up to the main floor. It also had a fully stocked wine cellar and liquor larder. The principal chef was imported from French Canada, and the haute cuisine was unparalleled and world-renowned.

The second floor provided sumptuous apartments for members and their guests, each handsomely furnished with hand-carved walnut bedsteads, Italian marble-topped dressers, and commodes—complete with china water jugs and honey-pots and ceiling-high walnut wardrobes. Each apartment included a large fireplace which was inscribed with a famous quotation from Shakespeare and topped with a white marble mantle. Thick woolen carpets and brocaded satin and velvet drapes further complemented the rooms.

For the sporting members, polo matches and tennis games were "de rigeur." The exclusive membership was originally restricted to fifty, but that was later ruled inadequate. High ranking military officers and their ladies from nearby Fort D.A. Russell and Camp Carlin were admitted for a modest charge per visit, without the necessity of formal membership.

Black tie or formal military dress was generally expected for dinner, and optional white tie (appropriately and light-heartedly dubbed "Herefords" by club members because of the open white front and the tails behind) frequently supplemented the regular dress code. If ladies were invited to the festivities, which was more frequently the case than not, full-length evening gowns were expected.

It was not at all unusual to witness a club member pulling up in front of the club with many of his friends in an attention getting fifteen-foot "tally-ho" or "drag" drawn by a half-dozen perfectly matched thoroughbred horses, as a prelude to the evening's entertainment. The gratuity, tossed to the boy who tied the horses to carved-top hitching posts, was generally five silver dollars (representing perhaps fifty dollars in today's currency).

After ordering drinks for the party from the imported carved walnut, crystal-mirrored back-bar, the party then adjourned to the dining room. The club steward was entrusted with overseeing every detail of dinner, which was served by attendants in formal attire.

One might very well choose to begin with pickled eel and black or stuffed green olives to titillate the cultured palate. Fresh oysters on the half shell, set in chopped ice and rock salt, were a regular staple. Expensive imported champagnes, wines, cognacs and other domestic and foreign liquors and exotic aperitifs from around the globe were offered from the beverage inventory.

To top off the meal, the party might then remove to the formal sitting room where they could relax comfortably in

The interior of the Cheyenne Club was sumptuous. This rare photograph shows the Reading Room. (UW American Heritage Center.)

the overstuffed chairs and sofas and chat over an after-dinner cordial. The men often chose to finish off the meal with light wrapper-leaf Havana cigars. In some other Eastern and European cities this might have been looked upon as pretentious, but Cheyenne was generally conceded to be the wealthiest city per capita on earth.[2]

One evening in 1883, some British members held a get-together for some of their American member-friends who were visiting at the club. Forty-one gentlemen sat down to the table. Sixty-six bottles of imported champagnes and twenty bottles of red wine were consumed during supper alone.

Another impromptu party was given to celebrate a particularly large and profitable livestock sale by one of the members. The price tag for that evening was over $5,000, with only twenty-five guests in attendance.

The club rules were strict and inviolate—no profanity, no drunkenness, no fisticuffs, no cheating at cards or games, no pipe smoking, no gambling, and absolutely no games of any kind on Sunday. The inflexible rules were dutifully posted. One evening, John Coble, a prominent cattleman from the Iron Mountain country north of Cheyenne, later a close friend of the notorious Tom Horn, became a bit inebriated. He drew his .45 caliber pistol and shot two holes through the painting behind the bar which depicted, rather unartistically, two purebred Shorthorn bulls which Mr. Coble did not believe reflected the high caliber of his own cattle. He was ordered to resign from the club, which he begrudgingly did shortly thereafter. This painting, complete with bullet holes, can today be viewed in the Wyoming State Museum in Cheyenne. Many other paintings in the club had considerably more artistic value and were created by artists such as Albert Bierstadt.

An elegant, brick opera house was soon built in downtown Cheyenne, and the finest operatic companies from America and Europe were engaged to perform.[3] On nights when no formal opera troupe was performing, other eminent theatrical personalities and entourages were enjoyed by Cheyenne residents. Opening night at the opera staggered the imagination with its display of wealth and social status.

The Opera House Ball held to open the premier season in 1882 was a lavish spectacular.[4] Each lady was presented with a white silk perfumed program, each accompanied with a white corsage. Scented, embossed menus were on each dinner plate. Black tie and "Herefords" were seen everywhere. As for the distaff side, large coiffures were surmounted by flouncy, feathered chapeaus complementing fancy brocaded and elaborately jeweled evening gowns, many with abbreviated trains.

Exquisitely prepared dishes such as Blue Winged Duck with Richelieu Ragout and Larded Tendons of Veal á la

Jacquemiere were served. Succulent desserts such as Whipped Syllabub and Peach Meringue á la Francis were typical of the gourmet fare served at these occasions. Post-opera parties regularly lasted till two in the morning, and many of them lasted much further into the night.

One of the most exclusive residential streets in Cheyenne was referred to as Cattlemen's Row. It was lined with expensive, multi-storied mansions of frame, brick or stone, or a combination of those. Each was styled by a different architect, and each was of different architectural design. Each strained desperately to outdo the other mansions in size, expense and design. They also included elaborate livery barns and stables in the rear which housed phaetons, buggies, and open and closed carriages which were drawn by the finest in blooded horses.

But let's not get too impressed with all this swaggering wealth yet. Something very serious was about to happen to that high-falutin bovine aristocracy, which almost nobody had anticipated.

Not everyone had an established herd or sufficient capital or borrowing power with which to purchase one. Among those without was the hand-to-mouth settler, the homesteader. However, the most enterprising of them soon discovered that the rich cattlemen had so many cattle, they didn't know how many cattle they had. The cattle monarchs' trusted foremen might not have divulged the correct information to their bosses anyway, even if they really knew, since sometimes they were already expropriating a few head for themselves. This led the wealthy cattlemen directly into a problem.

The grim-faced, hard-working pioneer/homesteader was able to drum up damned little sympathy for the foreign cattle kings, who had their employees do all the difficult work while they themselves raced across the range to play cowboy. So some of the settlers (also called nesters, and synonymously called rustlers early on in cattle country) began expropriating a few unbranded calves to begin spreads of their own.

Parenthetically, the reader ought to know that unbranded calves were called "dogies" (not doggies), "mavericks," "slicks," or "bums." At any rate, since the big boys were raking in such huge profits, they didn't notice, or maybe didn't care, that quite a few of their calves were choosing new masters.

So, the practice of casually filching a few head from an employer or someone else's herd evolved into a kind of tongue-in-cheek game—an understood code of range ethics. It was called "the longest rope." Anybody who stumbled onto an unbranded calf could expropriate it with impunity and put his own brand on it. It was, however, considered "sticky wicket" to go about openly beating the bushes for them.

In Wyoming it is commonly rumored that many of the most prestigious cattle ranches got their start that way. People just looked the other way—that is at first. It was simply playing the game, and many pulled up a chair at the table.

Things kept cruising along fine and dandy until one day those cattle barons discovered something else. They found out that they shouldn't have blabbed about their good fortune to all their relatives and friends, who jumped on the bandwagon. Soon there were one hell of a lot of cattle on the open public ranges of Wyoming, and before long this overpopulation of the range led to the near extinction of the thick, nutritious mountain grass.

This overpopulation of cattle began to weave the dreadful fabric of disaster. Even though the stockman grumbled, he still didn't acknowledge the extent of the problem until too late. Even if he had confronted the problem earlier, he could have done little about it, and it would have meant facing up to the reality—the end of the cattle business as he had know it.

3. THE WEATHER

The economic pinnacle of the cattle business arrived about 1883.[1] There seemed no way to stem the growing numbers of cattle being driven in from outside onto the free, open ranges of Wyoming. As a result, increasing amounts of beef were shoveled onto the Eastern meat markets each fall. This predictably resulted in a severe glut on the meat markets back East. The price of beef plummeted to around a half, or even a third, of what it had been. And another cataclysm was just around the corner.

In the late summer and fall of 1886, the cattlemen began quietly discussing the lack of adequate rainfall during spring and summer, only half of what it had been in previous years. The grass wasn't recovering the way everybody expected, the way it always had before, because of the overgrazing. Cattle had to move on half a lope to get enough to eat. The livestock were facing winter without that nice, thick layer of grass-fat that they usually put on in the summer.

Cattlemen began to uneasily predict that they might suffer a little larger calving loss than usual in the spring. The hay crop was less than ever before. Actually not everybody thought it necessary to put up much hay, anyway. There was little sense of any serious impending danger. The livestock had come through every other winter in pretty good shape, hadn't they?

But, the cattlemen didn't remember about the winter of 1871-1872 or the blizzard of March 1878. So they relaxed and had another Red Dog whiskey highball and Havana cigar at the Cheyenne Club. Everything would turn out all right, right?

On November 9, 1886, the winter[2] began ominously with an unusually early four-inch crust of snow cover. Even most of the old-time stockmen couldn't remember seeing it begin quite as early. It was followed by rain and more snow. Old-timers began to have an uneasy feeling about this particular winter. The Laramie newspapers, however, predicted that there was nothing much to worry about; "nothing really unusual," they said. It was hard to put a finger on it, but most everyone felt it, even though no one talked much about it. The skies seemed darker than usual. The snow and freezing rain wouldn't let up.

Often the sun didn't come out for weeks at a time. It seemed, too, as though the biting, whistling wind was never going to let up. The snow became unusually deep, and the wind kept up its never-ending howl. It became tougher for the men to work at their outdoor chores. They worried about going too far from the ranch buildings for fear of getting lost. It was getting pretty near impossible to check on the cattle.

A pall hovered heavily over thoughts of the ranchers and townspeople alike. The snow drifted in so deep that, in some places, ranchers had to dig a pathway from the ranch house to get to the well. Fighting their way to the shed for firewood became an agonizing experience. The snow burned eyeballs, and a person could get lost going to the privy unless he strung out a trail of hemp twine. Then, beginning during the last days of November, the temperature suddenly dropped to ten or twenty degrees below zero.

Would the sun never come out again? Would the storm never relent? What if no one could get out to feed the horses?

What if the food ran out? People didn't dare travel anywhere. What if...? Every question cascaded over every other one in a mind-boggling search for answers no one really wanted to face.

Finally, on February 20, after a particularly severe night, the weather broke. Heavenly sunshine smothered the earth in its warm embrace. Not a single cloud was left to tell of the nightmare which preceded this magnificent day. It wasn't just sunny, it was truly delightful. At long last, the men could get out onto the prairie to see whether their imaginations had been playing tricks on them, or whether things were really as bad as they had envisioned. But no one looked forward to what they were afraid they would find out there.

But, Hallelujah! The results of the storm turned out to be less severe than anybody thought. The livestock were weaker for sure, and they had lost some flesh, but they could put it back again in the spring. It was not a bone-crushing catastrophe. Everyone dared to smile again, just a little—crookedly. Spirits sort of improved.

That lovely, warm sun continued to pour down day after day. The hard snow cover was melting away fast, and the gaunt livestock found it easier now to scratch up forage and dig down to water. After all, stock could actually stay alive on very little forage, but they couldn't survive without water. Little by little it really began to feel more like spring. Spring! Blessed spring! Soon rivulets of water ran everywhere, the ice melted off the creeks and streams, and slush began to show up all over. Maybe it was going to be an early spring. It was hard to look forward to that prospect so early, but following all the depression, to have an early spring...! It was almost too much to hope for.

It didn't happen all at once. At first it was just a vague feeling, like last fall. The still, wet air didn't seem to smell quite like it had before. The muddy snow slowly turned into a clinging, crunchy slush that stuck to galoshes. The rivulets of water slowly started to thin out, and the weather, which had been so toasty in recent days, seemed to chill off a little more again. Even putting on more clothes didn't seem to help. Little by little, the wind crept back into the valley, and the men started buttoning up their outer clothes again. The horses sensed it, too. They weren't venturing so far out for forage any longer. They stuck closer to the corrals and hung around the hay manger more. The men stopped smiling at each other and pulled their hats down farther over their faces. Something strange was going on, and everyone sensed it.

Then the sky turned jet black, just as before a tornado. The wind started to blow even harder. Snow started falling again, heavily, and the temperature suddenly cascaded down below zero. Not even old timers could remember all those things happening together like that before. It was spooky, and people began to feel damned uneasy about it. Then suddenly the temperature plummeted straight down. The snow stopped abruptly. But the wind continued to blow, and everything froze over solid as a gravestone. The livestock couldn't break through the ice-crust to running water. They couldn't paw up anything to feed on. After several days the cattle began to bellow hoarsely and scream like stuck pigs. And then the slinky wolves and coyotes began to laugh and sing!

When the weather cleared up long enough, cattlemen peered out through holes scratched in frosty window panes and saw that the stock was losing one hell of a lot more weight. Some of the poorer ones began to collapse from exhaustion and exposure. Cattle slid around on the icy snow cover and fell down heavily. The weakest ones gave up, lay there and died.

Cows began to abort. The poor beasts began to chew on willows and eat the bark off the cottonwood trees as high up as they could reach. They even chewed chunks out of fence posts and ate the corners of log buildings. This incessant effort to get something into their stomachs left the cattle's lips and gums cut and bloody. They looked like hollow, skin-covered skeletons. Cowboys cringed as they listened to the creatures calling out, knowing nothing could be done to help them. The men decided that hell wasn't at all what the preachers said it was. It wasn't fire and brimstone and hot as hell. It was snow and ice and razor-sharp winds—and it was *cold* as hell!

When spring did arrive at last, the rancher knew what he would find on the prairie. When he finally got out on the flats and down into the swales, he stared at what he saw in horror, and everywhere it stared back at him with black, empty eye-sockets. Buzzing, fetid death was everywhere. The consequences of the winter struck him like a thirteen-pound fencing maul. Wyoming has never since seen such savage death and mutilation.

It has been said that in the spring of 1887 some ranchers could walk across their spreads without ever stepping on the ground. The soggy earth was strewn with the rotting bodies of dead cattle. They were piled up three and four deep against the fences where they had drifted in their search for food. The draws and gulches, where cattle had sought water and shelter, were full of carcasses.

Many ranchers lost as much as three-quarters of their herds that winter, some even more. The Winter of 1887 altered forever the way cattle are raised in Wyoming. It was never again the devil-may-care, easy-money pursuit it had been before. The Eastern, Southwestern and foreign interests that had known the affluence of Cheyenne and Laramie were never to see those halcyon days again.

Most of them, now broke and broken, salvaged what they could or simply abandoned their gigantic spreads to the four winds. The formerly arrogant cattle barons stumbled back home to the Southwest, or the Midwest, New England, Prussia, or the British Isles, or wherever they came from, to explain away the unexplainable to their shocked, but unconvinced, co-investor friends. The co-investors, too, lost wealth through their venture into the unpredictable livestock business. A few of the cattle kings tried, some only halfheartedly, to stick it out, but it was largely a losing battle. It seemed every imaginable adversity had conspired to wipe them out. The carefree days of the high-riding "playboys of the prairie" were gone forever.

But wait just a minute! Contrary to the plight of the cattle barons, many homesteaders managed to hang on in Wyoming. After all, except for their cherished 160 acres, they had hardly anything to lose. In fact, many soon found themselves better off.

And not all the cattle barons quit the state. Thereby hangs the ominous prelude to what Agnes Wright Spring called "the most revolting crime" in the entire annals of the West—most certainly in Wyoming.

Over the last century every imaginable excuse has been put forward to try to excuse the inexcusable and to disguise the truth. Now, however, after the passage of a hundred years, it is high time to expunge the record of what is downright apocryphal, often ghoulishly light-hearted, yellow journalism ignorantly put forth as history. It is time to reevaluate what has previously been tossed off as fact regarding this execrable episode in Wyoming's past.

Long forgotten facts have shown up in brittle newspapers, in books with faded covers and broken spines, in dusty archives, in little-known and almost forgotten personal files, and in personal interviews with surviving relatives, friends and neighbors of the actual participants. For the first time actual on-site research and exploration have revealed new, hitherto unknown information. Also included within these pages is information from dog-eared sketches and from rediscovered specifications, maps and diagrams. Some very old, faded photographs of the people and the places where the terrifying events took place have been unearthed in family collections and photo archives and are printed here, some for the first time.

PART TWO: THE CAST

4. ELLEN WATSON

Her full name was Ellen Liddy Watson,[1] but her family called her "Ellie" and her friends later knew her as "Ella."[2] Her father, Thomas Lewis Watson, was born in 1837 in Hamilton, Scotland, before her grandfather, John Watson, brought the family to America. Thomas was just a boy when they came to America and settled in Ohio.

Thomas remained with his parents in Ohio for five years before running away and working his way to Canada where he met and married Frances. Ellie's mother was the former Frances Close whose family had come from Ireland to eastern Canada.Their first daughter, Ellie, one of the two principal characters in our story, was born on a farm, July 2, 1861, near Arran Lake in Arran Township, Bruce County, Ontario, Canada, on a beautiful, heavily-wooded and sparsely-settled peninsula overlooking Owen Sound and Georgian Bay on one side and Lake Huron on the other.

After Ellie was born the Civil War broke out and Thomas volunteered for the Ninety-ninth New York Volunteers, who were made up primarily of Scottish emigrants. He served briefly in a medical unit, but discovered he hated blood and returned to Canada. Ellie was the oldest child of a family of ten children. She and six other brothers and sisters were born in Canada. Only the last three children were born in Kansas.[3]

It may have been the enticement of free farm land in western America that motivated Thomas, in 1877, to bring his young family across the border to America. He moved his wife and seven children, including Ellie, to Kansas where he filed his formal intention to become an American citizen. The family settled on a homestead claim only a few miles northeast of what is now Lebanon, Pawnee Township, Jewell County, Kansas. Lebanon was just a few miles east of Smith Center, the county seat. The little town of Lebanon is the very heart, the geographical center, of the continental United States.

Thomas filed on a homestead claim[4] and the family moved onto the land, built a modest farmhouse, and, as the Indians expressed it, "turned the grass upside down," and seeded their rich, virgin soil to grain. After becoming an American citizen and fulfilling his five-year residency requirement, Thomas was granted fee simple to the homestead land they had worked so hard to prove up on. He later proved up on and sold several additional homesteads. Ellie's mother, however, never became a naturalized citizen. Also Thomas and Frances overlooked a very important detail. They forgot to naturalize Ellie, an oversight which later caused their daughter a great deal of anguish.

During those early, back-breaking years in the opening of the West, there was little time for children's education. That was more the rule than the exception in those days, for it was important that everyone in the family work the land. Hard work was a necessary part of every poor family's survival, and not just in the West, either. It was a matter of working from before sunup into the nighttime, with just barely enough time out to eat and sleep, and very often for a full seven days a week. Children routinely worked alongside their parents. Producing many children provided more labor.

Ellen's parents, Thomas and Frances (Close) Watson, immigrated to Kansas from Canada. (Photo courtesy of Daniel Brumbaugh.)

In the early West, the study of the Bible was often the only education the children of homesteaders received. Frequently parents were illiterate, as were both Ellie's parents.

Ellie reached womanhood without a very extensive education. Since her father and mother were illiterate, however, they were determined that their children would be able to read and write. After their daily chores were done, the children attended a small one-room elementary school nearby. The whole family possessed a very thick Celtic brogue which, it was said, often made it difficult to communicate with others. Ellie spoke with a thick, colorful brogue for the balance of her life.[5]

Somewhere around the age of sixteen, Ellie was shuffled off by her parents to nearby Smith Center, where she was

This photo of Ellen Watson is from the Watson family collection and is believed to have been taken near the time of her marriage to Pickell in 1879. (Courtesy of Ruth Nelson.)

engaged as a cook and housekeeper by a local banker and farmer, H. R. Stone. Soon Ellie fell within the view of a young man who farmed adjacent to the Watson's homestead. His name was William A. Pickell[6] and before long he began to court Ellie. His courtship was eventually successful because on November 24, 1879, Ellie and Bill were married on the Watson farm. After the wedding the young couple moved to Bill Pickell's homestead.

Unfortunately the new bride was not able to enjoy her marital bliss for very long. It seemed to be common knowledge within the tiny, typically nosy settlement, that Pickell beat Ellie unmercifully during alcoholic fits of rage. Furthermore it was whispered that Pickell was impotent. To make matters worse, someone advised Ellie that Pickell had been unfaithful to her.[7] During one of those brutal beatings, Bill struck her repeatedly with a horsewhip leaving her covered with nasty red welts. Terrified and badly hurt, Ellie finally ran screaming from her husband and fled headlong across the flat farmland to the sanctuary of her parents' home. She had been married for only two short years.[8]

Ellie then secured employment for several years on another neighbor's farm as a cook and domestic.[9] In 1883, against her mother's wishes, she decided to escape the constant entreaties of her husband, and she left the family to move twelve miles north across the state border to the nearby town of Red Cloud, Nebraska, where she had often shopped with her family. Upon her arrival there she secured a job as a cook and domestic in the Royal Hotel.[10] Her relatives testify that Ellie was known as a marvelous cook, as was Ellie's mother and the other Watson girls, as well.

It has been said by some who knew her, that Ellie was extremely bright.[11] But her father said that there was not a trace of "fastness" in her personality.[12] Upon examining Ellie's only known photographs, talking with the Watson family and studying written descriptions of her during her lifetime, it is evident that Ellen Pickell had matured into a pretty, buxom, blue-eyed, auburn-haired young lady, with a soft smile. According to the beauty standards of the time, she was attractive indeed.

She was also tall, about five feet eight inches or so, which by yesterday's standards was unusually tall for a woman.[13] All the Watson children were tall, although neither the father nor mother were as tall as their children.[14]

Ellie left home for good. She established legal residency in Red Cloud, a town of about three hundred people, and filed for divorce on February 26, 1884, on the grounds of extreme cruelty and infidelity.[15] Curiously, the divorce was not finalized until late March 1886 and then on Pickell's grounds of desertion.[16] However, this date was still in advance of her later remarriage in Wyoming. While still living in Red Cloud, she kept in close touch with her family. After all, she was only twelve miles away.[17]

According to letters she wrote home, Ellie decided to leave Red Cloud. She went first to Denver City, Colorado.[18] To get there she probably traveled northwest by stage to the newly-completed rails of the Denver City and St. Joseph Railroad and took the train to Kearney Junction. From there her train would have taken the Union Pacific tracks west across Nebraska to Julesburg, Colorado. Then the route left the Union Pacific rails and veered southwest to Denver City. That was the cheapest and most convenient route.[19] Although we don't know the exact date of her arrival there, we do know her brother was a resident of Denver City around that time, and it is possible that she went there to pay him a visit.

She then moved north about 120 miles to the boomtown of Cheyenne, Wyoming, where she again wrote letters home. It was a logical place to look for a job because at this time it was purported to be the wealthiest city per capita on earth. Money gushed and bubbled like champagne.[20]

At this juncture in the story we reach a dilemma. We must decide whether or not to include another woman whose name for a whole century has been linked to and confused with Ellen Watson. This new woman was a prostitute. This is exactly what reporter Ed Towse told us to believe about Ellen

William A. Pickell and Ellen Watson were married November 24, 1879, on the Watson farm. They were together only two years before Ellen moved out. Pickell was said to have been an alcoholic who beat Ellen. This photo, never before published, was taken in Red Cloud, Nebraska, probably at or near the time of their wedding. (Courtesy of Lola Van Wey.)

Watson in his first article after the lynching. Towse knew of a woman named Ella Wilson, erroneously named as Ella Watson in a medical report, who was involved in a real "shoot 'em up, Charlie" at the notorious bawdy house in Fetterman, Wyoming. The shoot-out was written up in the *Cheyenne Daily Leader*, so Towse may have remembered the name similarity and referred back to this earlier article.

After this fracas at Fetterman, involving death, maiming, and extensive destruction of property, the deputy sheriff of that part of Albany County turned matters over to the local courts. Now here's where the dilemma arises. Ella Wilson (Watson) was a prime witness to the shoot-out. In every instance during the depositions, she signed her name "Ella Wilson, 'X' her mark." She was therefore apparently illiterate.

In all depositions and indictments before District Judge John D. O'Brien, Clerk of District Court Richard Butler, and Prosecuting Attorney William J. McIntyre, this woman's name was given as Ella Wilson. During the gunfight Ella Wilson was actually shot in the neck and shoulder, only a bad flesh wound to be sure, but requiring substantial medical attention. The examining physician, J.N. Bradley, inadvertently recorded her name as Ella Watson instead of Wilson.

A simple clerical error? Yes, but it seems the source of much misinformation, so we cannot dismiss this confusion easily. We must try to put this piece of evidence to bed (perhaps a bad metaphor) once and for all. So let's examine the facts and let the reader judge whether this woman is indeed Ellen L. Watson-Pickell or some other woman.

First, our original Ellen was literate. When she signed her name, she always signed it Ellen L. Watson, except, of course, during her marriage when she signed Ellen Pickell. She never signed "Ella" on any known document. However, Ella Wilson (Watson) of Fetterman was unable to sign her own name.

Since the original Ellen L. Watson was married during the time of the events at Fetterman, it was likely she would have signed her name Ellen Pickell or, perhaps, Ellen L. Watson—certainly not Ella Watson and never Ella Wilson.

Second, the woman at Fetterman seems to have been well established. Ellen Watson Pickell, being newly arrived in Wyoming, could not have had time enough to accomplish this. The events at Fetterman occurred in August 1884, six months after Ellen Pickell filed for divorce in Red Cloud.

Third, the name Watson was a very popular name in America at that time. "Ella" was also one of the most popular end-of-the-century first names. Ellen Watson Pickell was never known to have worked at anything but marriage, cooking, cleaning, and housekeeping. It seems probable that Ed Towse and Ed Slack of the *Cheyenne Sun* intentionally or inadvertently confused two women with similar names.

Fourth, an article in the *Cheyenne Daily Sun* of September 2, 1884, gives us a physical description of the Ellen Wilson (Watson) at Fetterman. It says "Miss Ellen Wilson, a fair but frail young half-breed of some forty summers, more or less, was also shot in the melee—in the shoulder." By contrast Ellen Watson Pickell was Scottish Anglo-Saxon, five foot eight or so inches tall, anything but frail at 165 pounds, and was twenty-three years of age.

Fifth, the Watson family back in Ohio received letters from Ellen Watson Pickell mailed from Denver City, Cheyenne and Rawlins, but they never received any from Fetterman.[21] Her family never mentioned knowledge of her living in Fetterman, even when her father came to Wyoming after her death and was interviewed extensively in newspapers.

Sixth, Towse also confused Ellen Watson Pickell with another real-life, notorious whore, this time from Bessemer Bend, Wyoming, whose name was Kate Maxwell and who was earlier called "Cattle Kate" in the press. Ed Towse and Ed Slack lifted the catchy nickname "Cattle Kate" from the earlier editorialized real Kate Maxwell and hybridized her into dead Ellen L. Watson. We learn more of this later.

Furthermore, Fetterman was not a likely destination for a traveler. Unlike Cheyenne which was on a main railroad thoroughfare and was a likely stopping point for someone looking for a job, Fetterman was an isolated, former military outpost. Travel to Fetterman from Cheyenne would have taken at least several extra-exhausting days of rough, bumpy travel around the mountains and over the sagebrush badlands in the customary slow bull wagon.[22]

And then, too, why in the world would an uninitiated young woman seek out an unfamiliar, raunchy, defunct military town like Fetterman as a place to experiment in the demimonde of prostitution? If Ellen Watson Pickell had desired initiation in the sad profession of prostitution, the rollicking boomtown of Cheyenne offered plenty of opportunities in a more convenient and profitable location.

It seems likely that Ellen Pickell logically continued farther west on the main Union Pacific route from Cheyenne on through Laramie, to Rawlins, Wyoming, the very next substantial stop on the railroad. In fact there hardly would have been time for a quick trip 160 miles each way back and forth up north to Fetterman to rush into a new endeavor as a novice prostitute in a completely unfamiliar whore house.

But because it is hard to put one hundred years of misinformation to rest and because we don't want to appear arbitrary, let's look at the entire story of Fetterman's Ella Wilson (Watson). Besides, this gives us an opportunity to examine one of the most unique, but nearly forgotten, trollop-house shoot-outs in all Western American history.

ẽ ẽ ẽ

The common soldier who frequented a "hog ranch" had precious little money to squander, even when "flush" after payday, so the cost of a soldier's "pig," hence the expression hog ranch, had to be minimal. The "soiled doves" catering to the military usually were in their late thirties or early forties, beyond their desirable prime, and very close indeed to the end of their careers.[23]

The original log cabin hog ranch that had entertained the soldiers of the military post of Fort Fetterman was called Brown's Ranche and was a rather distant seven miles north of the fort,[24] across the North Platte River and outside the military reservation on a little trickle of water called Currant Creek. (It earlier had a much more colorful name which will be left to the imagination of the reader.) It was owned by a tough hombre by the name of William Brown, who called himself an "innkeeper." Together with his wife (incidentally also named Ella), he kept and boarded four "hogs" on the premises, who were the misses Lydia O'Brien, Alice Beam, Hattie Hatter, and Ida Hamilton, the latter of whom may have been the famous, but egregious, prostitute formerly from Denver, Colorado.[25]

After the army's abandonment of the fort, a new frame dance hall was built only one mile north of the raunchy, now civilian town of Fetterman. At the dance hall four to six girls regularly attended to business.[26]

Following the abandonment of the military post, the local citizenry took over the buildings and put them to civilian use. Since there was no railroad through that part of the country, the town soon became a busy and lusty distribution point for freighters, wealthy cattle barons, and poor cowboys. Cowboys irregularly had money to spend and no other place anywhere nearby to spend it. So Fetterman became a crossroads of trade. It was also halfway between Fort Russell, adjacent to Cheyenne in the south, and Fort McKinney near Buffalo, in the north—a convenient halfway stop.

However, the new east-west Fremont, Elkhorn, and Missouri Valley Railroad soon callously, but intentionally, bypassed Fetterman by laying its tracks about five miles to the south. With that unexpected and devastating development, most of the citizens abandoned the old town. Almost everything, including the buildings, was moved south to the supplanting new railroad town of Douglas, whose town lots were already being sold by none other than the railroad itself, of course. Rollicking, raucous Fetterman just wilted away.[27]

But before the advent of the railroad, Ella Wilson (Watson) was an inmate of the newly-built, infamous, frame buildings on the northern outskirts of Fort Fetterman. And here Ella Wilson was an eye witness to one of the least publicized, but most unusual, gunfights in the West. It took place on the afternoon of August 29, 1884 [28] at Sanders' and Lawrence's combination whore house, dance hall, gambling den and saloon. Let's sneak a look at the first-hand description of a shoot-out in a frontier bawdy house.

Some of the story was told by Deputy Sheriff Malcolm Campbell, who later to won election as the principal county sheriff, and who still later wrote a fabulous book about his experiences as a lawman on the wild and woolly Wyoming frontier. Additional facts have been gleaned from contemporary newspaper accounts and court records.[29] We have a detailed description of the hog ranches, written down in a letter from an unabashed early-day patron by the name of Abe Abrahams. In a nostalgic cowboy poem appended to the letter, he claimed very warm and affectionate memories for both the earlier log and subsequent frame hog ranches.[30]

He describes the first location seven miles north of Fetterman as consisting of:

"...two log buildings. The main building comprised the dance hall, bar, and separate rooms for the women. It was about 40 feet long and 18 feet wide, with a stand on the north end for the fiddler. The south end of the bar opened into a room, where Jack Sanders, the proprietor, and his wife Vi slept. Across the road about 20 feet there was another log building. It housed the kitchen and dining room, with a long table in the center covered with oil cloth, which would seat about 20 people. There were only two chairs that I ever saw there, just long benches for the girls and guests. Sanders and his wife used the chairs. Now at one end of the cook house there was a room, also logs, which was always kept locked. It was the liquor room. Jack Sanders built this Hog ranch near a small trickling creek called Currant Creek. Jack Sanders had his brother with him for a while. He tended bar."

The writer then goes on to say:

"A few years later...I don't remember when [but after the military moved out]...William Brown abandoned the old Hog ranch. Then Jack Sanders, in partnership with a man named Billy Bacon [His memory is faulty here. He should have said John Lawrence. Bacon comes later.], put up two new buildings made out of native lumber on the Fetterman side of the [North Platte] river about 1/2 mile out. It was a big structure of the same lines as the [earlier] log one 7 miles north, on the other side of the river."

A couple of weeks previous to the main fracas, there had been a shooting spree at Lawrence's new, frame hog ranch. Three devil-may-care cowboys by the names of John Fenix [pronounced Phoenix],[31] "Pretty Frank" Wallace and Harry Crosby, who were flush from payday, were patronizing Lawrence's place. Frank Wallace was called "pretty" because he wasn't, a typical humorous Western contradiction in terms. According to Deputy Sheriff Malcolm Campbell, he was as homely as a mud fence, with pale blue eyes and a huge, thick mass of a nose that Campbell said "stood out like a landmark."

On that earlier visit these three drunken companions shot up all the mirrors in the back bar, blew out most of the windows in the place, shot holes in the bedroom doors, and generally terrorized the owners, gamblers, bartenders, and all the screaming, hysterical female inmates, including one whose name was Ella Wilson (Watson). The proprietor of the place, who was a tough and surly hombre, had an even tougher and surlier partner by the name of Jack Sanders. The two owners quickly tossed the three drunks out on their ears, accompanied by the admonishment never to darken their doorstep again—or else.

A couple of weeks later, however, the three companions rode merrily into Fetterman and proceeded to get drunk at a different establishment, Billy Bacon's saloon, located in the middle of town. Subsequently they began drinking and gambling at the Faro table, after which the three decided to ride on out to the "ES" ranch where they had been offered the chance to hole up for the winter. Fenix, after struggling drunkenly up onto his horse, turned to his two buddies and shouted that they ought to take a slight detour and repay a visit to the hog ranch.

Deputy Campbell, who knew about their previous boisterous goings-on, was sitting on the front steps of Billy Bacon's saloon, chatting with some of the boys, and overheard the noisy challenge. He realized that there would be one hell of a lot of bad blood if they persisted in their announced mission, so he loudly warned the jousty triumvirate that such a course of action might not be in their best interests.

Pretty Frank and Harry Crosby seemed reluctant, but Fenix hollered defiantly that he was not afraid of Lawrence and Sanders, and besides, he said, somebody ought to have guts enough to clean out the whole filthy hole. He whirled his handsome white horse around and raced off toward the forbidden establishment. The other two cowboys, realizing that Fenix would not fare well alone, screwed up their courage and reluctantly galloped along.

According to the testimony later given in the case brought against Lawrence and Sanders by Pretty Frank Wallace and Harry Crosby,[32] the drunken trio galloped to the hog ranch where they reigned their horses up in a cloud of dust. They were confronted by the two grim owners. The three troublemakers swung off their mounts and shouldered their way past the owners and into the bar, where a shouting match ensued.

Proprietor Lawrence, in a towering rage, shouted that he would give Fenix "twenty dollars if he would spit in his face!" That was an unmistakable, out-and-out challenge, but Fenix apparently was slow to meet it. Lawrence shoved his face into Fenix's and, in even greater volume, proffered the proposition a second time. Fenix was aware that proprietor Sanders was fingering a shotgun and that Lawrence had his hand on a cocked pistol in his pocket, but so did Fenix. So Fenix complied—by expectorating a huge mouthful of wet gob in Lawrence's face. He then hossed out his gun and started shooting. From that moment on it was not easy to tell what happened or in what sequence.

The noisy shooting and loud profanity alerted the people in Fetterman, and they began to watch the hog ranch with much anticipation. Soon a trio of horsemen rode toward town, all hunched up in a curious way. As they approached it could be seen that Fenix was riding in the middle slumped over on his saddle horn with a cowboy riding on either side holding him up. Jack Fenix had been fatally wounded in the abdomen.

The abandoned soldiers' barracks had a room that the townspeople used as a combination hotel and hospital. As the trio reached town, Deputy Campbell helped the men carry the dying Fenix to a bed in the hospital. Someone then shouted out that Pretty Frank was lying dead in the doorway of the dance hall, so Campbell deputized Charlie Cobb, a friend who was handy, and the two set out at a gallop toward the scene of the gunfight.

They had hardly gotten started when they ran into Sanders and Lawrence who were also riding hard and fast, but toward town. When they saw the deputy and Cobb, they halted their horses, dismounted and stood menacingly in the middle of the road with their guns at the ready, Lawrence with a shotgun and Sanders with two six-shooters. The deputy shouted out to them that he only wanted to talk, and the two lawmen rode cautiously forward and stopped.

The two proprietors told of their previous warning to the three "ringy" cowboys after the first incident and how the three drunken cowboys had ignored their warning, showed up, started arguing and shot the place up again. They further claimed they had killed Pretty Frank and were going into town to finish off Fenix and Crosby, whether anybody gave a damn or not. The two owners then mounted up again, wheeled around their horses and raced wildly off around the lawmen toward town. Campbell noticed that Lawrence had been wounded in the shoulder.

Deputy Campbell and Cobb spun their horses around, and Campbell, by spurring his much swifter horse unmercifully, managed to beat everyone back to Fetterman, with

Cobb racing right behind him. Campbell leaped off his quivering horse and bounded over to the hospital. He yanked out his pistols and wheeled around to fill the doorway with his body. Seconds later Lawrence and Sanders ran up with fire in their eyes and their guns drawn.

Deputy Sheriff Campbell's young wife was frightened when she overheard the shooting and shouting nearby. She watched her husband and Cobb ride crazily through town, pursued hotly by Lawrence and Sanders. Concerned for her husband's safety, she scooped up their baby from its crib, ran out of the house, and swished over to the hospital room where her husband stood barring the door with Cobb braced to back him up. She frantically begged Lawrence and Sanders not to shoot her husband. They assured her that they were not after her husband, but that the deputy had better damned well let them have Fenix; they then lunged again toward Campbell and Cobb. Campbell shouted that he had helped carry Fenix to a bed and that he was sure there was no need to pump any more lead into the dying man.

Lawrence and Sanders gradually relaxed their hostile demeanor, and soon relinquished their weapons, but not before Campbell gave them his solemn promise that they would be under his official protection. At the deputy sheriff's invitation then, the four men calmly strolled over to Billy Bacon's saloon to get a drink (which certainly seems logical under the circumstances), and sent for Dr. Bradley to look at Fenix and fix up Lawrence's wound (which also seems damned logical, too—and in just that order!).

Now back to the hog ranch. Pretty Frank was not dead at all, but just badly wounded. Buckshot from one of the shotgun blasts had torn through the upper and lower eyelids of one eye, blinding him in that eye. Other fragments from the same blast lodged in his huge nose. The shot had knocked him down and he was temporarily unconscious.[33] And a good thing it was, too, because, according to witnesses, if Lawrence and Sanders had known he was still alive, they surely would have shot him dead right where he lay. As it was, however, when he revived, he made sure everybody had gone, crawled unsteadily onto his horse, rode away and hid in the back of an abandoned building just outside Fetterman, where he was eventually discovered and arrested by Deputy Sheriff Campbell.

Harry Crosby, the all-but-forgotten member of the triumvirate, had also been slightly wounded, but had slipped away by rushing outside the saloon during the confusion, jumping onto his horse, and racing off to the "ES" ranch where he hid out till spring. A suit was subsequently filed by Pretty Frank against Lawrence for attempted murder.[34] The resulting inquest was held six miles south of town on Judge J.P. O'Brien's ranch. Lawrence, however, was acquitted on the grounds of self-defense.[35]

As a kind of postmortem to these wild past events, after the inquest at Judge O'Brien's ranch, Lawrence returned home to Fetterman, and before too long, again involved himself in a bitter argument. It may even perhaps have been related to the previous fight. This time the trouble involved Billy Bacon, who, the reader will recall, owned the saloon in town, and the trouble occurred again at Lawrence's dance hall and saloon on the outskirts of Fetterman. For an unknown reason, both men hauled out their hand guns and fired point blank at one another. Bacon was shot in the throat while Lawrence was shot in the abdomen. Bacon survived for two days and Lawrence three. Bacon, however, might have survived his wounds, except that while Dr. Bradley was probing for the bullet in his neck, the bullet came loose, lodged in his windpipe and he choked to death.[36]

Through the court records, we discover that Ella Wilson (Watson) was smack dab in the middle of the Fenix-Lawrence fray. She was wounded in the neck and shoulder[37] and she was not the only witness. There were lots of others. There were several unnamed (of course) patrons, some other female inmates, and several fancy gamblers who were all there during the frenetic proceedings. Most of them immediately disappeared, of course, and could not be found to testify at the subsequent inquest.[38]

None of these events happened at nighttime, when things more naturally would be expected to be busy. This whole episode happened in the middle of the afternoon. This, then, was seemingly a very busy place—not just a sleepy, little out-of-the-way marginal enterprise somewhere out in the boonies. No, sir. This was clearly a very popular place.

At any rate Ella Wilson (Watson) became the prime witness for a suit by the Territory of Wyoming against Pretty Frank Wallace on the charge of "Assault with Intent to Commit Murder." Her written deposition, outlining the facts of the case, was made on the same afternoon as the shooting. Here she signed her name "Ella Wilson-X-her mark."[39] Whoever she was, this woman's official deposition splashes even more light on the case. She testified:

> Before the shooting Fenix and Lawrence went outside to talk. Lawrence was standing at the end of the counter. I saw [Pretty] Frank Wallace walk up to [proprietor] Lawrence and say 'What in the hell is wrong with you? You look scared to death!' And then when they came in, I heard Lawrence say to John Fenix 'I heard you came over to clean the place out!' and then Fenix put his hand back and cocked his six shooter before he pulled it out of his pocket. He shot twice at Lawrence before he

could get out of the door, and he turned around and shot me! I then saw Frank Wallace shoot at George Belden [a professional gambler] and then at Lawrence. I did not see Lawrence any more. I heard John Fenix say 'Shoot the son of a bitch!' I saw no one shoot but Fenix and Wallace.[40]

The doctor's report described Ella's wound as a:

"Flesh wound in neck and shoulder. Ball grazed left shoulder and entered neck on a line drawn from lobe of left ear to the spine of the second servicle [cervical] vertebrae, about two inches from lobe of ear, passed back of spine and came out nearly over the middle of upper line of right scapula. Powder marks on back of hand.

Signed J. N. Bradley, MD."

Ella Wilson (Watson) must have been right in the thick of things. With remarks such as "powder marks" and "in the doorway," it is clear she obviously came very close to death in this shoot-out.

Soon after these affairs, in 1886, Fetterman was bypassed by the Fremont, Elkhorn and Missouri Valley Railroad[41] and we hear nothing more of the hog ranch, because, a couple of weeks after the shooting, on the death of Lawrence, it closed its doors forever.

ﻉﻉﻉ

While the tale of this shoot-out at Fetterman is fascinating, there is absolutely nothing, except the similarity of names of Ella Wilson and Ellen Watson, to indicate that our original Ellen L. Watson ever went into the demimonde of prostitution.

In fact, we find that Ellen L. Watson has arrived in Rawlins, Wyoming, and has been engaged as a cook and domestic

Ellen Watson worked at the Rawlins House for about two years, from 1884 to 1886. This photo was taken a few years later in 1890. (Carbon County Historical Museum.)

in the Rawlins House which was indisputably the leading hostelry in town. It was owned by Mr. Larry Hayes and his wife Mary who, together with several pious and straight-laced women, operated the finest room-and-board facility in town. It had forty immaculate rooms with which to accommodate their guests. Ellen worked there about two years from 1884 until 1886.

Now, however, something else should be brought forward, so as not to omit even the tiniest piece of tawdry information. The police records of Cheyenne show that an Ella Watson was arrested June 23, 1888, in Cheyenne for drunkenness by Police Officer Ingles. It seems difficult to believe that this could be our Ellen L. Watson from what we know about her. But some authors have used this arrest to accuse Ellen L.

Watson of prostitution and unseemly conduct. One author even definitely declared that this arrest was on charges of prostitution. This is unfounded, however, since the police records state only "drunkenness" and further, there were no laws against prostitution at this time. In fact, according to historians and the census records of the time, prostitution was openly flaunted and rampant all over Cheyenne. It was an accepted business practice and arrests were not made.

It is highly improbable that our Ellen Watson was in Cheyenne because her father stated in his Rock Springs, Wyoming, newspaper interview immediately after his daughter's death, that Ellen had been visiting with her family in Lebanon, Kansas, for two months, June and July of 1888. It is impossible for her to have been in Cheyenne, unless her father lied about Ellen's visit to his Kansas homestead. Knowing Thomas Watson's highly-structured Presbyterian character and background makes this assumption unlikely.

Secondly, be reminded Ellen never used any other name but Ellen L. Watson on any document officially attributed to her. If Ellen had been in Cheyenne and had been arrested, she might have tried to hide her arrest from her family by using another name, but that hardly seems probable and would have been the flimsiest of veils anyway. Had she wanted to hide her identity, she would certainly have used some utterly fictitious name.

Lastly, it is likely that Ellen was actually a teetotaler insofar as her whole straight-laced upbringing and future conduct points only to such benign behavior. Her first husband's alcoholism must have further turned her against drinking. There was never any evidence that she imbibed at all, except for the editorial diatribes against her by newspapermen Ed Towse and Ed Slack following her death, which are far from accurate.

To this point in Ellen's life, we have been following the advancing footsteps of a fairly average, unnoteworthy young woman. But soon other threads will irrevocably intertwine with hers to weave a frightening historic fabric of murder and destruction. Her young life is soon to be snuffed out by unjustified violence.

5. JAMES AVERELL

His name was James Averell. He was born to John and Sarah Ann (née Oliver) Averell on March 20, 1851, near the town of Renfrew (about fifty miles west of Ottawa) in Horton Township, Renfrew County, Ontario, Canada of an English father and Scottish mother.[1] Ironically, Jim was born no farther than one hundred fifty miles from where Ellen L. Watson was born.

Jimmy, as his friends called him even in maturity, was the youngest of seven children. Practically nothing is known about Jim's early youth in Canada, but his father died around 1851, shortly after Jim was born and shortly after having immigrated into northern New York state. A couple of years later, his mother remarried a younger man named Philip Cahill, by whom she bore three more children, one of whom, Willie, shall later enter this story in an altogether strange and different way.

Around 1864, Jim's older sister, Sarah, met and married a young New York farmer named Able Cole.[2] Before long, the newlyweds moved west to Wisconsin, where they resumed farming in a relatively new and hostile midwestern environment. The area was heavily wooded and required a great deal of timber clearing before any farming could begin. They settled in the township of Rushford in Winnebago County near

Eureka.[3] To Sarah and Able Cole's marriage was born their first son, their second child, whom they named Ralph E. Cole. The threads of his tragically short life will also be intertwined with others to become part of this story.[4]

Young Jimmy Averell left his parents and became the ward of his sister and her new husband. Sarah and Able accepted the responsibility as Jim's legal guardians,[5] although Jim never changed his last name. It is not clear what became of Jim's mother, step-father, and the rest of the Averell and Cahill children, although evidence points to their having moved farther west to the area around Tacoma, Washington.

Upon Jim's new family's arrival in Rushford Township, Jim was enrolled in a tiny elementary school in Eureka, where he had the only schooling he was ever to acquire. Although motivated and bright, he was never to have the advantage of more than a year of high school education, for around age sixteen Jim left school and went to work as a sawmill hand[6] at the Alom Trow sawmill near Waukau about four miles east of Eureka. His employer indicated that during the four years Jim worked for him, he was a very dependable worker.

Previous authors have written that Jim Averell was a graduate of Harvard, Yale or Columbia. That was quite impossible. While Jim had no more than a ninth grade education at best, that was more than many of his contemporaries received. Jim was highly intelligent, had a handsome script, was considered rather more articulate than many of his peers, was extremely ambitious, and was a gentleman. These things must have led previous writers to speculate that Jim came from an upper strata background and obtained an Ivy League college education.

At age twenty, Jim joined the United States Army. A possible relative, General William Woods Averell of Civil War fame and who later served with the cavalry in the West, may

Jim Averell was an articulate man with a handsome script, but he was not Harvard educated as some have alleged. (Wyoming State Museum.)

have inspired Jimmy to also volunteer for military service in the West. Jim must have been anxious to try his wings. Under Able's and Sarah's signatures as Jim's legal guardians, Jim signed on at Oshkosh, Wisconsin, fifteen miles east of Eureka, for the first of two five-year hitches in the frontier army of the West. Many members of the Cole family were present at Jim's enlistment; in addition to Able's and Sarah's signatures as legal guardians, the papers were signed by Eddy Cole and M.A. Cole, his stepbrother and stepsister. Jim enlisted as a musician.[7]

He was assigned to Company H of the Thirteenth Infantry. His enlistment papers described him as five feet, six and three-fourths inches tall with light complexion, grey-blue eyes and black hair.[8]

He was ordered out to Fort Douglas, Utah, on the outskirts of Salt Lake City, where he no sooner arrived than he was marched off to Fort Fred Steele,[9] fifteen miles east of Rawlins, in the south-central part of the new Territory of Wyoming.[10]

The first part of his first five-year hitch was spent in relative tedium guarding the Union Pacific Railroad and visiting various other military and civilian outposts in the area.[11] There is no evidence that Jim's musical talent was ever used by the army, so we do not even know which instrument he played.

During this first hitch, the infantry in Wyoming was not engaged in any particularly hazardous duty. However while Jim was billeted in Wyoming Territory, he was engaged in several forays after livestock and horses stolen by Indians and white renegades. Later Jim used this skill in recovering livestock with distinction at Fort McKinney.[12] At Fort Fred Steele, Jim almost certainly made the acquaintance of Joe Rankin, one of the three famous Rankin brothers. Joe Rankin was the famous and trusted army scout for the Thirteenth Infantry during Jim's tenure there. Ironically, at Fort Fred Steele, he probably saw or met another well-known scout named Tom Sun, who will reappear in our story later.[13]

After about a year and a half, on November 25, 1873, Jim's unit was reassigned to Fort Douglas on the outskirts of Salt Lake City.[14] As fate would have it, they were soon again reassigned to Fort Steele and then north to the Sioux and Big Horn Expeditions. After the completion of the expeditions, in

October 1874 the troops were reassigned to Louisiana, and Jim was discharged at Port Gibson, Mississippi on May 22, 1876.[15] The remarks column of his discharge papers in 1876 refer to Jim as "a good, honest and reliable soldier." It is significant, however, that he received his first taste of Wyoming while still a very young man.

After Jim's discharge and return home in 1876, he apparently did not find life around Rushford very stimulating, because, during a trip to nearby Chicago, Illinois, after just a few weeks of civilian life, Jim re-enlisted on June 20, 1876, for another five year tour of duty.[16] On his second enlistment papers, he signed up not as a musician, but as a "laborer." The recruiting officer's name was Lieutenant Clayton Cole.[17] Although there is no evidence that they were related, it is a possibility as it was customary in those days for soldiers to recruit their relatives.

As odd as it may seem today, keep in mind that Jim never gave up his Canadian citizenship.

This time he was assigned to Company D of the Ninth Infantry, under legendary General George Crook whose military division seemed continually in pursuit of hostile Indians and distinguished itself at the Battles of the Rosebud and Twin Buttes. Except for a strange irony of fate, his old unit, the Thirteenth Infantry, almost certainly would have fought alongside Custer at the Battle of the Little Big Horn.[18] But so far, Jim's fortunes remained under a lucky star, and some time after his second enlistment Jim was promoted to the rank of sergeant.

As a member of Company D, Jim was engaged in reconnaissance and fighting Indians and renegade whites.[19] He was also assigned to duty in the construction of Cantonment Reno and subsequently its replacement posts, first Depot McKinney and then Fort McKinney proper. Fort McKinney was forty

Fort Reno where Jim began to learn the craft of surveying. (Wyoming State Museum.)

miles north of Cantonment Reno in north-central Wyoming. During the surveying and construction of these forts, Jim was exposed to the craft of surveying.[20]

During 1877, Jim's outfit was assigned to construct a telegraph line from Fort Fetterman to Fort McKinney along the Bozeman Trail. The line was completed on January 17, 1878, when the first message was sent across the wires. It was the first time wire communication had been established north of Fort Fetterman into Powder River country.

Soon Sergeant Averell and a corporal received an assignment off the miliary reservation at Fort McKinney to recover illegally acquired heating stoves from O'Dell's dance hall, the closest of the disreputable business establishments east of the fort in the fledgling town of Buffalo. They returned immediately with the confiscated property without incident.

In October 1879, Jim was given a new command. He was placed in charge of the troops still stationed at Depot McKinney. He returned there with two privates to guard and defend the buildings, together with the remaining material and supplies, until they could be shipped on to Fort McKinney. On

December 1, 1879, Depot McKinney was abandoned, and Jim delivered his troops back to the main fort.

Jim was then selected for several special assignments against Arapahoes and Crows, as well as against marauding white renegades. At the special request of the famous interpreter and military scout, Frank Grouard, Jim was handpicked to accompany Grouard and a teamster on sorties north into Montana, even though Jim was in the *infantry*. Jim must have impressed Grouard as both a fine horseman and a good soldier. One of these sorties was documented in April 1880. It is most curious indeed that Jim was chosen over all the men of the seasoned, crack *cavalry* unit, both commissioned and non-commissioned officers, who were stationed at the fort.[21]

To be singled out and chosen by Frank Grouard in particular is not to be taken lightly. General Crook believed Frank Grouard was the finest and most indispensable man in his entire command.[22] Their mission was to pursue, attack and capture renegade bands of both Indians and whites, who were preying upon and stealing civilian horses and other military property. They were to capture the offenders, recapture the stolen property and return all to the fort. The thieves were then prosecuted and the property returned to its rightful owners. Jim later received official recognition for his part in the work.[23] It was further stated by his superior officers that he was a "good soldier and excellent with his men."[24]

The soldiers often found relief from the tedium of military life by visiting the little town of Buffalo which had sprung up along Clear Creek, a few miles east of the fort. On February 12, 1880, Jim purchased a small house in Buffalo from David and Kittie Mills which had apparently been used partly as a bar, or at least it stored some of the accoutrements of a bar. Jim converted it to a one family dwelling which he rented out to the town jailer, Robert B. Rankin and his family. Rosa,

Rosa Rankin and her husband, jailer Robert Rankin, rented Jim's house in Buffalo. Later Rosa Rankin foiled the escape attempt of Big Nose George from the Carbon County jail. (Carbon County Historical Museum.)

Rankin's wife, also cooked the meals for the prisoners. According to the 1880 census, Averell kept one room for himself and another boarder and must have slept there on overnight visits to town. So Jim became a property owner. He didn't squander all his army pay the way most unmarried enlisted men did, for apparently he had saved enough to buy the building without floating a loan.

Jim Rankin was a lawman in Buffalo and later in Rawlins and was a friend of Jim Averell. His brother Robert served as jailer and his sister-in-law Rosa fed the prisoners in both towns. (Carbon County Historical Museum.)

He soon became a long-lasting personal friend of both the Robert and Jim Rankin families, who lived near each other in Buffalo. The Rankin family left a substantial mark on the history of Wyoming. Another Rankin brother, Joe, was the famous guide and scout mentioned earlier in connection with Fort Fred Steele, where he may have been acquainted with Averell. Jim Rankin was a deputy sheriff in Buffalo, and soon became sheriff of Carbon county and later U.S. Marshal. Jim's tenant, Robert Rankin, who was the town jailer in Buffalo, later assumed the same job at the Carbon county seat in Rawlins.[25]

At some point before 1881, the Jim and Robert Rankin families were offered more important positions in the rapidly-growing railroad town of Rawlins. Since Averell's hitch was just about up, he sold his Buffalo building. In those days, it was customary to sell a building together with all the furnishings as one unit. On November 1, 1881, Jim completed the sale of the house with its furnishings to Henry B. Robertson.[26]

Probably as a result of reporter Ed Towse's later articles, some present-day historians have mistakenly equated this property with that of an early dance hall, saloon and house of prostitution owned by another Mills on the other side of Buffalo and surmised that Averell ran a bawdy house.

Let's dispel the confusion. Jim's property was occupied by the town jailer and his family, whose brother was the deputy sheriff of Buffalo. It is unlikely that the town's law enforcement officials would live in a house of ill repute.

Second, the house was in the early residential section in the south part of town, somewhat outside the business district, hardly a place to run a bar in competition with others like the famous Occidental Hotel and Saloon which was certainly the place in town where the action was. The established red-light district was on Laurel Street, more than a block away

Third, Jim's house, which is still in use, is far too small for the suggested illicit occupancy. The interior is quite clearly a one-family residence, with living (sitting) room, kitchen, three bedrooms, of which one was used to sleep a boarder or two—hardly a suitable arrangement for a place of wild debauchery. The Rankin home at 130 South Main Street, at this writing, houses a prestigious law firm. According to

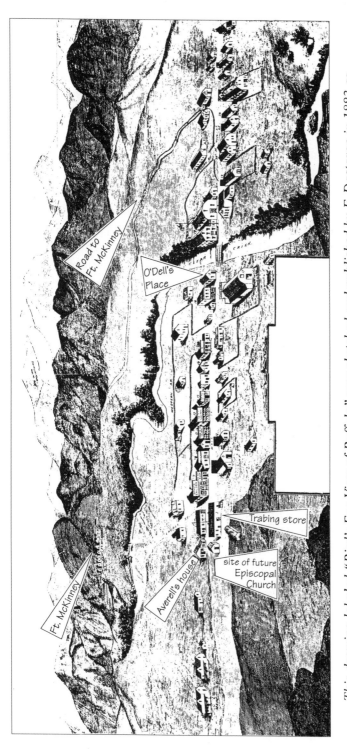

Road to Ft. McKinney

O'Dell's Place

Trabing store

site of future Episcopal Church

Averell's house

Ft. McKinney

This drawing labeled "Bird's Eye View of Buffalo" was sketched and published by F. Dastarac in 1883 as a part of an advertising sheet. Relevant locations are identified. (Courtesy of Johnson County Library.)

the present occupants, the room divisions are still pretty much as they were when Jim Averell owned it. Almost all of the windows and interior doors still sport the original wavy glass, brass door knobs and hardware, although the brass is now painted white.

The actual Mills Saloon, which was apparently part of, or right next door to Mrs. O'Dell's clandestine pleasure palace, was situated where the present-day Johnson County court house stands, on the other end of town from Jim's building.

Jim's one-family residence was north across the street from the future Saint Luke's Episcopal church and southeast from the Trabing General Store. One would hardly think of the clergy and congregation of the Episcopal church choosing a location across from a recent bawdy house, nor would such a location have been likely to win the approval of the ultimate church authority in the area, Bishop Ethlebert Talbot.

Somewhere in this previous period, Jim foolishly went "absent without leave" from the fort. He was court martialed, fined fifty dollars and demoted to private.[27] This kind of conduct and disregard for post discipline, however, was more the rule than the exception with soldiers stationed at lonely, isolated Western outposts.[28]

During the time Jim owned his house in Buffalo, he became embroiled in a controversy which led to his indictment on murder charges. A rough and ready local named Charles Johnson came to town from his nearby ranch fairly regularly, got drunk and started fights. He was a man of substantial proportions who enjoyed a brawl. He had a conspicuous police record and had killed a man named Charlie McLeod.[29]

There was bad blood between Jimmy Averell and Charlie Johnson. Later testimony revealed that people at the fort and in town knew about the threats Johnson made against Averell's life. At least that was the testimony of George Wanhamer and Almira J. Swalley, both residents of Buffalo and witnesses to the fight which took place.[30] Averell must have been seriously concerned about those threats, because he went to his new post commander, Colonel George W. Van Horn, with the problem. The Colonel was later to be summoned for jury duty and was elected foreman for the preliminary hearing which investigated the affair.[31] From witnesses' reports, this is what seems to have happened:

Somewhere around March 20, 1880, Jim must have insulted this bully named Charlie Johnson. Whatever the trouble was, Charlie was damned angry. Jim declared later he tried to stay completely out of Charlie's way. About a month later, however, on the afternoon of May 2[32] on his way to pay a visit to Buffalo, Averell confided to one of his buddies, Private Daniel Sleeper, that he was increasingly uneasy about Johnson's threats against him, but hoped nothing would come of them. However, sometime between one and two o'clock that afternoon, Jim was visiting Mrs. O'Dell's place, which was apparently directly adjoining the Mills Saloon,[33] when Johnson appeared in the doorway with fire in his eyes and liquor on his breath.

While Averell's back was to the door, Johnson came crashing into the bar. On hearing Johnson's noisy approach, Averell swung around and Johnson lunged heavily at him. Averell quickly pulled out his army revolver and told Charlie to keep back, that he didn't want a fight. Johnson kept coming and told Jim to put up his pistol, so he could beat the hell out of him. Johnson filled the room with his grumbling profanity.

Jim protested again that he didn't want a fight. It would hardly have been much of a contest, since Johnson was a big, muscular man and Averell was slight of build and only a little over five-and-a-half feet tall. Johnson then called Averell "a cowardly son of a bitch" and lunged forward again.

Upon those final intimidating words, Jim was said to have become "greatly excited" and fired a warning shot through the roof. Averell again told Johnson he didn't want to fight him but that he would not stand still for being called a "cowardly son of a bitch" again. Seemingly undaunted, Johnson kept on coming. Jim warned him again, but when Johnson got too close, Jim fired a second shot downward which stuck Johnson in the left leg. Johnson wheeled around, or was wheeled around by the force of the heavy military bullet, and a third round struck Johnson in the back. The subsequent doctor's report said the bullet "just missed the spine and entered his body to a depth of ten inches and a width of one half inch."[34] Whether Johnson was armed was never established. Johnson was put to bed by a friend, Frances S. Murphy, and a doctor was summoned. Johnson lived for another eight days before expiring.

The very next day after the shooting Jim hastily wrote a letter to N.L. Andrews, a Laramie attorney who had earlier lived in Buffalo and to whom Jim had already spoken about Johnson's threats. Jim obviously believed the attorney was planning to return to Buffalo to seek the position of County Attorney (later Andrews did). Jim wrote:

My dear Mr. Andrews,

You will no doubt be surprised to hear of my having shot Charlie Johnson, but I was compelled to do so, or be shot myself, according to his own words, which were not only spoken to me, but to others and the people at large. I sincerely regret that such things have to happen, but I avoided it by keeping out of his way since March 20, until yesterday, when he met me where I could not get out of his way in safety. You know the character of this

man. I want to know when you will be here, and if
you can assist me by counsel. I would like to see
you here, and, if you had been here, this awful affair
would not have happened, and you know I inti-
mated to you that I wanted to put him under bond to
keep the peace and leave me alone. Please let me
hear from you soon as possible, as your advice
[could] be of assistance to me, I believe.

   Respectfully yours,

   Jim Averell

Within two days of the shooting, Charlie Johnson's friend,
Frances Murphy, filed charges against Averell on Johnson's
behalf. Three days after the shooting, on May 5, a warrant
was issued for Jim which was served by Special Constable
John Spering. Jim was then detained in the Buffalo town jail
with bond set at $1,200 which was immediately posted by
Jim's close friends M. E. Hocker and Deputy Sheriff Jim G.
Rankin.[35] The next day Justice of the Peace O.T. McAllen
held a preliminary hearing under which Jim Averell was
found "guilty of assault with attempt to kill," and Jim was
again incarcerated in the local jail with new bail set at $2,000.
That bail was immediately posted by Thomas Cook, George
Powell, and by one of the pillars of Wyoming society, August
Trabing, a prestigious Buffalo merchant who later played a
prominent role in creating Wyoming's first constitution and
also was elected to the Wyoming Legislature.[36]

Bonds of one hundred dollars apiece were slapped on all
the various witnesses to try to guarantee their later appear-
ances. There were over a dozen of them—all but one favorable to Jim's defense.[37]

Let's clarify what that preliminary hearing was. It was
held to determine whether or not there was "probable cause,"

that is to say, sufficient evidence to bind Jim over to a formal inquiry by the district court. The "guilty" decision was actually improper at a simple preliminary hearing. The decision as to whether or not to indict for probable cause is the only proper function of such a preliminary hearing, but after all, these were territorial days and judges were lax concerning legal procedures. In Averell's case, Justice McAllen concluded in the preliminary hearing that there was sufficient evidence to bind over Averell to a grand jury hearing at the county seat at Rawlins.

At about the same time the Rankin brothers moved to Rawlins to accept more important, more prestigious and better paying appointive positions. After fulfilling their jobs as deputy sheriff and jailer to the satisfaction of the local constituency, Jim Rankin soon ran for and was elected sheriff of Carbon County and his brother, Bob, was reappointed jailer.[38]

As sheriff, Rankin ordered two deputy sheriffs, a man named Cook, who had already helped post bail for Jim, and another man named Flavin, to proceed to Buffalo and escort Averell to Rawlins for a formal hearing. They arrived back in Rawlins on May 26. Jim was still out on $2,000 bail, but he voluntarily housed himself in the Rawlins jail, where he was delighted to find Robert Rankin serving as jailer and his wife, Rosa, cooking for the prisoners just as she had back in Buffalo. Jim was invited to live with the Rankins at their new home in Rawlins, and he gratefully accepted. It seems that the jail was overcrowded in anticipation of the next session of the court which was to begin almost immediately.

In addition to being overcrowded, the Carbon County jail was about to receive an infamous and notorious inmate— "Big Nose" George Parrott. Sheriff Rankin was moving him under heavy guard from the territorial penitentiary in Laramie to Rawlins for trial on charges of murdering two well-liked

TERRITORY OF WYOMING, \ ss.
County of Carbon.   /

The District Court for said County and Territory, in the name of the United States, to any Sheriff in the Territory of Wyoming:

An indictment having been found on the ___14th___ day of ___September___ A. D. 188_0_ in the District Court for the County of Carbon, charging ___

James Averell

with the crime of ___

Murder

You are therefore commanded forthwith to arrest the above named ___James Averell___ and bring him before this Court to answer the indictment.

By order of the Court.

WITNESS ___J. W. Meldrum___ Clerk of said Court, and the Seal thereof, at Rawlins, this ___14th___ day of ___Sept___ A. D. 188_0_.

J. W. Meldrum
Clerk District Court Carbon County.

Deputy Clerk.

This bench warrant was issued for the arrest of Jim Averell on the charge of murdering Charlie Johnson. It was delivered to Averell by his friend Sheriff Jim Rankin in Rankin's own home where Averell was staying. (Wyoming State Museum.)

police officers from Rawlins. It is logical that jailer Bob Rankin wanted to have as few prisoners as possible, so as not to interfere with his careful guarding of the egregious Parrott. The townspeople were already plotting to greet Parrott with a lynching bee, and the Rankin brothers knew it.

A year or so earlier, not too far back east along the railroad tracks, the citizens of the "Hell on Wheels" coal mining town of Carbon had already lynched Parrott's former partner in crime, "Dutch" Charlie Bates, by violently yanking him off the train and perfunctorily lynching him from a telegraph pole by the station, before the authorities could get him safely back to Rawlins for trial. Neither of the Rankin brothers wanted a repeat of such an act in Rawlins.

Because Averell had been unable to round up a sufficient number of his important witnesses, his Rawlins attorney, Homer Merrell, also a justice of the peace, and soon to be the district judge, kept filing petitions for continuance to the next regular session of the district court, which were regularly granted.[39] On September 17, the Carbon County judge in Rawlins again issued a bench warrant for Jim's arrest and appearance, which was delivered by his good friend and former neighbor Jim Rankin, right in Rankin's own home. Averell promptly accompanied the sheriff down the street and into the courthouse, together with as many of the available witnesses as they had been able to round up.[40] Apparently neither Rankin's position as sheriff nor the charges against Averell had altered the warm regard the two men had always shared for each other.

At the next grand jury hearing in Rawlins, Jim was re-indicted and placed in jail again, this time with a new $1,200 bail. It was promptly posted by two more good friends, M.E. Hocker, who had previously posted Jim's earlier $1,200 bail in Buffalo, and a Mr. Powell of Rawlins. Judge Jacob B. Blair then adjourned the grand jury until the next regular session. The grand jury was regularly reconvened again on October 8, but there was a full docket of other serious cases which caused another delay in Jim's trial.

Somehow, because of the inordinate delays caused by the granting of continuances, one after another, together with the court's desperate search for Jim's supporting witnesses, his bond expired, and he was again temporarily incarcerated, this time with Big Nose George during Parrott's widely publicized murder trial. Big Nose was finally convicted on December 15,

1880, of the first degree murder of two exemplary and well-liked Carbon County law enforcement officers and sentenced to die on the gallows on April 2 of the next spring. Jim Averell was still in jail during Big Nose's famous jail-break attempt, when he used a penknife to saw through his shackles and clubbed jailer Bob Rankin completely senseless with them as Rankin tried to keep him from escaping. Rankin's wife, Rosa, who had arrived to deliver the prisoners' meals, rushed over, slammed and locked the iron cell door in Parrott's face, thereby frustrating Big Nose George's last chance to escape. She then ran screaming into the street shouting for help.

The people of Rawlins became outraged with what had happened to Bob and Rosa Rankin and a vigilance committee, now convinced that a hanging date of April 2 was much too distant, forced their way into the jail house, subdued the Rankin brothers, and dragged Big Nose outside where they pushed and shoved him down the street to a telegraph pole next to the railroad depot. He begged them with tears in his eyes not to strangle him, but they were unmoved by his pleas for mercy and roughly put a hemp rope around his neck and the telegraph pole, forced him to stand on a barrel, and summarily kicked the barrel out from under him.

Parrott was a big man of six foot, two inches and when the barrel was kicked away, Big Nose's feet rested on the ground. Someone shouted for a ladder, one quickly appeared and was leaned up against the telegraph pole. This time Big Nose George was forced to climb the ladder. When part way up it was rudely yanked out from under him, and he dangled helplessly in midair.

In the haste of the moment, however, the amateur vigilantes had neglected to tie his hands. Big Nose desperately wrapped his big arms around the pole, but because of the heavy hand-made shackles around his ankles, he was unable to climb up the pole. Before long he inevitably tired, relaxed his arms, slowly slid down the pole and strangled to death in plain view of the hundreds of people who had gathered to watch the final grisly moments of the lynching. Jim may very well have witnessed these events from his cell window. In any event, whether he actually saw the events or not, he could not have helped but hear the raucous shouting and screaming. It would have been impossible to have misinterpreted their meaning.

Later, a death mask was made of Big Nose George's face and head. It was then that it was discovered that he had rubbed his ear off against the coarse hemp rope during his death struggles. It must have been a frightening time for Jim Averell. He may well have wondered if he were to be next. After all, he too was incarcerated for alleged murder.

Jim's attorney, Homer Merrell, soon to be District Judge, kept gaining further continuances. Sufficient witnesses, who were essential to Jim's defense, still could not be located. Finally, on April 12, Jim's loyal friend, Sheriff Jim Rankin again posted bail, and this time Jim was out of jail for good.

Eventually Jim's case was dismissed because the court ruled that, since he was an enlisted man, his case was a matter for the military courts and that the civil courts therefore had "no jurisdiction."[41] Jim Averell was finally freed and was never found guilty of the charge. He must have felt very happy, indeed, after such a long period under arrest. As a military man, he reported to the commandant at nearby Fort Fred Steele, where he had been stationed during his first hitch nearly ten years previous. He requested transportation back to Fort McKinney. However, because he had nearly completed his second hitch, which expired on June 19, 1881, he was assigned to work in quartermaster's supplies there at Fort Fred Steele until his honorable discharge.[42] As far as

Jim was honorably discharged at Fort Fred Steele where he had earlier been stationed. (Wyoming State Museum.)

can be determined, Jim never received a court martial from the military.

During Jim's ten years in the army in Wyoming, he had often traversed the beautiful, green-grass valley of the Sweetwater River north of Rawlins.[43] The army made regular and frequent wagon trips through that country carrying supplies, rotating personnel and packing the mail southwest or northeast up and down the military road between Fort McKinney and Fort Fred Steele. About fifteen miles north of Rawlins at a stage station known as Separation, the road divided and an alternate civilian route went directly south to Rawlins Springs which was also along the railroad but situated fifteen miles west of Fort Fred Steele. Since there were apparently never more than two infantry sergeants at Fort McKinney at any one time and such trips seldom required a fully-commissioned officer, Sergeant Averell quite possibly would have been assigned to escort and oversee these transportation details on a regular basis.

Jim must have become thoroughly enchanted with this beautiful, nearly virgin Sweetwater country which was begging to be settled up. In addition to that, he could not have avoided hearing about the Timber Culture Act, the other homestead laws and the Desert Land Act opportunities and about the tantalizing fortunes being made in the agriculture and livestock business in Wyoming. He must have longed to own his very own farm and be his very own boss free from military overview. Since he was soon to be a civilian again, he made plans for his future.

After his discharge, Jim took a job to supplement what he had saved from his army pay so that he could file for a homestead. He purchased the necessary supplies to build a house and bought a wagon, horses, barbed-wire and farm machinery with which to earn a living while proving up on his claim. Even then he didn't have sufficient money for everything.

Then, Jim took the bull by the horns and filed as a former serviceman on his first 160 acres of virgin grassland on Cherry Creek under imposing Ferris Mountain in the beckoning Sweetwater River Valley north of Rawlins. He must have been almost electrically charged about the future. But Jim's luck was soon to change.

6. Homesteading

After his discharge in 1881,[1] Jim stayed on at Fort Steele, working for the sutler, John William Hugus, who also operated as a banker. One year the store alone did a business of $350,000, so it was by no means a small operation. It was the largest business in Carbon County at the time. Encouraged by the success of his Fort Steele operation, Hugus started another successful bank and general store in Rawlins. Soon he had other business locations in Saratoga and South Pass City, Wyoming.

While Averell worked there, the sutler's operation at Fort Fred Steele was managed by a green, twenty-year-old accountant from the East, later to become Wyoming's Acting Governor, stuffy Fenimore Chatterton.[2] After only six months, Jim apparently had a "craw-full" of Chatterton and quit. Later it became clear that Chatterton was only a fair weather friend, although John Hugus himself would remain Jim's lifelong friend. Jim collected his pay and returned home on the railroad to his sister and brother-in-law's farm outside of Eureka, Winnebago County, Wisconsin.

During this visit Jim was stunned to meet a young lady by the name of Sophia Medora Jaeger, whom he remembered from years before as a cute, little gangling girl in grade school. During his decade in the army she had blossomed into

This photograph of Sophia Jaeger is believed to have been taken about the time of her marriage to Jim Averell in 1882. (Courtesy of Lawrence Jaeger.)

a most attractive young woman. Sophia was the ninth child of a family of twelve children. The family had spent some time in New York State, as did the Cahills, before moving west to Wisconsin. One of Sophia's older sisters, who had earlier been in the same class with Jim, said she remembered him as a fine young man.

Jim was so smitten with this young lady that he set about courting her ardently, and before many moons had elapsed, the two of them had fallen in love. She was twenty-one and Jim was thirty. Following a whirlwind courtship, the two lovers were engaged. Sophia's iron-willed Prussian father, Johann (John) Philip Jaeger, disapproved of the marriage, although her mother, Maria (Mary) M. Jaeger [née Durr] seems not to have shared the same sentiment. But in true Victorian Prussian style, Mary yielded to her husband's absolute authority. Sophia's parents had immigrated from Prussia. Her father was from Wurtemburg, and her mother from Baden.[3] Sophia therefore spoke fluent German, although she didn't write or spell it very well.[4] She may have acquired her German language skills at home, although schools were often taught in German in the widespread Prussian-American communities of that era.

Papa was apparently a highly-structured, straight-laced, nineteenth-century Victorian. No clear reason for his disapproval has been discovered, except, perhaps, for the difference in ages of Jim and Sophia, although such an age differential was not uncommon either in Prussia or in America. But the father's disapproval was adamant indeed.[5] Her father swore to disown her if she married Jim, and adjured her further that if she persisted in marrying Jim Averell she would never again be welcome under his paternal roof, unless, as he prophetically announced...unless or until she were to "return home in a box!"[6] That dreadful and ominous proclamation came back to torment the uncompromising father for the balance of his seventy-six years, for young Sophia had only a little over six months of living ahead of her.

In spite of her mother's pleadings, Sophia's angry father expelled her from his house, and Sophia went to live nearby with her brother Ed's family. The two young lovers doggedly proceeded with their wedding plans. Sophia chose the material and made her own wedding dress. The nuptial date was set for February 23, 1882, on the occasion of Sophia's twenty-second birthday.

They were married on a snowy day at three in the afternoon by the Reverend Robert Blackburn in her brother Ed's

This photo of the first Averell homestead was taken after the Butler Brothers acquired it. Averell's original one-room home was the right front portion of the larger building on the left. The Butlers added onto the house as well as adding the additional outbuildings. (Courtesy of Ruth Beebe.)

home.[7] Sophia's mother, her many brothers and sisters and their spouses were in attendance, together with the entire Cole family. Sophia's father, however, stubbornly boycotted the wedding. All in all, it must have been a very bittersweet day for Sophia and Jim.

After a short honeymoon, Jim entrained back to Rawlins alone to get his new Wyoming homestead in shape and make preparations for his bride's arrival.[8] As soon as possible Jim sent for Sophia, and they were reunited in early May 1882 at the railroad depot in Rawlins, a town of about twelve hundred residents.[9] It was raining heavily, and Jim wisely decided to wait before starting out across the soaking wet prairie for their new homestead. They stayed over in Rawlins for two days at the home of Jim's close friends, the Charles Lawry family, while the weather and roads dried up. Charlie and Jim had known one another several decades before when they were boyhood friends back in Ontario.

On May 7, the newlyweds climbed into their buggy and drove fifty-five miles north-northeast to the tiny, but thriving and prosperous, hamlet of Sand Creek (also known as Ferris Post Office) in the Sweetwater Valley just north of the Seminoe Mountains. Sophia wrote in letters home to her sister that it was so much nicer there than in Rawlins, which she remarked was too noisy [because of the railroad], had no sidewalks and had sandy, alkaline soil which didn't seem to grow anything.

Jim had already started to improve his new 160-acre Desert Land Act homestead and was anxious to show it to his new bride. Jim had not yet finished with the house, so Sophia was invited to stay in Sand Creek with the family of Jim's friend, influential rancher James V. Cantlin. Cantlin ran a herd of about 250 cattle nearby and was Carbon County Deputy Sheriff and had been since 1878. He was also the postmaster of the Ferris Post Office in Sand Creek. The Cantlins greeted Sophia with hugs and kisses and, according to Sophia, made her feel just like family. Before the day was out at least a dozen couples had paid her a visit and made her feel at home, and, according to her letters, Sophia was deliriously happy.

In a letter to her sister and brother-in-law, the Bradleys, Sophia confided that it was Jim's plan to improve the claim sufficiently to sell it, then to move on and repeat the process.[10] That summer Jim took a job on the ranch of a cattleman friend named Sharais on Pete Creek, a mile or two east of Jim's homestead, where he helped put up hay and worked as an all around ranch hand. The surveying skills he had learned at Fort McKinney soon came in handy, because, for the following summer or two, he accepted the invitation of state surveyor William (Billy) Owens to help survey the lower Sweetwater

Valley. Interestingly, later Billy Owens arguably became the first person to climb the almost 14,000 foot peak of the Grand Teton in what became Grand Teton National Park, Wyoming.

The Averells' new home was a pleasant thirty-foot by thirty-two foot one-room house, with a covered front porch which faced east toward the morning sun.[11] That way the front door also faced away from the prevailing southwest winter winds. It was in the middle of a slowly rolling, grassy plain, on Cherry Creek which supplied abundant year-round water for irrigation and domestic use.

According to Ruth Beebe, daughter of Stewart Joe Sharp who later purchased the ranch [Sharp bought the ranch from the Butler brothers who had earlier purchased it from Jim Averell], the house was fitted out with comfortable furnishings, most of which were purchased second-hand from Averell's friends, the Charles Lawrys in Rawlins, upon the Lawrys' decision to return to the state of Maine. Jim wanted to buy a pump organ for his musically talented bride, but she talked him out of it, because, she avowed, that would be far too extravagant. Sophia raved about the furniture. Some of the other furnishings had been shipped out from Eureka. Jim's new bride did not face the hard-packed dirt floors covered with gunny sacks and the inside walls covered with old newspapers that many frontier women tolerated.

The pioneers often moved furniture, pianos and delicate, breakable items across the bumpy prairie in an interesting way. Loose grain was shoveled in, under, around and over whatever was being shipped in the freight wagon. Two cargoes could then be shipped safely at the same time.

Still treasured by Ruth Beebe's family is Jim and Sophia's lovely Prussian-made, brass-pendulum wall clock in handsome black walnut with frosted-glass swans and artwork. It may have been a wedding gift from Sophia's mother or perhaps her brothers and sisters. Beebe inherited it from her father, Stewart Joe Sharp.[12] Ruth Beebe's daughter, Virginia MacIntosh, and son-in-law, Bill, still live and ranch on Averell's first homestead and occupy the original house, which is now part of a much expanded ranch home.[13]

Before long, Sophia discovered they were to be blessed with a baby.[14] The young couple was overjoyed. Preparations were made for the baby. The joy and excitement, however, was crushed by a premature birth.

On August 28, 1882, Jim wrote the following lachrymose letter to Sophia's sister and brother-in-law:

> Dear Bro. and Sister Bradley,
>
> Well, my dear folks, I must tell you our little 5 months old boy came on the 23rd inst. at 6:30 AM and stayed with us until 1 PM that day. We were visiting Mr. Cantlin's folks at the time, although I had gone over to my own place and was not with her that night. However, I was sent for, and it drove me to bed until today. Phila [probably pronounced "pheela," the way Sophia pronounced her name as a little child] is doing well, and we have a good house we rented to live in town [Rawlins] soon as she is able to ride in.
>
> You can imagine how bad we both feel. We miss our dear little boy. We loved him as much as if he was older. He cried from the time he was born until he died. Seemed as if he was fighting for his life for a long time; and when he died he put a little hand over each eye, and, according as he left us, his little body turned white commencing at the points of his little fingers. You probably know how to sympathize with us. And I believe

You can immagine how bad we both feel, we miss our dear little boy, we loved him as much as if he was older. He cried from the time he was born until he died, seemed as if he was fighting for his life for a very long time, and when he died he put a little hand . each eye and according as he left us his little boddy turned white commencing at the points of his little fingers, You probably know how to sympathize with us. and I believe you are both true-hearted toward us both, I will have to go to Rawlins tomorrow or the next day and as soon as Phila is   in   and   she and I will live there.

Love to the babe and you both

Jim Averell wrote home to Sophia's sister and brother-in-law reporting the death of the baby. This is the second page of a two-and-a-half page letter. (Courtesy Lawrence Jaeger.)

you are both true hearted toward both of us. I will have to go to Rawlins tomorrow or the next day, and as soon as Phila is good and well, she and I will live there.

Love to the babe and you both,

Jimmy.

P.S. We have not wrote to anyone on the subject but you and Min's folks [Min was Sophia's sister], but of course we will tell them in time.

Your loving brother and sister,

James Averell

Soon the young couple discovered that the bereaved mother was beginning to exhibit the symptoms of what was then called "child bed fever," a common aftermath of birth even into this century. Mrs. Cantlin and Jim tried everything they knew to do, but still Sophia did not respond well. The nearest doctor was in Rawlins. It was not uncommon for a frontier doctor to travel one hundred miles on horseback or by buggy to fulfill his duties. Even then, if he were fortunate enough to arrive in time, the tools he used, his primitive medicines, the crude facilities at hand, and the knowledge he possessed, often proved inadequate.

Jim disconsolately returned briefly to the homestead, packed up a few things in their buggy and drove back to the little hamlet of Sand Creek. In the meantime Mrs. Jim (Cora) Cantlin got her sister-in-law, Mrs. William (Jane) Granger, to help, and the two women did everything they knew how.[15] Knowing that Sophia was in the kindest of hands, Jim rode to Rawlins to find a doctor.

Three doctors practiced in Rawlins, but only one, Dr. Thomas Maghee, routinely made such long journeys to treat patients. Maghee was an unselfish doctor who was on retainer to the Union Pacific Railroad. Jim prayed he would

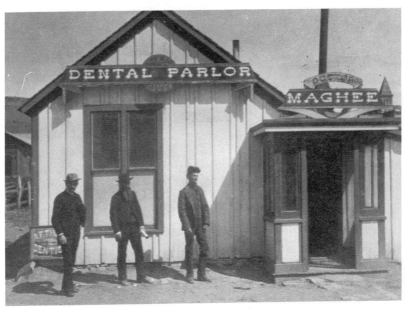

Doctor Thomas Maghee (in center) attended Sophia Averell. He is shown in front of his Rawlins office. (Carbon County Historical Museum.)

be available. His prayers were answered. After learning of Sophia's illness, the doctor snatched up his black bag, and the two men hurriedly set out together for Sand Creek, forty-five miles away. Upon his arrival the good doctor determined that there was very little he could do to help Sophia. He confided to Jim that, in his best medical opinion, there was precious little time left for her.

On September 6, 1882, Jim summoned his courage and wrote the following soul-shattering letter to Sophia's mother, which Dr. Maghee delivered to the post office in Rawlins:

> My dear mother, and all who love my dear darling wife,
>
> Phila lost her little child by miscarriage on the 23rd inst., and I am heart broken to say it, but, the chances are against her living very long. 'Tis sad

news for you, but I am heart broken, and loathe to
tell you. O, my only beloved one on earth. I know
I will follow her soon.

> Your loving son,
> James Averell[16]

Jim could not have known how prophetic his closing
words would prove to be.

Thoughtful Mrs. Cantlin, who, together with her sister-in-
law, Mrs. Granger, had ministered day and night to Sophia,
sat down at her desk and wrote the following unsolicited letter
to Sophia's parents:

> Mr. and Mrs. Jager,
> When your daughter first came to this country
> her husband brought her to our house, and so our
> acquaintance began and we were the best of
> friends. When she heard that my babe was born,
> she was very anxious to see him, and she came to
> make me a visit.
> Her and her husband, thinking it would be for
> the best for her, for them to move to town [Rawl-
> ins] this winter, he brought her [to Sand Creek] and
> left her for a visit. That is, I mean, my sister in law
> [Jane Granger] and myself. He left her and went in
> town [Rawlins] and rented a house and bought fur-
> niture and all and when he came back she was not
> well, but we did not think of what was coming.
> Nor after she was taken worse dast we think she
> was dangerous until the Dr. told us, and then
> Jimmy wrote you and sent it by the Dr. to the P.O.
> Dear friends if she had been at home you would
> not feel near so bad, but her husband done all that
> could be done. He stayed by her night and day,

In 1882 Sophia Jaeger and her mother and father posed in the family cemetery plot. Six months later, Sophia died in Wyoming. Her body was returned to Eureka, Wisconsin and was buried in the same plot. (Courtesy Lawrence Jaeger.)

never left, and we done all we could for her. She was sick in a very comfortable room and had everything she asked for. She was sensible [awake and aware] when she left this world of care and told Jimmie to tell you she loved you all till the last.

But God does all things well. Sometimes in our sorrow we don't think that it is so, but He will send over the poor stricken heart peace and a blessing if we ask for it, and that is all we need.

I will close with love and prayer for you all.

I remain, Mrs. Jas. V. Cantlin[17]

Jim's grief at the loss of both his baby son and the wife he adored must have been intense. He drove to Rawlins with the bodies with him in the buggy. He sorrowfully left his two loved ones with his friend, Coroner James A. Bennett, who prepared them for the rail trip home to Eureka. Such a short time ago, there had been such happiness. Now all of that had vanished.

Before long Jim received a note from Sophia's brother Ed advising him that he would reimburse Jim for shipping the bodies back to Eureka. Jim accompanied the bodies by rail to Sophia's parent's home in Wisconsin, where they were laid to rest in the family plot. The funeral services were performed by Mrs. Sedgwick, a Second Day Advent minister from the little town of Portage, Wisconsin.[18] Sophia's father's ominous and prophetic admonition to his daughter never to return home except "in a box" was tragically carried out.

Years later Minnie, one of Sophia's nieces wrote:

> It was such a tragic heart breaking time for them all. Grandpa [Sophia's father] was so mad he turned her out, and she went to Ed's home and was married there and went away. Then he [Sophia's father] had the nerve to bring her back dead. I wonder why he did that & then exacted that promise from Grandma not to look at her. He told Min [Sophia's sister] it was the Old Man's idea and he was disappointed after he went to the expense to bring her home. Said he looked at her the morning they got there and she looked real nice.
>
> Oh, it's all so heartbreaking to even think of now. Poor Grandma! Uncle Lew said when he got home [from the funeral], grandpa was pacing the yard behind the horse barn and poor grandma was walking the kitchen floor with her apron over her eyes. Only God could comfort them!

Two weeks after the funeral, on October 5, Jim returned to Wyoming. He tried to put his life back in order by throwing himself headlong into continuous, hard ranch work. On January 10, 1884, at the courthouse in Rawlins, he filled out the necessary papers to apply for U.S. citizenship and declared his formal intention to become a naturalized American citizen.[19] We find the following in Rawlins' Carbon County Journal of January 19, 1884. It reported:

"Mr. James Averell came in from the Sweetwater Saturday evening. He reports no snow in the Sweetwater valley. Cattle fat and stockmen happy."

With no loving family now to bind him to his first homestead, and with much to make him wish to leave it, Jim finished the house, completed the fencing and other earlier begun improvements to the land, and sold it to a couple of wealthy Philadelphia brothers, Frederic C. and Robert C. Butler, together with a partner named Horton.[20] Jim then packed up his things, put them in his two-horse farm wagon, and drove away, towing his buggy behind.

On July 22, 1885, Jim filed on his next claim about fifteen miles north of his first one, this time under the Homestead Act.[21] It was situated almost equidistant from and just between Horse Creek and the Sweetwater River, at the very east end of what was later called Averell Mountain.[22] It was distant from any other road ranch. Jim had learned that farming in the sandy Sweetwater Valley was difficult, and so this time he planned to supplement his farming income by serving meals, running a small general store with a bar in one corner, and selling the scarce fresh vegetables he raised. Jim not only planned to cater to the hungry civilian and military travelers with hot meals, but also to sell general merchandise and fresh farm produce for miles around to his neighbors, the scattered ranchers and cowboys.

Averell first built two sturdy, one-story, log buildings adjacent to the Rawlins-Fort McKinney military road that he had travelled while in the army. The dwelling consisted of sitting room, kitchen, dining room, two bedrooms and a large storage room in the back. The other log building housed the one-room general store, cafe and bar.[23] A third building, a rather different frame structure, will be discussed later. His was the classic Western road ranch, of which there were hundreds, and which were designed to serve an enormously scattered and varied clientele. A plan of the home and store is still extant which was sketched by John Fales, a Sweetwater resident and friend of the Averells who was a jack-of-all-trades. However, in later years, his sense of proportion must have failed him because the dimensions he outlined were too large. He described the log home as one thousand feet in length, certainly a miscalculation. The rooms would all have been gymnasiums. If scaled down, however, the proportions of the building and layout of the rooms appear to be about right. The actual dimensions of the home were fourteen feet by seventeen feet with a log addition of twelve feet by eighteen feet.[24]

Jim fenced in some parts of his land to keep the neighboring livestock out of his vegetable gardens. The operation must have kept him busy, with constructing new buildings, operating the store, trips to far away supply centers, and farming.

Jim had picked a strikingly beautiful location for his home and business. Miles of rich, level, green prairie extended down to a point where the Sweetwater ran into the larger North Platte River. The Seminoe and Ferris Mountains rose to the south, the Shirley and Laramie Ranges to the southwest, the Deer Creek Range to the northeast and the Rattlesnake Range to the northwest. Finally the Sentinel[25] and Sweetwater Rocks filled the extraordinary panorama. A dramatic setting.

Another important reason for selecting this location was the shelter afforded by the nearby Sentinel Rocks to the southwest in a valley noted for its prevailing southwest winds, especially bitter in winter. It was also close to the site Central Pacific was proposing for a connecting railroad.[26] The tracks were to run from Wyoming's southwest corner, northeast through the Sweetwater Valley, finally connecting with the westward moving Fremont, Elkhorn, and Missouri Valley Railroad.[27] Also deposits of almost pure natrona (soda ash) were found in the Sweetwater Valley just a couple of miles south of Jim's place. Fifteen miles northeast of Jim's homestead, an extravagant European style health spa was planned at Alcova Hot Springs. Finally an oil pipeline already had been surveyed to parallel the proposed Central Pacific railroad spur line. Jim's homestead site had many advantages.

However bad luck continued to stalk Jim Averell. This new Central Pacific railroad spur never materialized. When the minerals were mined, the soda deposits proved to be inadequate to warrant the spur line. Furthermore, although enormous capital was raised for the health spa, it was never developed because the project depended upon the spur line to bring tourists and health seekers and, to make things worse, the developers absconded for parts unknown with all the investors' money. To top things off, the pipeline plans were also put to bed for several decades with the loss of the proposed accompanying railroad spur line.

But still, Jim's venture was not a complete disaster. At first things went well for the little store. After all, it had the advantage of being brand new and it soon became a gathering place for the cowboys on the open range. In such a sparsely-settled area it could not, at best, have generated a large stream of traffic, but roundups involving plenty of cowhands were still held, and the military road bore frequent, but irregular,

traffic. Cattlemen and cowboys regularly resupplied themselves at the store with the basics, such as canned goods and
tobacco, and perhaps even a little something to wet their
whistles, as time and money allowed.

The next nearest road ranch was at Sand Creek[28] nearly
twenty miles south along the military road to Rawlins. There
was nothing along the road north of the Averell place for
twenty-five miles, till the tiny town of Bessemer. The Oregon,
California and Mormon trails passed by a mile or so east of
Jim's place, and they were still occasionally traveled.[29] Jim
had thought long and hard about this particular location before
investing his money in supplies, equipment and buildings.

The little store continued to do modestly well, but cowboys were notoriously short of cash and were only "in the
money" right after payday. Out on the range payday was often
held only at the end of a roundup, once or twice a year. Ranch
hands' wages included board and room, so the waddies[30]
never really lacked for much, but, on the other hand, they
never had very much either. Life on the open range was Spar-
tan indeed. Cowmen were notoriously self-reliant.

There was not yet a regular stage or mail line from Rawlins or Lander which connected to any of the newly evolving
communities like Casper, Glenrock or Douglas. This was very
much an isolated part of the world.

Before long, Jim had to borrow money from saloon proprietor and money-lender, John Dyer, as well as from J.W.
Hugus and Company, the bank of his friend John Hugus, for
whom he had previously worked at Fort Fred Steele.[31] Both
locations were in Rawlins which was the closest, and, initially, the only nearby resupply town.

During those days in Wyoming it was not unusual for a
person to run up a long credit tab to be paid off at some inex-
act future date, if the person was considered a good risk.[32]

Averell's credit and integrity must have been satisfactory, although sometimes, in letters, Jim complained that expenses and debts created a hardship on his limited finances.

As an example of Jim's occasional difficulties in paying his bills, the following is a letter to newly-elected Sheriff F. A. Hadsell[33] from the Sweetwater post office dated March 25, 1888. It is evident that his creditors were hounding him. Jim wrote:

> Dear Sheriff,
>
> Please deposit to the credit of E.A. Leuroot in the Bank of J.W. [Hugus] & Co. $35.00. Get certificate of deposit and send it to Mr. E.A. Leuroot of Box Elder P. O, Box Elder Co., Utah for me, as you will see by the enclosed bill of sale.
>
> Pay W.J. Smith of Rawlins for me $15.00. Pay R.H. Magor $10.00 and I will pay all my debts as soon as I can, but it is hard to make all ends meet. My dear sheriff, I will do the same for you some time.
>
> Very respectfully,
> James Averell

It would appear that, although Averell was getting along all right, he was still having trouble keeping up with his obligations. Certainly his business was not the "goose that laid the golden egg."

But a windfall occurred at this time to supplement Jim's income. On June 29, 1886, as an active Democrat, and through the efforts of newly-elected Democratic Governor Moonlight, Jim received a presidential appointment as the postmaster of the newly-created Sweetwater Post Office, and he received an additional appointment as a justice of the peace. At about the same time he was further awarded an

Devil's Gate, where the Sweetwater River passes through a chasm cut in granite, has been an important landmark in central Wyoming since the earliest days. (Author.)

appointment as a notary public. These appointments would create additional traffic through his little restaurant and store. Things were looking up for Jimmy Averell.

During his time on the range, Jim also learned about some flagrant illegal practices that were used by many cattle barons to acquire thousands of acres of public land. It was the practice of filing on 160-acre pieces under either the Homestead Act, the Timber Culture Act, or the Desert Land Act [the last of which was usually 160 acres, but could be up to 640 acres], and "ostensibly" performing all of the required prerequisites for future ownership—building a flimsy, portable, frame cabin to give the appearance of establishing necessary residency, filing for water rights, and pretending to irrigate the land. After five years, the "homesteader" obtained fee simple to the public's land.[34]

The key word, of course, is ostensibly. It was very difficult for the bureaucrats to administer the land acts properly from as far away as Washington. It also was possible for homesteaders to secure earlier title to the land by buying it outright after a minimum required length of residence of at least a year and a half. The price was $1.25 an acre, which in today's buying power would be about $12.50 an acre or around $2000 for an entire 160-acre parcel. Few homesteaders had that kind of money, so most of the homesteaders had to fulfill the five-year residency requirement.

Although a person could officially file on the land at regional points, such as Rawlins, the final administration of public lands was done in Cheyenne and Washington. The entire program was typical bureaucratic bungling. Because 160-acres was enough land for an adequate farm on the east coast , the men making decisions in Washington assumed 160-acres plots in Wyoming were also adequate. It was virtually impossible to survive on only 160 acres in Wyoming. So some way had to be found to circumvent Congress's ignorance.

So portable one-room, frame cabins were skidded from one claim to another. They were moved away from one newly-proven-up claim, over to a new one. These portable cabins were not set on permanent foundations, but on a few loose rocks. Then stove ashes, together with a wide selection of old bottles and tin cans, were thrown around the cabin as though it had been lived in for five years.[35] A horse-drawn ditcher[36] was used to make ditches, giving sufficient appearance that the land had been irrigated to satisfy the inspector.

All of these theatrics were simply to satisfy the state and federal bureaucrats who approved or disapproved ownership. If a question were raised by the bureaucrat, it was sometimes possible to bribe the inspector. In fact the process was so rampant, so out in the open, that many inspectors were simply paid off with a regular, periodic gratuity which served as a retainer assuring approval of all claims made by the cattle kings. Some inspectors gave preference to the huge landowners over the little homesteader, who was truly doing his double damnedest to prove up honestly on his claim. There was no money for the inspector in working with little homesteaders. No incentive.

Jim legally filed on an additional 160-acre claim on Horse Creek, under the Desert Land Act.[37] [A separate 160-acre claim could be filed under each of the land acquisition acts. Another filing under the same act was permitted if the previous claim under that act had been relinquished.] He then applied for and was granted water rights on Horse Creek for his new claim and proceeded to build four miles of irrigation ditches which meandered across Albert John Bothwell's illegally fenced-in pasture and hay meadow to Jim's road ranch a mile and a half away.[38] This move, although legal, did not further endear him to Bothwell who had previously controlled most of the land in that area. We will hear lots more about Al Bothwell in the pages to come.

Jim's filing was on an "L" shaped string of four, square forty-acre pieces which cleverly straddled the abundant, year-round, spring-fed waters of Horse Creek together with another unnamed intermittent stream just east of it. This effectively controlled the water out of Horse Creek from this point downstream.[39] It tied the water up, not only for Jim's irrigation, but also made it difficult for others to make use of it for either irrigation or stock watering, without Jim's express permission.

It is possible that Averell planned to sell his new homestead for the right price. Sophia, in her letter home to her sister in Eureka, Wisconsin, said Jim planned to establish, improve and then sell homesteads. That was common practice by clever homesteaders in the West. But Jim obviously did not want to face up to reality. He did not conceive of the explosive hatred that the location of his homestead would generate in the stubborn poseur, Albert John Bothwell.

Water is life in Wyoming. Make no mistake about it. This new homestead filing on Horse Creek, together with several other clever, but intimidating maneuvers to come, inevitably and irreconcilably nailed down the lid on Jim Averell's and Ellen Watson's coffins.

7. The Lynchers

JOHN HENRY DURBIN
(U T Ranch) [1]

John Henry Durbin was born in 1842 in Fayette County, Pennsylvania, one of six children of Irish Methodist parents, although John later attended the Congregational church.

He attended elementary school for only a few years.[2] As a young man he moved to Ohio where his first marriage ended with the death of his wife. He then moved to Aurora, Indiana, where he purchased a small farm and married again. His second wife also died; this marriage produced two daughters. During the Civil War, he joined one of the native Indiana companies and was commissioned a second lieutenant. After the war, he decided to move west and brought his daughters to Colorado in January of 1868. Sometime thereafter he married for a third time, and this marriage produced four sons.

He first settled in northern Colorado, where, with the money he saved from the sale of his Indiana farm, he invested in a herd of longhorn cattle which had been driven up from Texas. Colorado, by this time, was pretty well settled up, and the parcels of land were getting smaller and less suitable for large herds of cattle. On a visit to Wyoming, he was offered an opportunity to manage one of Amos Peacock's two Cheyenne butcher shops.[3] There he learned slaughtering and butchering. Soon his brother Tom also was encouraged to learn the trade and began to manage Peacock's other Cheyenne butcher shop.

After the devastating Cheyenne fire of 1870, Peacock became discouraged and sold his interests to the two Durbin brothers. Along with the purchase of Peacock's butcher shops, the brothers bought five hundred additional cattle and Peacock's slaughterhouse. Soon they secured meat contracts from the military to supply Wyoming's military forts with fresh beef. These five hundred head, in addition to the earlier herd of Texas longhorns, together with the slaughterhouse, was the beginning of a livestock empire which became famous in the Rocky Mountain West. In 1872, John permanently relocated his family to Cheyenne and built a substantial home at 2016 House Street. A third brother, George, followed the Durbin brothers to Wyoming.

In November 1876, John and his brother Tom moved to the Lead-Deadwood area of South Dakota during the Black Hills gold rush. They were successful at mining, and they purchased the Golden Terra mine, which was later sold to William Randolph Hearst. The mine was then renamed the Homestake Mine. The Durbin brothers sold it for a fortune, but it was only a fraction of its subsequent value after Hearst developed it. While the two brothers still owned the mine, John imported and operated the first gold stamp-mill in South Dakota. He also opened one of the first banks in Deadwood, but soon decided he was not cut out for the sedentary banker's life and sold his interest.

An exciting episode at this time involved a shipment of gold bullion from John's bank.[4] He had heard that Indians [nobody knew for sure whether it really was Indians] had learned of the shipment and were lying in wait for the stage along the route so they could rob it of its precious cargo.

This photograph, from a vintage newspaper, is one of the few photographs of John Henry Durbin. (Wyoming State Museum.)

Durbin then loaded a second coach with the actual bullion, allowing the regular stage to precede the other. Upon seeing the regular stage, the robbers attacked it, killing the driver and robbing all the terrified passengers, who then escaped by running into the brush and scattering to the four winds.

Finding nothing of the sought-after gold, the thieves suspected trickery and retreated just before the second stage arrived at the site of the ambush with Durbin's actual gold shipment. The brothers soon thereafter sold their varied interests and moved back to Cheyenne.

John seemed to have had the Croesus touch, even more so than his brothers. Every new project he began made profits. His venture into the livestock business proved to be his quickest and easiest money-making proposition. At first, his brother Tom was a rather reluctant partner in the cattle business. He decided not to follow John's footsteps exactly, although he participated passively, and even actively on occasion when it was necessary. One reason for his foot dragging may have been his strong interest in politics and the Republican Party.[5] Both John and Tom signed up in Cheyenne as charter members of the Laramie County Stock Association which soon became the Wyoming Stock Growers Association, the real future political powerhouse in Wyoming.[6]

Politics, however, apparently had no such stimulating effect on John. Brother Tom was not very tall and of slight build. John was also short, but more robust, and he took the bit in his mouth and worked the cattle business on the open ranges of southeastern and central Wyoming.

The third brother, George, never exhibited any desire to become involved in the cattle business. His interest was in sheep raising and, in his own right, he accumulated enormous spreads of land and livestock.[7] The Durbin brothers' livestock interests were to become among the most important in the Territory. A project that was started simply to resupply their own meat market made all the Durbin brothers multimillionaires. When John Durbin later sold his livestock interests, he purportedly owned over a million head. John later reverted to his earlier business interests and started a large meat packing enterprise located in several of the most important Western cities.

John Durbin was ruthlessly ambitious. He associated with the cattle thieves and rustlers in the Sweetwater country. He allied himself with two notorious cattle rustler brothers by the names of Nate and Clabe Young.[8] They were both long, lean Texans with sharp, granitic facial features. They purportedly had shifty eyes and seemed always to be looking around. Clabe, the foreman of Tom Sun's vast "Hub and Spoke" ranch, was wanted back in Texas for murder.

An investigator from Captain Turtle's Chicago Detective Agency named John M. Finkbone, formerly a range detective for the Wyoming Stock Grower's Association in 1883, was appointed to find and arrest Nate and Clabe Young.[9] As Finkbone traveled to the lower Sweetwater Valley, he ran into John Durbin and confided his mission to him. Durbin rushed back to the Sweetwater Valley and advised Nate and Clabe of Finkbone's mission and tried to frustrate the arrest of the two brothers.

Because of this forewarning, Finkbone was able to apprehend only Clabe. Finkbone took Clabe to Sand Creek where he slapped him in irons. Then he took Clabe on the stage to Rawlins where they boarded the train for Cheyenne. Clabe was held in the Cheyenne jail prior to his eventual railroad trip back to Texas under heavy guard. Durbin clandestinely followed Finkbone and Clabe to Cheyenne and promised Clabe that he would help get him off. Durbin even sent help to Clabe later while he was in his Texas jail cell.

Tom Collins, John Durbin's foreman, also a Texan expatriate, was known to be an out-and-out rustler—not only for Durbin, but even for himself. He often placed his own "Spectacle" brand on slick calves for his own fledgling herd. This met with stiff disapproval from Durbin, but he could do little without fear that Collins would blab to the Association about Durbin's illicit activity in retaliation. Collins was finally blacklisted by the Wyoming Stock Growers Association for rustling; Durbin was strongly chastised by his peers and was finally forced to discharge Collins.[10]

Robert M. GALBRAITH
(T Bar T Ranch)[11]

Robert M. Galbraith, or "Captain" as he preferred to be called,[12] was not a tall man, perhaps five feet, nine inches. He was of Scottish parentage, but had been born in England in 1844. He apparently received little education. His parents came to America in 1849 and settled in Alton, Illinois, where he lived till he was twenty-two. During the Civil War, he worked as a locomotive engineer on military railroads.[13]

He then moved to the West where opportunities were more numerous and exciting. Galbraith secured a job at the headquarters of the Union Pacific Railroad in Omaha, Nebraska, in 1866. His workmanship came to the attention of company executives, and at the age of twenty-two, he was put in charge of the railroad yards there. In 1867 he moved with his job to Cheyenne. The Union Pacific Railroad finally finished its link up with the Central Pacific Railroad at Promontory, Utah, in 1869. Galbraith was then placed in charge of developing and managing the newly-opened railroad yards at Laramie, Wyoming.

His next assignment was eighty-five miles west of Laramie at the new problem coal mining town of Benton, three miles west of Fort Fred Steele.[15] The mines at Benton supplied the puffing steam engines with fuel. Nothing is left there today but a few eerie mine shafts, some crumbling foundations and an almost forgotten and lonely little cemetery. But in 1869 it was a true "Hell on Wheels" tent town and was unchallenged as the raunchiest town in all the West. It lasted only three months. But what a summer!

Benton businesses included the Desert Hotel, Queen Hotel, North Star Saloon, Buffalo Hump Corral and the Belle Marie which vied for attention with other businesses adorned with red-bordered, self-explanatory signs. The Big Tent was a

Robert Galbraith was called "Cap'n" by his acquaintances. He came to Wyoming with Union Pacific and later was a member of the Wyoming legislature. (Wyoming State Museum.)

frame building forty-by-one-hundred-feet with a canvas roof. Altogether there were five dancehalls and twenty-three saloons in this festering town of three thousand. On weekends an additional thousand or so men came to town. And, when off duty, the soldiers from nearby Fort Steele helped swell the town's numbers. Fully one hundred lives were snuffed out during Benton's few days and nights which was reflected in the name of one popular establishment, Widow's Restaurant! But the railroad facilities still had to be managed seven days a week and, as the new superintendent of the railroad facilities there, "Cap'n" Galbraith struggled to maintain order—at least at the railroad yards.

After that successful assignment, he was sent even farther west to the mushrooming railroad town of Rawlins Springs, whose name was later shortened to Rawlins. Captain Galbraith was put in charge of all railroad operations there. In September 1870, he married Ophelia Smith of Jacksonville, Illinois, and they eventually produced three sons.[14] He became a pillar of the Presbyterian Church in Rawlins.

In 1870, Galbraith severed his employment with Union Pacific and tried his hand at mining. He relocated in the Seminoe mining district about thirty-five miles north of Rawlins. Here, he probably first saw the Sweetwater country which was only a short distance north of this mining district. He must have been impressed with the livestock potential of this grassy prairie land because he soon returned to it in a big way.

As a member of the Wyoming Legislature[16] from Carbon County, he was invited to escort a party of dignitaries, including Thomas A. Edison, on a special scientific expedition to witness the coming solar eclipse on July 29, 1878. The Separation Stage Station, thirteen miles north of Rawlins, allegedly afforded the most advantageous location in America from which to view the eclipse.[17]

After viewing the eclipse at Separation, Galbraith helped guide Thomas Edison on a fishing trip into the Sierra Madre Mountains in south-central Wyoming close to the border with Colorado. A famous Wyoming legend recounts that Edison broke his bamboo fishing rod on the heavy brush surrounding a wonderful fishing spot called Battle Lake. That evening Edison tossed his broken rod into the campfire and noticed how very long the fibers glowed without disintegrating. That event supposedly inspired Edison with the idea of a glowing filament within an incandescent light bulb and led to his experiments with the light bulb, back home at his laboratory.[18]

Some time later Galbraith gave up mining, left the Seminoe mining district, and returned to Rawlins. In 1882 he purchased a mercantile business. Apparently, Galbraith did not take to the sedentary nature of a businessman's life and longed for something more exciting. He was probably also enticed by the astounding profits being made in the cattle business around him.

He sold his interest in the store in 1884 and entered the livestock business. He took on a partner named Blake, hired Henry Hayworth as his foreman,[19] and began ranging cattle thirty miles southwest of Rawlins near the Sierra Madre Mountains in the dry south-central part of Wyoming. Galbraith soon experienced success and expanded his livestock holdings and land. This was not unusual. The cattle business was booming. The trick was to gain control to as much public domain grazing land as possible.

The Federal government suddenly cracked down on the use of the open range. The stockmen were stunned. They couldn't allow the open range which they had used without fees to be hacked up into 160-acre homesteads. The cattlemen had to do something, and do it fast. In order to secure ownership of the necessary giant tracts of range, the cattleman invented a device to circumvent the law.

Many big cattlemen required each of their cowboys, as a condition of their employment, to file on a 160-acre claim. Most cowboys were footloose and generally had no interest in being tied down to a piece of real estate. To reward a cowboy for filing, he was given a bonus of around fifty cents an acre.[20]

Now anyone with a grain of savvy, however, could easily see a much bigger opportunity than that. So the cowboys also started filing on dozens of 160-acre pieces of land in the names of their sisters and brothers and mothers and fathers and cousins and aunts and uncles and friends. The practice became so flagrant that even the dead began filing on and proving up on 160-acre homesteads. Before long, even dull-headed Washington discovered the extent of the fraud and put a moratorium on nearly all homestead patents. In 1886, for example, there were only two homestead approvals granted in all of Wyoming.

But the moratorium was too late. Nearly all the desirable lands had already been swallowed up by the cattle monarchs except in less desirable or less known areas. The Sweetwater country was one of these less known areas. But, the government pondered, what could be done at this late date about cattlemen having appropriated all this public rangeland illegally?

It could slap all the cattle kings in jail, but that was impractical. The government would have to put the richest and most politically powerful territorial magnates behind bars. That didn't make good political sense. Besides, a very large number of federal and state employees in Wyoming were somehow involved in this extralegal scheme. If the cattlemen, the cowboys, and the government employees were all involved, nearly everyone in the territory would have to be incarcerated! And if the government expected to get convictions, it would be necessary to get everybody to testify against everybody else. It became evident that nothing could be done, so the matter was quietly pigeonholed, over the objection of the usual noisy minority of do-gooders.

Galbraith became a wealthy man and acquired an interest in politics, the way many men do when they become very wealthy. After all, few poor men have the time or the money to run for office. So in 1884, Galbraith successfully ran for the Territorial Legislature representing Carbon County.

About that time Galbraith must have recalled the lush, native grass of the Sweetwater country, because just before the government cracked down on all those illegal filings, Galbraith expanded his operation in southern Wyoming into the Sweetwater Valley and began to run more cattle on the public domain. At that time there were hardly any cattlemen in the Sweetwater Valley, but the newcomers were increasing and beginning to file on rangeland there with gusto. In comparison to the rest of Wyoming, there was still quite a lot up for grabs there, and Galbraith was frantically grabbing.

Later in 1889, after dropping out of politics for a couple of years, he was elected to the Council, today's equivalent of the State Senate. Since the sessions only lasted a little over a month during the winter, politics didn't interfere with his spring, summer and fall range duties, but it certainly did allow him to introduce special interest legislation for himself and his livestock cronies.[21]

ALBERT JOHN BOTHWELL
(TW And Broken Box Ranches)[22]

His name was Albert John Bothwell, and he was born in 1855[23] in Iowa where he grew up. It was said his father was a wealthy merchant and early in life Al had all the benefits of his father's affluence, including an education at Yale or Harvard as a civil engineer with accompanying studies in law.[24] Many people have testified to his extensive knowledge of law, but there is no record that he attended Yale or Harvard at any time. A George W. Bothwell did attend Yale Divinity School in 1871, and he would have been the correct age to have been Al's brother by that name who came to Sweetwater country to co-invest with Al in his oil exploration fiasco.

Al may have led his acquaintances to believe he had studied at a big New England university to radiate additional prestige among his peers, although such an education would not likely have impressed the under-educated, but fiercely

Albert John Bothwell, seated in chair in foreground, ran cattle on public domain land where Averell and Watson each filed for homesteads. (Robert David Collection, Casper College Library.)

individualistic cowboys at all. If anything, it might have had the completely opposite effect. Pretentiousness has never been looked upon with favor by Wyomingites—not then or now.

Al Bothwell's trail seems to show that as a young man he first moved to southern California before moving to Colorado in 1880 to try his hand at ranching. Before long, though, he discovered that Colorado was becoming chopped up into little homesteads, and those who wanted to expand had no room in which to do it. He decided to move to relatively undiscovered

Wyoming where farming homesteaders were not yet arriving in droves and where he could still run his cattle on the free open range, so he sold his interests in eastern Colorado. Sometime around 1883, or perhaps even a little earlier, he moved into southeastern Wyoming and soon began to use huge sections of the open range. Before long he decided to expand into the area around the Sweetwater River in central Wyoming.[25]

Bothwell's main sphere of influence in the Sweetwater Valley was the country around the confluence of Horse Creek and the Sweetwater and North Platte Rivers, where he built his first ranch building at the northwestern end of Steamboat Rock.[26] He ran cattle in this valley extending up north to where the Sweetwater River finally dumped into the North Platte River. On the northwest, the land he used ran back up against the foothills of the Rattlesnake Range. To the south his spread extended more than twenty miles clear down to Arkansas Creek south of the Sentinel Rocks, and even south of Ferris Mountain to Bothwell Creek. The Sentinel Rocks will later assume an important role in this story. On the northeast, the range extended up from Horse Creek to within about twenty miles of where the Military Road crossed over the North Platte River on the old Government Bridge—a truly humongous hunk of land.[27] Now, Al Bothwell didn't actually own all this land; he just acted like it. And he sure as hell did that!

Al was not an altogether unlikable kind of person, especially if one were near his social strata, but he was just too puffed up to be genuinely warm and friendly with anyone but those of his own economic and cultural background. He was fairly tall for that time, perhaps six feet, with a reasonably big-boned, but trim physique. He sported a well-trimmed Van Dyke and mustache and, all in all, he made a very handsome and striking first impression.[28] He even had some of the locals believing that he was English aristocracy. He played the part to the hilt and regularly wore a red hunting vest beneath his jacket. His employees irreverently called him "Robin Red Vest" behind his back.[29]

Underneath he was a real promoter. He tried every imaginable scheme to gouge money out of Wyoming.[30] He even convinced his own brothers, John and George,[31] to come to Wyoming and invest in the Wyoming Land and Improvement Company, and tried to attract outside capital into what may likely have been a phony oil exploration enterprise. The *Casper Weekly Mail* said tongue in cheek:

> Bothwell's legacy to the Carbon county oil fields, in the shape of a fine piece of machinery going to waste, entirely deserted, and a thousand foot hole. This hole was bored some five years ago, and as nothing was struck it was abandoned and everything left on the ground.[32]

The three Bothwell brothers created the appearance of being engaged in both oil and gold, in part by referring to the dormant drilling equipment. The geological experts who had discovered both gold and oil in the Rattlesnake Range area, simply laughed at them.[33] Al Bothwell quietly and conveniently forgot about the dry hole he had put down. It seems to have been simply a ploy to bilk others out of their hard-earned savings. His brothers soon left Wyoming never to return, with George staying on a little longer than John.[34]

Al kept dreaming up ever wilder schemes. He plotted a new town a few dozen feet from his ranch buildings to which he gave his own name, "Bothwell," and he promoted Bothwell as the future capital of Wyoming.[35] He even unloaded a few lots. At its height, Bothwell consisted of a stable, a small blacksmith shop, Bothwell's primitive ranch buildings, and another building we will describe in a moment. He also tried to sell shares in two enormous irrigation projects, one involving Bear Lake, which straddles the border between Idaho and Utah, and the other project in the Sweetwater Valley,[36] and a gold mine which appears never to have existed.

The *Casper Weekly Mail* of August 16, 1889 wrote:

> The Sweetwater Land and Improvement Company, which proposes to deal in land and water rights in the Sweetwater Valley, has been incorporated with a capital of $300,000. The incorporators are John R. Bothwell, John C. Baird, J.C. Davis, E. P. Schoonmaker and Albert J. Bothwell.

Bothwell seems to have sucked several monied lambs into his sacrificial scheme. He was not only enterprising, he was devilishly clever.

He somehow convinced a young bachelor editor, named H.B. Fetz, and his assistant editor, J.N. Speer, to get in on the ground floor of his new town of Bothwell. After all, Al declared in promotional literature broadly distributed around the area, Bothwell was going to be the new state capital when Wyoming was admitted to the Union.[37] The two editors put up a frame newspaper office, set up their printing presses, and went to work. Heaven only knows who they thought they were going to sell their papers to or where their news would come from.

So, for the few months of its brief existence, the *Sweetwater Chief* [38] published a weekly newspaper. From comments made in the *Carbon County Journal* in Rawlins, it appears the *Sweetwater Chief* began publishing about April 1889.[39] This is not to suggest that Fetz and Speer were idiots. They were not. Upon the demise of the town of Bothwell, they moved their presses to Rawlins and successfully published a new rag under the name of the *Rawlins Republican*. Perhaps they had

Although Bothwell's wolves were kept penned, they seemed relatively tame. The man and woman are believed to be members of the Bothwell family. (David Collection, Casper College Library.)

fallen under the influence of Bothwell's imposing personality. Or it is possible that Al Bothwell underwrote their expenses at the town of Bothwell.[40]

Al Bothwell's wife, Margaretta, was pleasant, articulate and fancied herself a writer. Her marriage to Al was her second. She had earlier been married to a man named Church by whom she had two children.[41] According to several locals, the Bothwell family had their winter home in Los Angeles and they regularly visited Al's Broken Box ranch on Horse Creek, but it was said that his wife professed a distaste for such primitive and uncultured surroundings, although it was also said the children loved it. While visiting at the ranch, his wife draped herself in large, floppy hats, and wore high heels and fashionable city finery,[42] and generally did not seem to, or perhaps wish to, fit in with the locals.[43] Her visits to Bothwell's ranch on the Sweetwater seem to have been short. After sojourning for a brief period she and her children would then return to Southern California[44] to await Al's winter visit after he had fulfilled his need to daddle in cattle ranching, or whatever else it was he was daddling in at the moment.

It seems then, that after one of Margaretta's visits to the ranch, Al began daddling in the family housekeeper, Miss Wadsworth,[45] who was nearly ten years younger than Al, but whom most agreed was a most exquisitely beautiful young woman.[46] Some time later, she surprised Al with twin daughters. His first wife then divorced or legally separated from Bothwell and Miss Wadsworth promptly moved in with Al.[47] She bore him two additional children, a son John Randolph in 1897 and a daughter Ada in 1906.[48]

The famous naturalist, conservationist and author, Hiram M. Chittenden stopped and visited with the Bothwells during a trip through the Sweetwater country. He was looking for a suitable place to dam up the waters of the Sweetwater River near Devil's Gate. In May 1897 he wrote in his book, *A Western Epic*:

> I set out on horseback for the ranch of Albert J. Bothwell. I was treated to one of the pleasantest surprises I have ever met. I found as delightful a family as one could meet in any city. Mr. B. is an exceptionally shrewd business man and at the same time a very excellent scholar, his particular studies being in the line of geology and evolution. For the great teachers, Spencer, Huxley, Darwin, and Tyndall, he has an admiration amounting almost to worship. He

has a remarkably well equipped library and is a most interesting conversationalist. [Both Ruth Beebe and Edith Sanford of the Sanford family which bought the remaining ranch from Bothwell, attest that although the ranch house furnishings were relatively primitive, the walls of Bothwell's living room were covered with books.]

There was living with them a lady by the name of Wadsworth who was like the other denizens of this delightful spot engaging and hospitable to the utmost degree.

Mr. B. has built up an extensive ranch in the very lower part of the beautiful Sweetwater valley. He farms out portions of his ranch to small farmers, but finds great difficulty in securing competent men. He has a large amount of ditches on his lands and, take it all in all, seemed to me to be very well "fixed".

In the evening the ladies sang and performed on the piano. At 10 PM I retired.[49]

TOM SUN
(Hub and Spoke Ranch)

Thomas de Beau Soleil was his original name.[50] The family was of French Canadian ancestry. The name was later Anglicized to Tom Sun. Tom was born in Vermont on February 28, 1846, and when he was only eleven years old his mother died, and Tom ran away from home.

Some time later he arrived in St. Louis, Missouri. A beaver trapper named Descoteaux, who had trapped in Wyoming as early as the 1830s, was also in St. Louis to sell his large cache of furs which he had floated down the Missouri River from Wyoming. One day he ran into a vagrant young boy of very dark complexion who appeared hungry, homeless and alone. It was young Tom Sun. Descoteaux took the boy under his wing with the assurance that if Tom stuck close by him, he would always be provided for. True to his word, Tom stuck close beside Descoteaux and became his loyal right arm. The two became inseparable friends, and trapped together up and down the Missouri River and its tributaries for several years.[51] Descoteaux, who had already trapped in what is now Wyoming, decided to bring the boy with him on another visit to trap beaver pelts. This was Tom Sun's first glimpse of Wyoming, and Wyoming subsequently became his lifetime home.

In 1858 Basil Lajeunesse, another fur trapper, chose to build a log fort and trading post where he would attract the most attention from the Indians and trade furs in relative security. That Indian trading post was situated just south of spectacular Devil's Gate of Oregon Trail notoriety on the cool, clear waters of the Sweetwater River. It is not more than one hundred yards south of the ranch buildings Tom Sun later built. That original ranch is still owned and operated by Sun's grandson, Bernard, and family, and Tom's original white-washed log buildings are still standing today.

Later, during the Pony Express days of 1860-61, a horrible incident happened close by at the Sweetwater Station only a couple of miles below Independence Rock. The Pony Express station was attacked by Indians and the resident agent was captured and staked out on the prairie with iron pins driven through his hands, feet and mouth, crucified by the Blackfeet.[52]

Tom enlisted during the Civil War and was assigned to a bridge gang and spent the balance of the war in that capacity. At the end of the war, he returned to Wyoming and continued to trap for furs. When the Union Pacific started laying tracks across Wyoming Territory in 1869, Tom jumped at the chance to earn extra money and got a job as a tie hack for the Union Pacific railroad. He learned to cut and finish ties for the rapidly moving construction crews near Fort Fred Steele. Soon he was hired, together with Buffalo Bill Cody and Joe Rankin, as an Indian scout and guide for the military at the same fort, and where he almost certainly met Jim Averell who was stationed there at the time. Homer Merrell, Carbon County District Judge at that time, said "he's a man worth knowing—one of the most interesting men in Wyoming. He has been raised by the Indians, you might say, and knows the chiefs of many tribes intimately. He knows their language and their signs and you will never tire listening to the narrative of his life...."

Billy Owen, Deputy U.S. Mineral Surveyor for Wyoming, had this to say about Tom Sun for whom he was surveying two gold claims: "He was indeed a most interesting man, a charming, delightful companion, surpassing even the high estimate I had made of him from the glowing description given to me by Judge Merrell."

After the country began to settle up, Tom moved back north to his beloved valley just above Devil's Gate on the Sweetwater River and built his first ranch buildings in 1872. He kept adding to the buildings on a fairly regular basis, someday to provide a home for a wife with whom he could share a lifetime of companionship and raise a family in comfort and security. Tom's hopes were finally realized when he went to Rawlins with his neighbor, Boney Earnest, who was at that time foreman of the Sand Creek Land and Cattle Company, Limited, of London, England, and Sand Creek, Wyoming. There he met Irish immigrant, Mary Agnes Hellihan, who was working at the Union Pacific Hotel owned and run by a Mrs. Larry Hays. [Mrs. Hays later built the Rawlins House hotel where Ellen Watson was employed.] Tom and

Mary were married in Rawlins in 1883, and this union produced four children.

Except for the earlier, but temporary, military outposts of Three Crossings and Sweetwater Station and Lajeunesse's even earlier Indian trading fort, Tom's ranch buildings were the first permanent settlements in the Sweetwater Valley, and still sturdily stand today.

A wealthy English hunter, named St. John Rae Reid, befriended Tom who was his guide, and during the summer of 1877 the two men became interested in the several large herds of cattle being moved through the Sweetwater country. They discussed the possibility of a joint venture in the cattle business. After Reid returned home to England, he sent a check for one thousand pounds sterling, and Tom purchased their first herd.

To bridge himself over, Tom had prospected at South Pass and other places in Wyoming. Before long he discovered two fine gold claims in the Seminoe Mountains which he called "Deserted Treasure" and "Emeletta." A close friend, William Owens, who surveyed the gold claims for Sun, later Surveyor General of Wyoming, wrote that the last named claim was named after an old girl friend. Tom sold both claims to an Easterner for $20,000, a near fortune in those days.

The cattle venture did not prosper; the price of beef fell drastically and bad weather and hard times compounded their difficulties. Further they had not prepared to put up hay and consecutive severe winters strained their capital reserves to the breaking point. Reid sold out to Tom.

During those difficult early years, Tom also supplemented his income by continuing to guide Eastern and European hunting parties. Wyoming was rich with wild game of all kinds, and there were trophies to be bagged. Tom gained a reputation for successful hunting sorties into the Big Horn

Tom (de Beau Soleil) Sun was a self-made man who protested the cattlemen's actions, but reluctantly became involved in the Cattle Kate affair. (Carbon County Historical Museum.)

Mountains and even farther west into the Yellowstone wilderness country. One of those hunters was Edwin C. Johnson, a wealthy hunter from Connecticut.

During one of Johnson's summer hunting trips, he witnessed the trailing of a herd of five thousand cattle from Idaho through the Sweetwater country. Then and there Tom and his Eastern hunter, Edwin, decided to become partners, and they ran even more stock on the Sweetwater open range country with mixed Durham cattle from Oregon. With Tom's experienced know-how, and the Connecticut Yankee's where-withal, they set out to build a significant herd. They hired two more men, went to eastern Oregon, hired three additional men there, bought a cavvy of one hundred horses, hired some experienced cowboys and trailed 2,800 head of cattle from Baker, Oregon, a marketing point for west coast cattle, to the Sweetwater country[53] One of the cattle wranglers, William (Billy) Johnson, Edwin's son, wrote: "In the bunch of cattle we had all kinds—some were Texas cattle, some were short horns, and one I remember had Mexican horns, I think it had come up from California."

They suffered the loss of two hundred head out of the entire herd and that to poison weed.[54] They grazed their rapidly growing cattle herds together on the open range south of Devil's Gate for several years.

Before long, with the beginning of the early onslaught of the new 160-acre granger/homesteaders,[55] Tom and his cattle-men neighbors realized the effect the homesteaders would have on the country and rushed to gobble up the remaining rangeland before it was all chopped up into little pieces. It became evident that quick acquisition of as much range as possible was first priority. Furthermore, additional gigantic herds of cattle had been brought in, and the range grass was suffering. In order to protect their large investments in cattle, the open range cattlemen had to gain title to large amounts of land, irrigate and fence it to avoid disaster.

Tom went about it with an integrity unusual among his neighboring foreign and Eastern opportunists who seemed interested only in profit. He had lived in Wyoming since he was a boy and felt far more than a passing affection for the land. He took the unusual step of building waterwheels on the Sweetwater River near Independence Rock and on lower Cherry Creek to raise the water high enough to irrigate the higher lands to comply with government homestead irrigation requirements.[56]

Sometimes, however, the unrealistic federal requirements were impossible to satisfy, especially with surface water as limited as it was in much of the valley, but Tom made an honest effort to comply. Many other cattlemen had a philosophy of get in, get the money, get out and let the devil take the hindmost.

ROBERT B. CONNER
Lazy UC Ranch

Robert B. Conner was born in Penn Haven Junction, Pennsylvania, on January 23, 1849. Toward the end of his childhood, the family moved to Hazelton before their final move to Mauch Chunk [later Jim Thorpe], Pennsylvania. He attended the Wooster Academy, a prestigious private boys' school in Danbury, Connecticut, where he received his late elementary and high school education. While in Mauch Chunk, he was a member of Saint Mark's Episcopal Church. He never married but was very close to his sister, Josephine V. Remmel, also of Mauch Chunk, and his brother, Philip B. Conner, as well as to several nieces and nephews who lived nearby. As a young man, Conner was first employed in Hazelton, Pennsylvania, by the Lehigh Valley Railroad as a freightman.[57]

Unlike Bob Galbraith, Conner found little future in the railroad, and before long he resigned his position in the freight department and moved to Wyoming. He must have arrived in Wyoming later than 1880, because he apparently did not ranch in the southeastern or south-central part of the territory first, which was typical of others who predated him. Also no early stock records can be found for him. By the time Conner arrived, he must have discovered that much of Wyoming's open range country was already swallowed up.

Sometime, in the early 1880s he learned about the Sweetwater Valley where some land was still available, and he proceeded to set up headquarters near the head of Horse Creek, situated about fifty miles southwest of the present town of Casper. Horse Creek meanders down into the Sweetwater Valley in a southwesterly direction from the Rattlesnake Range. It originates from some very large, warm mineral springs about ten miles up in the mountains where it flows from a large, gaping hole in the rocks. Conner built his ranch buildings about five miles downstream from Horse Creek's origin. Most of his original log buildings are standing today. Conner's first known filing was made under the Desert Land Act on February 14, 1881.

Like plenty of others who wanted to get into the cattle business, he began to accumulate ownership of cattle and land illegally. There was just hardly any legal way to do it in a hurry, unless you had a fortune to purchase somebody's already-existing land and stock. And why would any large outfit sell out if they were making good profits with little investment?

Now, not all cattlemen slid into profitability with little investment. Some of the cattle giants brought tons of capital to Wyoming, bought hundreds of thousands of cattle and oodles and oodles of grassland. But some achieved ownership to the land the same tried and true way. Some would-be cattlemen simply hired cattle thieves to help them increase their herd and blamed the rustling on the homesteaders.

Bob Conner was another example of a man playing the game. You were a damned fool if you didn't try it, and Bob Conner tried hard.

Conner had to discharge his foreman, Tom Collins, when the Wyoming Stock Growers Association took the extraordinary action of blackballing Collins for rustling.[58] Conner replaced him with a man named Ordway, whose reputation as a rustler was just as bad. Conner was cagey, but he was also militantly loyal to those who worked for him.

It was not unusual for a cattleman on the Sweetwater to hire skilled rustlers to work the ranges. During one particular year which is well documented, the Goose Egg ranch had been targeted for large scale rustling. One of the Goose Egg's enormous herds was located about twenty or twenty-five miles northeast of Conner's ranch and very close to the Bessemer Bend of the North Platte River. The Goose Egg was controlled by an extremely wealthy English nobleman whose name was George A. Searight.[59] It was an easy target for all who wanted to increase their herds at someone else's expense. The thinking seemed to be that Searight was first of all an Englishman and so was considered fair game. Second, he was aristocracy which also made him a target, and third he had so many cattle throughout the eastern and central part of Wyoming, he literally didn't know how many cattle he had, so he probably wouldn't notice even a fairly large loss.

The trouble was, the stock thieves did not settle for just a few head. Over a thousand cattle were stolen one spring from Searight alone, a lot of which ended up down in the Sweetwater Valley.[60] Clabe Young, who, it will be remembered, was Tom Sun's foreman, and who was being returned to Texas for trial, said that Searight would be lucky if he ended up "with any cows at all." He said he heard Conner tell his later foreman, Lew Smith, another notorious rustler, to go out on the range and brand all the mavericks they could lay their hands on, and to "give Searight's range particular hell!" Clabe then broke down and sobbed because, he confessed, there ought to be a lot of other cowmen in jail with him, like John Durbin and Bob Conner, and that those two were largely responsible for all his troubles with the law.[61]

M. ERNEST McLEAN
EM Bar Ranch

Little is known about M. Ernest McLean, except his brand. He remains a shadowy figure. It was said he hailed from somewhere around Chicago, Illinois.[62] In proportion to the others involved in the lynching, he owned a rather small ranch. It was situated just south of the famous Oregon Trail landmark, Split Rock, on the Sweetwater River.[63] That prominent Oregon Trail landmark is a huge, granite mountain with a one hundred foot vertical notch right out of the center top. It could be likened to the rear buckhorn sight on a hunting rifle.

McLean's ranch was on the north side of the Sweetwater River near the Three Crossings of the Oregon Trail.[64] The crossing was so named because the Oregon Trail squeezed narrowly between two mountains, and the trail had to cross the river three times, one right after another, where the river bends sharply back and forth like a monster python in agony. A military post and telegraph station there once guarded Creighton's first transcontinental telegraph line. McLean's ranch bordered John Clay's enormous Quarter Circle 71 spread on the east side of Split Rock. Charles Countryman's big 6 H 9 ranch was on the opposite, west side of Split Rock. McLean had one hundred fifty head of beautiful, purebred Durham milk cows driven in from the west coast. Durhams produce less milk than a Holstein, but the milk is richer. So, in addition to raising a few cattle for beef, McLean's operation included dairy products.[65] It featured butter, cheese, buttermilk and other milk products quite rare in those parts. Heaven only knows how Ernie got himself involved in this awful affair, but he surely did, and with both boots.

PART THREE: THE ACTION

8. BEGINNING OF THE END

O n February 24, 1886, on a trip to Rawlins to file on his second homestead, Jim Averell met Ellen Watson Pickell, and they quickly became fond of one another. It wasn't long after the final approval of Ellen's divorce in March 1886, that Ellen and Jim traveled incognito to the out-of-the-way town of Lander, Wyoming, and got hitched. We discover them there on May 11, 1886, where they filled out the "Application for a Marriage License."[1] For unknown reasons, the actual marriage license was not issued until May 17, six days later.

Many questions have been raised concerning this license. The names on the document are James Averell, age 31, of Sweetwater, Wyoming, and Ellen Liddy Andrews, age 24, also of Sweetwater. Logic leads us to assume that Ellen Liddy Andrews was actually Ellen Liddy Watson Pickell, but we'll get back to that in a minute.

Another point of conjecture is the document itself. The license is composed of three parts: an Application for Marriage License, a Marriage License, and a Certificate of Marriage. The application is dated May 11, the license is dated May 17, and the lower portion, the Certificate of Marriage, is not filled in. Let's take a look at this document and decide if it indicates that Jim Averell and Ellen Watson were married.

Why would Jim and Ellen have traveled to the unfamiliar hamlet of Lander on the Shoshone Indian Reservation to marry? It would have been much closer and more convenient for them to marry in Rawlins where everybody knew them. This question actually answers itself.

If they had been married in Rawlins, everyone would have known about it, and that is the very point. Marriage would have made it impossible to file separately on individual homestead claims. Only one person per family was entitled to file on a homestead. However, in Lander where chances were good that no one knew them, their marriage could be kept a secret. Ellen could file independently on her own claim. Virtually everybody did it. If the marriage were discovered by the authorities regulating homesteads, it would bring a slap on the wrist, perhaps a little fine, revocation of the claim, maybe—and that would be the end of it.

Now let's look a little closer at the details on Jim's and Ellen's marriage certificate. The Application for Marriage License was filed on May 11, a little more than two months after Ellen's "in absentia" divorce was finalized. But notice further, that the actual Marriage License was not issued until six days after the application. Why the six-day delay? Did state law require a waiting period after application?

There is no evidence concerning what Jim and Ellen did during those six days. It would have been possible, I suppose, for them to race back and forth to Jim's homestead during that interval, but what for? Jim would certainly have used his buggy for a wedding trip. It seems unlikely that Ellen would have ridden side-saddle for 105 miles each way back and forth or that she would have been a passenger in Jim's springless Bain freight wagon. The route from Lander to the Sweetwater post office followed the Rawlins-Fort Washakie stage road for forty-five miles east, then went up and over

FREMONT COUNTY, WYOMING.

Application for a Marriage License,

TERRITORY OF WYOMING,
COUNTY OF FREMONT.

I, *James Averell*, place, an applicant for a Marriage License, do solemnly swear that my full name is *James Averell*; that I am a resident of *Sweetwater, Wyoming Terr.*; that the name of my intended wife is *Ellen Liddy Andrews* that she is *twenty (24) four* years of age and is a resident of *Sweetwater, Wyoming* that there is no legal impediment to our marriage.

James Averell Applicant.

Subscribed and sworn to before me this *11th* day of *May*
A. D. 1886 *P. J. McNamara* notary Public for *Carbon County* (Seal)
License issued to above Applicant this *17th* day of *May*
A. D. 1886 *J. A. McAvoy* County Clerk.

MARRIAGE LICENSE.

Territory of Wyoming, County of Fremont, ss.

The People of the Territory of Wyoming to any Person Legally Authorized to Solemnize Marriage, Greeting:

YOU ARE HEREBY AUTHORIZED to join in the Holy Bonds of Matrimony, and to Celebrate within this County the Rites and Ceremonies of Marriage between Mr. *James Averell* and *Ellen Liddy Andrews* and this shall be your good and sufficient warrant for the same; and you are by law required to return to me for record, within ninety days from the celebration of such marriage, your certificate properly filled up and signed by you, showing in what manner you executed the same. A penalty of Five Hundred Dollars being imposed by law should you fail to make the return.

IN WITNESS WHEREOF, I have hereunto set my hand and the Seal of said County at Lander, this *17th* day of *May* A. D. 1886

Fremont Co.
Seal

J. A. McAvoy
County Clerk.

CERTIFICATE OF MARRIAGE.

I HEREBY CERTIFY, That on the _____ day of _____ A. D. 188__ at _____ in Fremont County, Wyoming Territory, I joined in Marriage Mr. _____ of _____ and M _____ in presence of _____ residing in _____

The document raises many questions, but it appears to indicate that Watson and Averell were married. (Courtesy Charles "Pat" Hall.)

precipitous thousand-foot Beaver Rim to the Rongis Stage Station, then followed the Oregon Trail back down the Sweetwater River eastward for another sixty miles to Jim's homestead.[2]

If you took no other consideration into account, for Jim and Ellen to have made such an exhausting trip, from Lander to Sweetwater and back again in six days, would have been a terrible hardship on the horse. Such a round trip would have taken at least five days. It seems most probable that Jim and Ellen spent the six days right there in Lander, or thereabouts, waiting to complete the required papers. Besides, while in Lander they were only fourteen miles east of Fort Washakie, where they could have gone to visit some of Jim's former military buddies now reassigned there with the closing of Fort McKinney.[3]

On studying the certificate, the writing appears to be done by one hand and possibly in one sitting. One cannot help but wonder if the May 11 date was a clerical error. The words May 17 appear twice on the certificate, making that date a less likely candidate for error.

Another controversial point is that, although Ellen used her first and second given names on the license, she used the last name of Andrews. Was this woman truly Ellen Liddy Watson Pickell? The name was signed Ellen as she always did, and she used her middle name for the first time. In an area with precious few women such as this thinly-populated wilderness, the odds of finding another woman with those first two names, who was acquainted with Jim Averell and exactly the same age as Ellen Watson, declaring her residence as Sweetwater, Wyoming, seems next to impossible. There is no record of another Ellen, or Ella, who was known to have lived in the Sweetwater country at that time. As a matter of fact, there were very few women at all in the

Sweetwater Valley. It seems certain that this woman was Ellen Liddy Watson Pickell.

Now let's look at what at first appears to be an oversight in the completion of those wedding papers. The final portion, the Certificate of Marriage, at the bottom of the page, was never completed. Frontier citizens were not all that concerned with dotting all the i's and crossing all the t's. Early homesteaders were less concerned with bureaucratic details than with survival. Besides, that last section of the contract afforded the applicants a ninety-day grace period in which to complete the transaction, although the law did require that they complete the marriage in the county where the license was granted. They may have delayed filling out the third part, planning to complete it later. Perhaps they never got around to making the long trip back to Lander. It is clearly unimportant whether Jim and Ellen ever had the last part of the certificate filled in or not. The lower part was only for a preacher to complete. The marriage was valid without having the last part completed anyway.

It has been put forth, however, that because of that detail, they were never properly married. Phooey! One can concede, however, that such nit-picking may have minor validity. But it is also possible that Ellen and Jim really didn't give a hoot about the last part! After all, the Marriage License itself was fully completed and registered. That's the most important part of the document. That's the part you hang on the wall! Besides, since they had both been married before, they may not have felt the need for the assistance of clergy. A justice of the peace would have been sufficient.

On the other hand, if they didn't really care about getting married, they could have just as well stayed at home, saved enormous wear and tear on their bodies, and lived together in harmony as man and wife without all the folderol. It's called "common law," and it was done all the time in the West. Frankly, although there is no evidence to support such a claim, it is possible that Jim and Ellen may have already struck up such a common law relationship. Ellen designated her residence as Sweetwater, and she may have already begun living at Jim's homestead. On the other hand, if they didn't want a marriage license, they sure went to a hell of a lot of trouble for nothing.

So Ellen and Jim were quietly united, and both parties could file on homestead claims. Later Ellen could claim another 160 acres under the Desert Land Act, making a total of 320 acres for Ellen, or a glorious total of 640 acres between them—a whole section of land on Horse Creek. That's the good news. The bad news was that their land and water were situated right in the middle of Al Bothwell's favorite pasture and hay meadow.

Upon their return to Jim's ranch, Ellen did the cooking and shared in the daily chores at the store and saloon. Reporter Ed Towse would have you believe that Ellen traded her affections to cowboys for maverick calves. Her pleasant and attractive feminine smile would have had a salutary effect on their business in that almost womanless country, without her having to leap into bed with every Tom, Dick and Harry who staggered through the door carrying a wriggling, bawling calf.

Not one shred of substantive evidence exists to show that those two settlers were anything but hard-working homesteaders, trying to eke out a living from a primitive and difficult environment. In fact, according to their neighbors and contemporaries, they were universally liked by nearly everyone who knew them, even including most of the valley cowmen, except Al Bothwell, of course, and his close friends whose free and legal use of rangeland Jim openly challenged.

Averell did his best to keep Bothwell, Conner and Durbin from illegally gaining title to the whole Sweetwater Valley. He allegedly did it through legal challenges to their filings under the various land acts. As an example of the stockmen's illegal practices, in late October 1889, almost immediately after the lynching of Jim Averell and Ellen Watson, Bothwell secured clandestine title to another 560 acres in one fell swoop.[4]

It is also evident that Jim did not take his office of Justice of the Peace lightly, for on September 17, 1886, just ten short months before his murder, he wrote the following official letter to the Carbon County sheriff in Rawlins:

> Sweetwater Wyoming September 17th 1888.
> Sheriff High
>
> Dear Sir:
>
> Mr. Mendenhall of Livingston, Wyo. was here today with a heard of horses enroute to North Park, Colorado.
>
> He says, on the 19th of Aug. he met a man 5 miles from Big Horn City, Wyo. with a wagon with bows on and a rough mess box in the hind end and same was hauled by two dark brown mules with one horse tied behind. He describes the driver as Mr. Jack Hassel, the man he saw with the outfit of the canon creek tragedy.
>
> I have told Mr. Mendenhall to confer with you when he reaches Rawlins which will be about Friday next.
>
> > Very Respectfully
> >
> > James Averell

Jim, of course, referred to Livingston, Montana, since there never was a Livingston, Wyoming. In the letter, "a wagon with bows on" refers to a covered wagon with the canvas cover removed, but with the supporting bows still erect and in place.

This letter to Carbon County Sheriff High adds still more convincing evidence that Jim was a diligent law-enforcement officer who took his gubernatorial appointment as a justice of the peace seriously. In remote areas, the early function of a justice of the peace was a very important arm of territorial law. In many areas it was the only semblance of civilized law and order for dozens of miles. In addition to regularly reporting the flagrant practices of the cattle barons' illegal acquisition of public rangeland, Jim carried out the duties of his appointive office by reporting new evidence relative to the Canon Creek (or Gulch) tragedy.

What Jim referred to as the "canon creek tragedy" took place not too far from the Ferris post office (located at the little community of Sand Creek) about twenty miles south of Jim's ranch, where a young "Italian" emigrant had been discovered dead with a bullet-hole in his head and wrapped up in a couple of comforters. The murdered man had earlier been seen crossing the North Platte River near Fort Caspar driving a camping wagon pulled by two dark mules exactly as described in Averell's letter. He had been accompanied by two travelling companions. It was suspected that the man had been done in by his two "hitchhikers" for his money and belongings. Those companions were further suspected of belonging to "Teton" Jackson's gang of horse thieves and murderers whose hideout was in the Jackson Hole country, then a haven for outlaws. Jim's letter advised Sheriff High of the whereabouts and direction of one of the possible murderers who seemed now to be in possession of the emigrant's mule team, camping outfit, chuckwagon and horse, and perhaps even his name. It has not been learned whether Jack Hassel was indeed one of the culprits or whether he was ever apprehended.

In 1887, to gain support for the Democratic governor's new initiative to weaken the large stockmen's hold on the territory and to advance the cause of farming and agriculture, newly-appointed Governor Thomas Moonlight and a close political companion toured the state in a buggy and lent an ear to thousands of citizen complaints. When he reached the Sweetwater country he listened to a new one. The stockmen— the "good ol' boys" of the Devil's Gate area—complained about the governor's appointment of James Averell as the justice of the peace and postmaster at Sweetwater. They whined that Averell was "a most disreputable character keeping a doggery of a saloon, and a disreputable woman." The Governor had not yet met Averell, but his next stop north would have been at the Sweetwater post office. If the Governor visited Sweetwater, he apparently did not find the occupants or the conditions as alleged by the stockmen, because Moonlight never requested the revocation of Jim Averell's appointments. If he did not go to Sweetwater personally, he surely asked around about James Averell and found him respected by many.

Let's take a look at what other stockmen, friends and neighbors said and wrote about Jim and Ellen.

First of all it is said by some of the local residents in the Sweetwater Valley today, as it has been passed down to them by earlier friends and neighbors, that Ellen was a most compassionate and unselfish young woman. It is reported that upon learning of a seriously ill neighbor's wife, she would pack up her things, hop into Jim's buggy and drive over to minister to the wife while performing the additional chores of cooking, washing, house cleaning, and the other multiple domestic chores required of frontier women until such time as the wife was restored to health.[5]

Several witnesses, luckily for us, actually wrote down what they remembered of the kindness and hospitality of both

Ellen and Jim. One was a young boy who lived with his family on one of the road ranches along the Rawlins-Fort McKinney military road south of the Sweetwater post office. His name was Harry Ward, and he was about ten years old at the time when he knew Averell. Later as a man, he was badly injured breaking wild horses and had to give up cowboying. Subsequently, he became one of the chuckwagon cooks for the roundup where Ellen and Jim were abducted by the lynchers. He wrote:

> My father ran a stage station halfway between Rawlins and Ferris post office,[6] known as the Lake Ranch. [It was two miles north of the then well-known Stone ranch and on top of Boulder Ridge on the old Rawlins/Fort McKinney military road.[7]] There were at that time many bull teams travelling the road. That was in '86 and '87. Much of the freight was hauled from Rawlins to Buffalo [and Fort McKinney] and many people stopped at my father's place and among them was James Averell. He gave me many a quarter. Then a little later Ella Watson came to stop there. I remember very well one time she came out from Rawlins and brought me a pair of striped socks. Boy, was I proud. There is one thing; James Averell was no hillbilly. He was a well educated man and of gentlemanly appearance. I have heard so many speak of him as a roughneck, but not so. Ella Watson was a fine looking woman. Other women looked down on her in those days, but no matter what she was or did, she had a big heart. Nobody went hungry around her.
>
> [Presumably, some wives in the surrounding country looked down their noses at Ellen because

they believed she and Jim were living together in sin or, perhaps, because of the rumors that the big cattlemen spread about her.]

Another declaration of Jim's and Ellen's generosity was from a cowboy, W.H. Harvey, who was hired August 27, 1887, by W.A. Carter, son of the sutler of Fort Bridger about one hundred fifty miles west of Rawlins. Harvey was helping to move a herd of cattle from the Cody area to Rock Creek where they were to be loaded onto the Union Pacific Railroad for shipment to Richland, Nebraska, for winter feeding. The outfit crossed the Sweetwater River at Jim Averell's road ranch in October 1887. The occasion was recorded by cattleman and author, John K. Rollinson, in his wonderful book, *Wyoming Cattle Trails*. He wrote that Harvey said:

We had good weather till we got to the Sweetwater River near Independence Rock. It rained here, and Fred [McDonald] and I rode to the ranch where we thought we might get in out of the rain. This ranch belonged to a man named Averill and his wife. There was a large shed not far from the house. I went to the door and asked Mrs. Averill if we could make our beds in the shed out of the rain. She said, "No, you boys come right in. No cowboy is going to make a bed in a cowshed while we have a house." [Notice she said "we."]

We were wet and cold. She gave us hot coffee, which was a treat. They kept some groceries. Uncle Peter McCullough had bought all they could spare as the herd went past. We were short of supplies. She showed us into a nice, clean room with a very nice bed and warm blankets, and said for us to sleep there, and she would call us in time to get to camp. I said "We can't get into that bed; we have been on the trail over a month and are too dirty." She replied "That's alright; nothing is too good for a cowboy." She called us up in time, and had a good meal ready when we got up, and refused to take any pay.

Still another first-hand experience came from the pen of Charles A. Guernsey, an historically influential cattleman, who was later to become a member of the Wyoming House of Representatives. He was in the company of Frank Lusk, another of the largest cattle barons in Wyoming; both men are now legendary. In his fascinating book, *Wyoming Cowboy Days*, obviously written after having read Reporter Towse's Cattle Kate article, Guernsey wrote:

> During the summer and fall of 1887, Frank S. Lusk, for whom the Town of Lusk was named, and I, with my broncs and buckboard, made two trips to the Sweetwater and Seminoe regions prospecting for coal for the Chicago & Northwestern Railroad. Which eventually terminated at Lander.
>
> On one of the trips we stopped at noon and had dinner with Bill Averill and Cattle Kate at their ranch on the Sweetwater not far from Independence Rock along the Oregon and Mormon trail. Averill was a Yale graduate, a civil engineer, capable and of good address. Kate, in her twenties, was far from being a bad-looking woman and was very bright.

Again we see someone who thinks of Averell as a very well-educated man, even though he only finished the first year of high school, and of Ellen as highly intelligent. In any event, Jim did write well and was undoubtedly more articulate than most of the cowboys in the area. From his only known photograph, which was probably the wedding picture from his first marriage to Sophia Jaeger, we observe his refined appearance, carriage, and tasteful dress.

Guernsey couldn't remember the exact names of their hosts, but even after nearly a half century he certainly did remember their unselfish kindnesses and gentility. He also remembered the name "Cattle Kate" from Reporter Towse's article which everyone remembered.

Next, wc have a different perspective from a John H. Fales, who built Ellen's log cabin. He resided in Sand Creek.[8] This is what he wrote:

> I knew Jimmy Averell and Ella Watson well. In fact, my mother made the bonnet which Ella wore when she was hanged.[9] And I built the cabin on Ella's homestead on Horse Creek. It was a single room, built of fir logs hauled by Jimmy Averell. It was fourteen by sixteen feet, had only one door, but there was a window in each side.
>
> I know Jimmy and Ella met in Rawlins where Jimmy had gone to file on his homestead which caused all the trouble later. Ella was working at the "Rawlins House", and was at that time a fine appearing woman. She was large, being about six feet two inches tall and weighing about one hundred-sixty pounds. She was not only a fine appearing woman, but a good woman.
>
> Averell, in contrast to Ella Watson, was a small man. He needed some one to run his road ranch, and he made this proposition to Ella: She was to take charge, and charge 50 cents a meal for all meals served there. Averell was to furnish supplies, and she could have what she made. Averell's

homestead lay inside of Bothwell's pasture, that
he [Bothwell] had fenced in illegally.[10] Later Ella
Watson took up a homestead on Horse Creek, and
above Bothwell's place and also obtained water
rights which included extensive irrigation ditches.

Then she took out a water right and shut Bothwell off from water. It was this fact, and the fact
that Averell [also] had homesteaded Bothwell's
pasture that brought on the trouble. It certainly
wasn't any rustling operations of Averell's and
Ella Watson's. Neither of them ever stole a cow.
And those who say that Ella Watson slept with the
cow-punchers, are slandering a good woman's
name. She and Averell were engaged to marry,
and were only waiting until she proved up on her
homestead. She even adopted an eleven year old
boy by the name of Decoy [DeCorey], because his
home was not very pleasant.

Fales may have been rather a short person because he
guesses Ellen Watson to be taller than she really was. Others
have said she was rather taller than average all right, but not
that tall! Fales' recollection of names is also a little off. John
DeCorey was working on the ranch with Ellen, but it was
Gene Crowder who was the eleven year old boy unofficially
adopted by Ellen and whose "home was not very pleasant."
DeCorey was closer to age fourteen, but that is an understandable error, since the statement was made decades later when
John Fales was an old man living in Mills, adjacent to Casper,
Wyoming, and the two boys' names are somewhat similar.
Gene Crowder's probable father, John M. Crowder, reportedly
a widower, was a footloose drifter and sometime freighter
who lived south of Whiskey Gap, and was allegedly a heavy

This sketch of Ellen's cabin first appeared in Alfred James Mokler's A History of Natrona County, 1888-1922, *which was originally published in 1923.* (Casper College Library Archives.)

drinker. As a widower with several young children, he probably was ill-equipped to take over the care of young Gene, so perhaps that was why Ellen took Gene under her wing.

An additional reason for Ellen's becoming a foster mother may have been, as some have alleged, that little Gene was "crippled" or "sickly." Gene and his immediate family were the only known Crowders within hundreds of miles of Sweetwater. Very little else has been learned about the man who may have been his father, except for one mighty important piece of information that we will learn about later. Notice that Fales mentioned again that Ellen's and Jim's homesteads cut Bothwell off from Horse Creek water. Fales continues:

As for her rustling cattle, she didn't. She bought her first bunch of twenty-eight head from an immigrant, named Engerman, at Independence Rock. [He was from Nebraska.] The man was trailing through to the Salt Lake basin [after which we have learned he continued on to the State of Washington] and these cattle became foot sore. He sold them to Ella Watson for a dollar a head, and I drove them from Independence Rock to Averell's ranch. Later, when the trouble over range arose, Ella Watson and Jimmy Averell were hung. Some one at Bothwell's ranch sent the two boys two custard pies. Something made Averell's nephew [Ralph Cole] suspicious. He would not eat them. Later they were analyzed in Rawlins and enough strychnine was found in them to poison half the people in Wyoming. [This is the only known reference to the custard pie story.]

This was a very instructive account, because it tells us a whole lot we didn't know before. First, it is evident again that many of Jim's friends still addressed him as "Jimmy" as his family and early friends did. Another man to call him Jimmy was Marc Countryman in the very next example. Such easy familiarity would tend to indicate that he was anything but stuffy and must have been a very pleasant and accessible young man. We have also learned where Ellen was earlier employed and what she was doing and even how the two of them met and when. We have also discovered that she was purportedly wearing a bonnet at the time of her death. That is not referred to anywhere else, but nobody else's mother made Ellen a bonnet, either. If anyone would have known this detail, it would have been Fales. We also learn some additional details about her homestead cabin. In Mokler's splendid *History of Natrona County*, he said that Ellen had flower window boxes which, together with the door and window casings were painted pale green. Six-foot-two, however, was an inadvertent exaggeration made at an advanced age many years later. Ellen's immediate family said she was about five-foot-eight.

In the account by Marc Countryman, the son of a friendly nearby cattle rancher, Marc, too, mentioned witnessing the same purchase of cattle from a passing immigrant in a covered wagon, who was trailing sore-footed cattle along the Oregon Trail.[11] So now we have two first-hand witnesses to Ellen's bona-fide purchase of cattle. At last we have testimony to reinforce the conclusion that she wasn't a rustler, more especially not with the lethal audacity to do it right under her neighbor's noses and especially, during their round-up.

Another letter was written by Dr. Frank O. Filbey, at sixty-six years of age, who had moved back to Peru, Indiana. He wrote regarding the middle 1880s on the Sweetwater when Ellen first arrived in the valley. He said:

> I was acquainted with Jim Averill and the lady, whose correct name was Ella Watson. They had claims of fine land below Independence Rock in Carbon County, Wyo. They had a store where we riders often purchased cartridges, socks, tobacco and little supplies needed. Jim also had a government license to sell liquor.
>
> I remember Jim as a pleasant little man ready to accommodate one at any time but a dangerous man if anyone tried to put anything over on him. [Ella Watson] was a very pretty woman and I can say I never seen a thing wrong with her or a bad move from her. These people both held valuable

homesteads in the valley, a thing not approved by
the cattle barons who was determined to keep the
range free and open for their own selfish benefit
and desires. These people [Ellen and Jim] so far as
I know were law abiding people. The alibi of the
stockmen was that Jim and Kate rustled cattle.
This I refuse to believe as I never knew them to
own a hoof. They were proving up on their claims
and selling goods to the cowpunchers. I was riding
at the time for the Bar Eleven ranch, Sam Johnson,
foreman. The other ranches were the U.T. [John
Durbin] up near Split Rock and the Hub and Spoke
[Tom Sun] at Devil's Gate and the small ranch of
the Butler Bros. [Averell's original 160 acre homestead on Cherry Creek] up near [north of] Whiskey
Gap. You know the big cattlemen objected to
homesteaders and nesters as they were called as it
broke up the great free range they enjoyed.[12]

We will hear again later about Sam Johnson, Dr. Filbey's
boss, but in an entirely different context. In another letter Dr.
Filbey wrote:

Jim Averill, I knew down on the Sweetwater
was a small man, perhaps 135 pounds...and Jim
was a very pleasing personality, almost always
smiling...I liked them very much, but I would not
want to have been the man to put anything over on
little Jim for he did not stampede for a penny.

Another Sweetwater acquaintance, Nathan Elledge, who
knew Jim while he was in the Sweetwater Valley, wrote:

...I knew them both [Jim and Ellen] very well. I
used to cart supplies to Wyoming to old Fort

Fittmer [Fetterman] and delivered mail to the Post
Office at Jim Averill's store at Sweetwater, Carbon
County, Wyoming. Jim was postmaster.

Jim Averill was a small man, but could always
be depended upon to take care of himself if given
half a chance, but he was a quiet, easy-going,
peaceable disposed person and had many friends
among the cowboys and settlers.

The next statement is from John Burke, written out in
pencil, now reposited in the archives of the Carbon County
Museum in Rawlins. It was written at the urging of his niece,
Mrs. Dorothy Kangas of Rawlins, who asked him to write
down what he remembered of the territorial days in Wyoming. Burke regularly drove a freight outfit back and forth on
the military road from Rawlins to the Sweetwater Valley
which passed through Jim's road ranch. Interestingly, he must
also have been a very close friend of Averell and Watson
because he was one of those who posted $500 bail each for
Frank Buchanan and "Tex" Healy, who were subpoenaed by
unsympathetic County Attorney Howard, who was foot-drag-
ging, at best, about getting witnesses to prosecute the lynchers. In addition to documenting many other interesting
historical events, Burke wrote:

> The first open and murderous attack made upon
> the settlers by the cattlemen of the then territory
> was in the summer of 1889 on the Sweetwater
> river in the then Carbon County. James Averell
> had taken a homestead on the rich valley lands.
> Adjoining Averell's claim Ella Watson had also
> taken a homestead claim. These claims were in the
> center of a large section of country occupied by a
> cattle ranch, & the presence of squatters or settlers

there was distasteful to the manager. Averill sold whiskey in connection with his small store but was a quiet, peaceably disposed person. He was never accused of cattle stealing, never owned a single head, so I will leave it to the reader to look for a motive for his murder.

Relative to Ellen's purchase of her cattle, Burke further has this to say: "Ella Watson had received a few mavericks. These she had purchased from the cowboys and ranchmen."

Burke was aware that perhaps Ellen did actually purchase a few of her cattle from friendly ranchers and cowboys, in which case it is possible she could have inadvertently bought some stolen mavericks. But in that case it would have been next to impossible to determine where they came from or whose they were, especially if, as Burke wrote, they were mavericks. It is also possible that Ellen may actually have been set up as a "patsy" and framed by an unfriendly rancher or one of his employees to make it appear as if she had stolen calves. Another possibility is that Burke really didn't know what he was talking about, but those who knew him well swear that he was uncompromisingly honest. In any event, his statement certainly opens up a Pandora's box of fascinating possibilities.

The final first-hand example of Ellen's and Jim's characters and personalities was written by a young Congregational missionary, who paid friendly visits to Ellen's and Jim's place on several occasions. He was the Reverend Frank Moore and he rose to be National Secretary of Missions of the Congregational Home Missionary Society. He writes about his extensive travels around central and south-central Wyoming on both foot and horseback developing new missions and Sunday schools around the territory.

One of his first visits north from Rawlins was to Averell's road ranch and the Sweetwater post office. As we know, Jim was an active and vocal Democrat and had been appointed postmaster by President Cleveland and appointed as a justice of the peace and a notary public on February 1, 1889, by Democratic Governor Thomas Moonlight. The Governor was loathed and despised by the cattle barons, primarily because he was from the east and was on the side of the farmers and grangers and against the large cattle interests. The governor thought the large ranchers were too overbearing and autocratic. Furthermore, nearly all the big cattlemen in Wyoming were Republicans. At any rate, the Reverend Moore wrote in his diary on May 31, 1889: "Went to Sweetwater P.O. [Received] good letters from Father and Coral. Went to Bothwell, a little town on a sandy plain."

Moore apparently found nothing illicit or out of the ordinary on the premises at Jim's road ranch. Certainly a Congregational missionary, of all people, would have noticed a bawdy house. He visited Averell's place again on June 10 and 11 and later wrote from Steamboat Springs, Colorado:

> This week came the news of another hanging in Carbon County, Wyo. This time all parties that I knew or had seen. In the little article I sent on the Sweetwater you remember the name of Tom Sun. He and A.J. Bothwell, the man with whom I took the ride past the soda lakes, and with whom I had stopped the night before. Mr. John Durbin a stock man whom I slept with another time with two or three other men, [Reverend Moore also slept overnight at Robert Conner's ranch earlier] are all charged with hanging Mr. James Averill, a man with whom I had stopped, and whom they charged

with calf stealing, and Ella Watson, who lived on a
ranch near Mr. Averill. They hanged both, I am
told, for the same crime. A pretty severe way of
dealing with a man and woman just for calf stealing. That seems to be the only value some people
place on life out here. It seems terrible when I
knew all the parties. Mr. Averill told me to come
again and he would give me his house to hold a
meeting in.[13]

Thus we have it from the pen of a man of the cloth, a missionary, that Averell's place was hardly a whorehouse or any
place which could not seriously be considered as a makeshift
place of worship. If Jim were running a house of ill repute, it
is unlikely he would have offered it as a suitable place for a
Sunday school or religious worship. It is also eerie to discover
that Reverend Moore said he stayed overnight at Al Bothwell's ranch the very "night before" the lynching. He apparently noticed nothing anxious or strange in Bothwell's
demeanor, at least nothing he noted in his letter. Bothwell was
evidently a very cool, calculated character.

Had Ellen Watson ever heard the name Cattle Kate? Probably not, unless perhaps she heard it in reference to the original, scandalous whore and murderess named Kate Maxwell, a
former seriocomic singer from Chicago, who operated a notorious gambling den, saloon, dance hall and brothel a day's
horseback ride northeast of the Sweetwater post office in the
fledgling town of Bessemer. Maxwell's escapades were written up in a long article in the *Bessemer Journal*, which we'll
refer to later.

9. THE BUSINESS OF RUSTLING

Before going any further we need to discuss how rustlers went about this business of rustling calves. First of all, anybody who knows anything about cows and calves knows that it is practically impossible to separate mommy from baby for very long. Not only is there an inseparable bond between mother and calf, even in the face of incredible adversity, which harkens back to primordial times, but there are other purely corporeal reasons for the cow and its calf to remain inseparable.

First, the cow who is suddenly separated from its calf soon begins to suffer pain from an increasing build-up of milk created by the absence of a suckling calf. In fact, the cow's bag can actually tear or rupture. Second, before long the calf begins to suffer from hunger pangs. With these two stimuli alone there is every reason for the pair to become inseparable.

A rustler also would have to deal with the primordial instinct of a cow to protect its young. Many a modern cowpoke ends up in the hospital by getting between a calf and its mother, and these early-day cows were not somebody's pet milk cow. They were basically wild animals who were near men only at branding time and weaning time, and those occasions did not create fond memories of mankind in their small cow brains. So it is not at all as easy as it may seem at first blush to tear a calf away from its progenitor and move it across the "lone prairie." So then, how did a rustler actually abscond with a calf or calves over miles and miles of open range country?

Unbranded calves were the booty of choice of rustlers. Cows were already branded and later rebranding or altering the brand could lead to suspicion. So, one regularly documented method was to shoot the cow, leave it where it fell, and take the calf—and that was that. This method, however, was probably not the best way to handle the problem because it was often a sure-fire way to attract attention to the dead cow, to the bawling calf and by extension, to the rustler himself. Furthermore, it was a terrible waste of beef.

Another less frequently used method, although not all that uncommon, was to shoot the cow in the bag itself, or shoot the teats off, which some rustlers thought was great sport. That of course, did not stop the calf from trying to suckle the mother, but it sure as hell stopped the mother from wanting her bag suckled. That method had the effect of weaning the calf from the cow without the cow being discovered dead, since it more often than not survived the wounds. Then the calf could be taken.

In some cases the rustler would rope and tie a calf and then slit its tongue which resulted in the early weaning of the calf from its mother since the calf found suckling on its mother an extremely painful experience. This effectively separated the cow from the calf since the calf quit suckling, and the mother's bag dried up making the subsequent appropriation of the calf a good deal easier.

Sometimes a mother cow died of natural causes or rejected her calf after birth, which happens infrequently, thereby leaving the calf to wander across the prairie half-starved. These orphan calves were sometimes adopted by a human. That was the kind of rustling that was occasionally resorted to by the homesteader.

Most serious rustling was done by groups of cowboys highly skilled in their clandestine occupation and bent on acquiring larger quantities of cattle. By rounding up a little herd of cattle, rustlers didn't have to separate individual animals from their familiar herd. It was quieter to move them since there was less bawling. This larger scale rustling was often done at night. Sometimes the mommies, who as branded animals were not as desirable as their unbranded calves, were brought along until they were no longer needed, then they were shot for their meat and their hides buried.

An alternative was to use a red-hot running iron to alter the brands, but then the rustlers had to keep the cattle out of sight until the fresh brands could heal up.

The best known method of rustling was to rope and drag a calf to its new destination, but this was a slow, one-at-a-time process. There were still more variations, but the point is that rustling was not as easy as it might appear to the uninitiated.

Finally it should be brought out that rustling was not limited to the exclusive stealing of calves only, but very often involved stealing a group of cattle. It involved moving the cattle, often in rather large groups of, say, around seventy-five head to a destination, perhaps a hundred miles away, where all or a part of the herd could be sold to a not-too-fussy rancher or cattle buyer. Or they were sold to a slaughterhouse or butcher shop and cut up for retail meat, destroying the evidence. Often the rustlers operated with relative impunity. The ranges were so enormous that the scattered herds were the natural target of these organized bands of rustlers.

With this short lesson in rustling, which most readers will not find particularly utilitarian, let's take a much closer look at the allegation that Ellen Watson was exchanging sexual favors for calves—a very bizarre charge to say the least.

In the mid 1880s, according to Holt's New Map of Wyoming, which shows every existing ranch in the territory, there could not have been over two hundred or so people— ranchers, wives, girlfriends, cowboys, rustlers and all— within a radius of fifty miles from Averell's homestead. No more than eighteen ranches were in that whole area.[1] The radius of fifty miles was arbitrarily chosen because a hundred mile round trip is about as far as any good horse should travel in a day at a good clip without foundering or killing the animal. It has to rest and it has to eat and drink.[2] Now then, if a fellow hoped to avail himself of those alleged erotic favors for dogies [again, not doggies] at the Averell place, he would first have to find a calf. Then he had to cut it out of the herd and drive it up to fifty miles across the prairie, across the mountains, "over the rivers, and through the woods," just simply to get to "grandma's" house of illicit pleasure.

I don't know, of course, how many readers have ever had to move calves, probably not many, but those of you who have, know how contrary a calf can be, especially when rudely yanked away from its mother and forced to abandon everything that has previously provided its warm security. I do not believe it is possible to move a bawling calf fifty miles in a day, even if nobody noticed you were trying to get away with a calf belonging to someone else. But let's table that idea for a moment and look at other alternatives.

If you were a rustler/paramour you could, of course, move the calf along more easily in the reassuring company of its mother. Again I don't know how many of you have cut a specific combination of cow and calf quietly and noiselessly out of a large herd all by yourself. Even with a splendidly trained cutting horse, it's not that easy.[3] Now then, suppose you did actually get the duo together. You still have to move that unhappy pair fifty miles to get to Averell's road ranch, when the only thing those two cloven-hoofed critters have on their elementary, one-track minds is to return at once to the herd they were just taken from. And, remember, you have to move them nonchalantly, without attracting any unwanted attention. After all, nobody wants to risk a necktie party in his own honor for a half hour in the sack.

Still another alternative is for you to pick up the unbranded calf, toss the calf over the saddle, mount up and ride up to fifty miles with that wriggling, fighting calf on your lap. First of all, if the calf is small enough to carry, it isn't yet weaned, which means that it's going to be bleating loudly with its tongue sticking out the whole time. Furthermore, it will be trying to suck on everything it can get its mouth on and slathering all over your front, to say nothing of relieving itself on your lap, saddle and horse, which will not help create a libidinous atmosphere. Also, when you look around, you will find the mother trotting along behind, bellowing like everything, partly because her teats and her bag are starting to ache from an absence of her suckling calf and partly because she is mad. She wants her baby back! All of this, remember, must be done quietly and in utter secrecy, so you won't attract anyone's attention while you're calf stealing, so you won't be strung up to the nearest cottonwood tree with a lasso around your breathing tube.

Another alternative might be a little better. You could rope the calf and tow it, hooves dragging, to Ellen's place, if it doesn't strangle first. Don't think for a moment that you are going to shake off that fiercely maternal, bag-sore mother cow. However, there is one definite advantage to this method. If the calf is roped around the neck, it will be able to utter only soft, strangulated, choking noises which cannot be heard over too great a distance. The disadvantage is that the anguished mother will be stentorian enough to more than make up the difference.

Now in cases where the mother tags along, contributing continuous wailing and bellowing, you could always put a large caliber bullet through her head. This has two serious drawbacks. The first is that somebody might hear the gun's report and come running to see what the trouble is. The second is that you have killed a cow for which, if you are caught, the customary open range punishment was to wrap a slip-knot, hemp contrivance just above your shoulders, toss the other end around a tree, and raise you up high enough to keep your feet from touching the ground. An alternative punishment was to summarily shoot the offender, which, if it didn't kill you, would certainly have a dampening effect on your libido.

I suppose also you might try hiding a calf inside a freight wagon pulled by a disinterested draft horse or two. That, however, is rather cumbersome, but it has the distinct advantage of muffling the bawling sounds and hiding the calves from prying eyes. The bad news is that your journey still will be accompanied by that loudly wailing mother cow.

I am sure I have quite inadvertently omitted many other possible alternatives, but I have addressed only those which I believe might somehow have an outside chance of success, unlikely though that may appear to be.

Let's just go out on a limb (perhaps not the best choice of metaphors) far enough to believe that one of these ploys actually succeeded. You would then arrive at the pleasure palace at last and, with a knowing wink, hand your calf over to Mrs. Averell to do with as she may find appropriate. All of this is done while trying desperately to keep anyone from noticing your soaked Levis and the interesting aroma that hauntingly accompanies you everywhere.

At that point, to celebrate, you really ought to have at least a libation or two with the "boys" first. Your comrades probably won't notice your unusual scent, since they are all radiating the same "eau de corral" as you are. Everything up to this point is very romantic.

But, after all, you've just arrived and the other cowboys in that smoky saloon make delightful company over a glass of "Old Moonlight," or two, or three, or more. After having socialized sufficiently, you bolt down your final shot, slam your glass down on the bar with masculine authority, and get down to the real business of your visit. You might even decide to add a little cash to the calf and spend the whole night. After all, it took you a whole day to get here.

Spend the night? Hell! You have to be back to the horse cavvy before 4 A.M. for a chuckwagon breakfast of pork-belly, coffee, biscuits and beans with the "boys." So you really ought to start thinking about getting back to the home-ranch before anybody notices that you've slipped away. So you hurriedly use up your calf privileges and then hop on your trusty but exhausted steed, who was not at all nutritionally satiated by having tongued the rusty, iron bit in his mouth, nor has he been sufficiently satisfied by nibbling on "post hay"[4] all day, all night, and now, all the way back to camp again.

Good news, though. By now your Levis have partly dried out. So you tighten the wet cinch strap, grab the saddle horn, swing up into the moist saddle, wheel joyously around, and ride back all those miles on your unhappy cayuse. But at least you are no longer confronted by the calf, nor do you feel duty bound to return the bawling cow which is still standing noisily in front of Averell's saloon angrily waiting for her offspring.

Now some may find it scandalous to be less than serious about the "calves for sex" allegation which has survived since 1889. But it's hard to be serious about something which is so ridiculous. Now, we must admit that a few of the potential customers probably live just a few miles away from Averell's place. In that case, for them at least, the whole complicated process is somewhat less difficult than it would be for the fellow who has to travel up to fifty miles. The only trouble is, cutting down the radius of operations will reduce the potential customer list by a large percentage. That really doesn't leave a gal with much of a steady clientele to work/sleep with.

The business would have been even less remunerative if the profits had been divvied up between a whole stable of soiled doves, as some authors and movie-makers would have us believe. We are now down to a little more than a few dozen hombres to draw from, and the visits, of necessity, would be on an infrequent basis and even less in winter.

In fact, the author has never heard of other such calves-for-sex enterprises being practiced, much less successfully, in the history of the West. It is difficult to imagine what an enterprising call girl far out on the prairie might do under these circumstances, but I am convinced that with only a couple of dozen clients, she would surely pack up and move on to greener pastures.

But for a moment let's dive headlong into the unknown and assume the impossible. Let's just assume for a moment, that prostitution in the wilderness really could be a profitable enterprise. If that were the case, it would have violated no known territorial statute to accept something in barter for something else. It would not even have been a misdemeanor. If such a project like harlotry on the purple sage were feasible, it certainly is no crime to take a calf, or a llama, or a gorilla, or a Flying Diana radiator cap in exchange for whatever you wanted to take it in exchange for. Prostitution was quietly and discreetly sanctioned in Wyoming. Most citizens just turned their heads. The laws avoided any statutory mention of it. It is evident then that the august male legislative body must have tacitly approved of prostitution, or they would certainly have done something more substantive about it. So such a bartering device is hardly justification for mayhem.

Let's hope the above illustrations finally put this calves-for-sex matter to bed for good (admittedly, perhaps another awkward metaphor), and let's get back to the real-life story of two very hard-working, newlywed homesteaders.

On August 30, 1886, Ellen L. Watson rode to Rawlins to sign the papers under the Pre-emptive Act (the so called "squatters rights" act) so that she could begin to improve her future 160-acre homestead. She was granted a formal federal permit to proceed. This also granted her precedence or first refusal against anyone who later tried to homestead on her property.[5] She returned home, moved out to Horse Creek, had John Fales and her husband build her a little log home, and moved in. At the time of her lynching, she had been a bona fide resident of the Sweetwater Valley for just about three years.

An additional problem was citizenship. Without it a homesteader could not be granted final ownership. Ellen perhaps struggled for some time with the difficult decision to renounce her cherished Canadian citizenship. But on May 24, 1887, just a year after her secret marriage to Jim, and perhaps even with her husband's encouragement since he had already filed for citizenship, she traveled the sixty miles to Rawlins to file the official document of intent. Early the next morning, she went to the Carbon County courthouse to appear before the federal authorities and signed her written intention to become a naturalized American citizen.[6]

At any rate we again find her signature, Ellen L. Watson, on the official papers. About a year later, on April 18, 1888,

Ellen Watson's signature appears on her application for citizenship filed in 1887. (Wyoming State Museum.)

we find Ellen back in Rawlins to finalize the papers on her pre-emptive rights homestead claim just north of and adjoining, the claim her husband had filed the previous year.[7]

As an experienced surveyor, Jim perfectly described his wife's adjacent claim by metes and bounds. It was the mirror image of his own earlier claim.[8] It enclosed an L shaped strip of land which swallowed up another 160 acres of Horse Creek.[9] Now both homesteaders were in a position to command a handsome price for their land, but they simply hadn't anticipated the explosive personality of unbending Albert John Bothwell, who saw himself as a leader of men and the personification of big money aristocracy. The two unsuspecting homesteaders would reap mortally diminished returns from their clever maneuver. It will turn out to be 180-degrees from what they had anticipated.

Of course, it was no accident that Ellen's land was the upside-down clone of Jim's. She had obviously consulted with her husband. It was a device other homesteaders had regularly and successfully employed.

On May 14, 1888, Averell sold Bothwell a water ease-ment out of the Sweetwater River, running in an easterly direction across Jim's road ranch property. It was exclusively for irrigation and made possible a Bothwell project to irrigate his huge meadows to the north and east. It was sold for the piddling price of thirty dollars.[10] Interestingly enough, the notary public who witnessed the right-of-way deed was none other than Homer Merrell, Jim's defense attorney in Rawlins, after Jim's shooting scrape in Buffalo.

Not long after Ellen formally filed on her own homestead, she, too, filed for an irrigation permit which took water out of Horse Creek just above where Jim took out his. Jim had built four miles of irrigation canals with which to water his road ranch property. Jim wrote the whole petition out in longhand and signed Ellen's name, which, as a Notary Public, he nota-rized himself. Although it sounds rather odd, it was legal enough. Now Ellen and Jim together controlled over a mile of Horse Creek. The author's visual inspection of the still exist-ing ditches indicates that these ditches were plenty large enough to completely reroute all the water out of Horse Creek. That, in itself would create a gigantic amount of bad blood between the newlyweds and Bothwell. This, however, is just one of the many things that irritated Al. Let's take a short moment to hypothesize at what must have been ferment-ing in Bothwell's head at this point. Although pure conjec-ture, it may have been something like this:

"Up until recently I had absolute control of all this land and water for twenty miles around, without any tenderfoot telling me what I could or couldn't do with it. The land was just lying here doing nothing until I came along. I'm the one that brought it into profitable, productive use. It wasn't worth a damn before I developed it. After all, agriculture is damned important to America. Now some stupid outsider comes

Homer Merrell defended Averell against the Buffalo murder charges, notarized the right-of-way document, and later helped with the prosecution's case against the lynchers. (Carbon County Historic Museum.)

traipsing in here and puts up a road ranch right in the middle of my land and tells me I don't have a right to that land any more. Why should he be entitled to that land? What's he done for it? I'm the one who worked it first. I took care of it like it was mine. I've spent a fortune putting up barbed-wire fences, and buying cattle and horses and trying to get enough land to graze them on. The federal government seemed glad to have me do it. Whether I owned the land didn't seem to be an issue then. Why are they changing the rules in midstream?

"First this Averell son-of-a-bitch got control of most of my water. And now he's brought in a whore to gobble up another 160-acres right over the top of Horse Creek, right in the middle of my best hay meadow. What the hell am I going to do if I can't water my stock and irrigate my meadows? It's obvious the federal government doesn't know right from wrong. Don't they realize what they're doing to me? If we cattlemen continue to let this sort of nonsense go on, these newcomer grangers will eventually steal everything we've worked so hard for. If I let these two nesters get away with this, every Tom, Dick and Harry will be homesteading before long, and that will mean disaster for all of us stockmen. I'll be damned if I'll let 'em take everything."

Now on first glance we can see how this logic might make sense, not only to Bothwell, but to many of the men who settled Wyoming. But let's look at it closer.

First of all, nobody was stealing anything. Bothwell and the open range cattlemen didn't own the land in the first place. Did the big cattlemen really think they were going to have free use of the open range forever? Yes, they owned many thousands of head of cattle. Cattle were commodities which they could sell for a profit. But Bothwell was right about the open-range cattle business; it was headed straight for its grave unless things turned around. And pronto!

About this time, in the late spring of 1888, Jim buggied Ellen down to Rawlins, and she caught the train back to Kansas to spend June and July with her family back on the farm just northeast of Lebanon. Things must have seemed just like old times again.

10. THE MAVERICK LAW

A piece of legislation was passed in 1884 by the stockmen-controlled Wyoming Legislature, during Galbraith's first term, which was more despised by most citizens of the Territory than any statute before or since in Wyoming law. It was the product of the lobbying efforts of the mighty Wyoming Stock Growers Association and was known as the Maverick Law.[1] It provided that mavericks, unbranded calves found alone on the open range, could not legally be appropriated by just anyone. They were to be branded with an "M" on the neck and became the exclusive property of the Wyoming Stock Growers Association, which was appointed the official law enforcement agency for the Wyoming cattle industry. This new law provided that those slick calves were auctioned off to the highest bidder only by appointed representatives of the association, and the proceeds went to the association to cover the costs of policing the range and enforcing the law.

In the legislative session of 1886, a provision was added that no one could brand calves except those receiving registered brands from the state. No small cattle rancher, or nester, or homesteader, or anybody else, was permitted to bid on mavericks, unless they had a registered brand.

What the cattlemen hoped to accomplish with the Maverick Law was obvious. They wanted to protect themselves from

167

rustlers on the range and from new homestead filings. But J.H. Hayford, editor of the *Laramie Sentinel,* wrote that the Maverick Law was "for the purpose of devising ways and means by which the 'big thieves' could head off the 'small thieves.'"

If the little operator had a registered brand, the large stock owners usually outbid him. In the bidding for an unbranded calf, it didn't make any difference how high the bid went, in the end, the large stockman was usually charged no more than $10 a head. It was a brand new way to steal at the expense of the poor homesteaders, who were usually honest, God-fearing citizens. In fact, it was often impossible for the homesteader to recover even his own calves if they strayed too far from home. The cattle-Caesars would have liked to eliminate the small herd owner altogether.

Before the advent of the Maverick Law, during spring and fall roundups, the cattlemen gathered in all the mavericks and then divided them up to the various large cattle owners participating in the roundup on the basis of the size of their herds. As homesteaders moved into the country, this became grossly unfair because the roundup also caught the strays belonging to small herd owners, and they were passed on to the large cattle kings with absolutely no recourse for the little guy.

With the advent of a new Republican governor and a change in partisan politics, the 1888 Legislature repealed the law under heavy popular pressure. They set up a new Board of Livestock Commissioners. This was pure window dressing. The territorial governor then appointed eight of the biggest and most politically powerful stock owners to the new board, one from each county. The device made virtually no difference in the way the law worked.[2] It was simply politics as usual.

The Maverick Law created countless problems for the homesteader. They were at the mercy of the cattlemen and that created special problems for the cattle kings. The first problem was the Maverick Law didn't stop the rustlers. That was unexpected. So although the cattle thieves continued unabated, the cattlemen began to blame the rustling on the little nesters and homesteaders, most of whom were simply trying to mind their own business. It is easy to see how the Maverick Law led to all sorts of problems and misunderstandings for both sides.

It must be remembered, too, that Jim was a feisty Democrat, and the cattle giants were nearly all Republicans. It's also well to remember that Jim was appointed to several positions by President Cleveland and Governor Moonlight, both Democrats. Jim even received two write-in votes for Sand Creek's Constable in 1886 in an overwhelmingly Republican precinct.[3] Perhaps because of that Jim began to feel encouraged and confident politically and, as a result, Jim made an unwise decision.

He decided to write a letter to the editor of the *Casper Weekly Mail* exposing the cattlemen's illegal land-grabbing practices in the Sweetwater Valley. This led to antagonism with his Sweetwater cattlemen neighbors. He also recklessly took sides against them on the issue of whether to split gigantic Carbon County into two smaller counties.

The settlers and homesteaders were very much in favor of dividing the county in two with the southern half remaining as Carbon and northern portion becoming the new county of Natrona. Naturally Jim took the side of the farmer/settler over the cattle monarchs who were trying to hold the enormous original county together. After all, the "good old boys" living in northern Carbon County had long-established relationships with the Carbon County officials, and they certainly didn't want to start all over again with new officials in a new county in which homesteader interests strongly prevailed. Jim's letter to the editor expressed the sentiments of the overwhelming majority of the new settlers. He wrote:

> We have now had some time to think the matter over and listen to both sides of the question, and we find two distinct views on the matter; namely the settlers who have come here to live and make Wyoming their homes, and the land grabber who is only here as a speculator in land under the Desert Land Act. The former are in favor of dividing Carbon County, believing it to be for the welfare and proper development of the country, and the latter opposed to the organization of Natrona county, or anything else that would settle and improve the country, or make it anything but a cow pasture for eastern speculators.
>
> It is wonderful how much land some of the land sharks own—in their minds, and how firmly they are organized to keep Wyoming from being settled up. Said one high toned land grabber, "If my name was added to your petition, it would have some weight, because I own some fifteen sections of land and fifty eight miles of barbed wire fence." In this he advances the idea that a poor man has no say in the affairs of his country, in which he is wrong, as the future land owner in Wyoming will be the people to come, as most of those large tracts are so fraudulently entered now, that it must ultimately change hands and give the public domain to the honest settler, and then the land will be cultivated.
>
> What better proof do we want of Wyoming's fertility than one acre will produce 400 bushels of potatoes or 75 bushels of the best oats in the world,

and then to hear the land grabber cry out that Wyoming is a desert. Is it not enough to excite one's prejudice to see the Sweetwater River owned or claimed for a distance of 75 miles from its mouth, by three or four men? Said a Rawlins visitor "The taxpayers of the town of Bothwell are anything but favorable to the organization of Natrona County."

Do not be misled by the matter of the town of Bothwell. There is not one house in that town, and you can with safety say, that the town of Bothwell is only a geographical expression, and its influence cannot go far against the new county organization. If something can be done to settle the county up and use the beautiful water of its many streams, which are now going to waste, have Natrona county organized. If not, leave the country as it is.

You may ask what can be done to better the situation? Change the irrigation laws so that every bona fide settler can have his share of the water; and as soon as possible, cancel the Desert Land Act, and then you will see orchards and farms in Wyoming as there are in Colorado. Who was it that in the year 1884 tried to have an act passed in the territorial legislature to bond each county in the territory to the amount of $300,000.00 to run a railroad tunnel through the Seminoe Mountains? It is one of the Sweetwater land-grabbers who is now opposed to the settlement of Wyoming or the organization of Natrona county. [He refers to Galbraith.] Not wishing to disguise myself in the matter, I remain yours truly,

James Averell, February 7, 1889.

Jim had just tossed grenades, lobbed mortars, fired an entire artillery barrage, and mined the lakes and streams of the entire Wyoming cattle industry, with a particular emphasis on the Sweetwater Valley. He also very specifically attacked Bob Galbraith, Al Bothwell, and Al's proposed namesake town. He was absolutely correct in everything he wrote, of course, except for one major mistake. Contrary to what he wrote, he definitely should have "disguised himself in the matter." Jim unwittingly signed his own death warrant. He also unwittingly added his new bride's name to the same instrument of death. Now, all hell would come down around their ears—actually it would come down a couple of inches below their ears.

11. More Difficulties

In 1887 Ellen ran into a problem with E. P. Schoonmaker, her neighbor at the Gate Ranch [now the Dumbell Ranch] located a few miles southwest of Ellen's homestead and downstream and across Devil's Gate from Tom Sun's Hub and Spoke Ranch. Schoonmaker filed a 160-acre Timber Culture Act claim right over the top of Ellen's claim. But in 1886, Ellen had taken the trouble to file formal squatter's rights under the federal Pre-emptive Land Act. Sometimes, however, even such formal action was not always successfully defended. So on May 18, 1887, in Rawlins, Ellen fought Schoonmaker's right to file a claim over hers, and defended her right to retain pre-emptive control of her land. She was successful, and Schoonmaker lost his challenge.

Why in the world would Schoonmaker, knowing of Ellen's existing homestead, start such a thorny legal dispute? What was the motive? Further, as Bothwell's friend and neighbor, why would he have filed on 160 acres right in the middle of Bothwell's hay meadow? Should we suspect that Bothwell put Schoonmaker up to it in order to rid himself of Ellen's homestead, or could it be that Schoonmaker was just land-greedy? People who knew him said he was a very civilized, gentle person who had earlier nearly completed his medical studies back east, but illness overtook him and he

173

moved to the high country of Wyoming for his health. We'll get back to these questions at a later time.

In July 1889, during the late spring roundup, centered at Bothwell's north ranch on Horse Creek, the cattle barons were still smarting from Averell's letter in the Casper paper. And to make things worse, it was reprinted word for word in the Rawlins paper by Jim's military comrade, editor John Friend. As a result Ellen and Jim began to discover skulls and crossbones tacked to their doors. Ellen and Jim certainly must have suspected Bothwell was behind this, but how could they prove it?[1] But there was little question as to what these symbols meant.

Don't forget that Ellen purchased twenty-eight head of cattle. She also built corrals and fenced in a 60-acre pasture enclosed by a three-wire, four-barbed "bobwire" fence, securely stapled to sturdy, new cedar posts,[2] but not until the summer of 1889 did Ellen finally brand her little herd. She must have had a reason for waiting so long before branding. Let's try to establish what that reason may have been.

First there was a clause in the "Maverick Law" which stated that it was actually illegal to brand neat (unbranded) cattle between February 15 and the beginning of the regular spring roundup. Ellen must have known this and didn't brand until *after* the local roundup had already begun.

Secondly Ellen had no registered brand until the fall of 1888. In October of 1888, she formally applied for the brand "LU." It has been impossible to determine the exact day because some of the Carbon County records pertinent to this story have either been destroyed, stolen, or mislaid

In researching this real-life story, the writer discovered that, on December 14, 1889, several months after the lynchings, George Durant, who was appointed administrator of Ellen's and Jim's estates by the Third Judicial District in

Ellen received this Bill of Sale from John Crowder five months after she registered her "LU" brand.

Rawlins, filed legal action against Bothwell and Durbin. In the action which was filed this was said: "The deceased was at the time of her death as aforesaid, the lawful owner and possessor of that certain livestock or cattle brand, to wit: 'LU', which brand was duly recorded in the office of the County Clerk."

Well, now we have learned that Ellen had a legal brand. But at this point we run into a very strange enigma. She registered her brand in the Rawlins courthouse in October 1888, but a "Bill of Sale" dated March 16, 1889, records that Ellen bought an "LU" brand from a John M. Crowder for ten dollars. This was five months after she registered it in Carbon County. Since the brand was already legally registered, why did Ellen feel she had to purchase the brand again from Crowder? Perhaps the bill of sale is for the actual branding irons, rather than ownership of the brand.

It is also interesting to speculate why she registered the letters "LU." Stockmen preferred simple brands that could be applied with a straight iron and perhaps a quarter-circle. Traditionally, they chose brands that had some significance, much like the personalized car license plates of today. They often registered their own initials or a shortened version of their names. Following that tradition, Ellen might have tried to get "EW" or "LN" (Ellen). But both those brands were already registered. However, she might have selected letters to represent the phonetic sounds of her nickname, Ella, or "LU" (El-Uh). Voila!

Now back to the matter of Ellen's having postponed the branding till summer. Her cattle were undoubtedly in very poor condition when she bought them because she allegedly paid only a dollar a head for them. Although it seems too cheap, that actually was the going rate for cattle in poor shape at that time.[3] Furthermore no emigrant in his right mind would part with his precious livestock after trailing them halfway across the West unless they had become so poor and footsore that selling them was the only way to salvage anything at all. This was a common occurrence on the Oregon Trail. If the cattle were in poor shape when she bought them, Ellen would have needed to give them time to recover before subjecting them to the hardships of a branding.

Another logical reason for the delay is that it is not a good idea to brand in the wintertime when the cattle are at their poorest, particularly if some of them are "calvy" (pregnant) which was almost certainly the case with Ellen's little herd, as it was with any mixed herd. Traditionally cattlemen try to breed their heifers and cows in the early summer so as to produce a calf crop the following spring. Feeding cows through the harsh winter months is unprofitable unless they are going to "calve" in the spring. If cows and heifers don't "take," as the rancher quaintly expresses a bovine pregnancy, they are considered "dry" cows (since they produce no milk) and are sent to market at shipping time the following fall.

In any event, assuming that at least some of Ellen's heifers and cows had "taken" and would calve in the spring, Ellen would surely have waited until the very last minute to brand, thereby allowing her cattle to continue to put on more weight and gain strength before risking hardship to both mother and unborn calf together and possibly losing some calves to miscarriage.

Evidence points toward Ellen's having bought a mixture of calvy heifers and cows, as well as steers. Just three days after the lynching, Bothwell and Durbin returned to Ellen's pasture, tore down her west pasture fence again, discovered forty-one head and divided them up between themselves. They then rebranded each person's half with his own brand. That was apparently done in a great hurry, since the cattle were precipitously moved out of the Sweetwater Valley and shipped off to the Cheyenne stockyards on the Union Pacific Railroad where they arrived on July 30 and were hastily disposed of, thus destroying any incriminating evidence against them.

Remember that the administrator of Ellen's estate, George W. Durant, swore that Bothwell and Durbin split forty-one, not twenty-eight head, when Durant took legal action to recover $1,100 for Ellen's estate. That was $600 for the estimated value of forty-one head of cattle, plus $250 for the wanton destruction of her pasture, new juniper fence posts and galvanized barbed-wire and corrals and $250 in legal fees. A logical conclusion would be that the difference between the original twenty-eight head that Ellen purchased and the later forty-one head resulted when thirteen of the cows calved that spring. Or we could take the more sensational route and conclude that Ellen had been busy at the bawdyhouse that winter with her alleged calves-for-sex scheme.

And what would have happened to her herd if Ellen had not branded them? Under the revised Maverick law, her slick (unbranded) cows and calves would have become the property of the Wyoming Stock Growers Association and, by extension, the property of Ellen's cattle baron neighbors who, under the law, had first refusal to buy her stock. But it is clear that Bothwell and Durbin decided not to wait around for legal formalities. They immediately took the law into their own hands and expropriated Ellen's cattle to themselves.

12. The Final Hours

Saturday morning, July 20, 1889, a particularly beautiful, warm and sunny day, a stock detective skulked around Ellen's pasture and observed newly-branded livestock.[1] It is logical to conclude that the stock detective was George Henderson since Henderson was the only stock detective employed in the area. Henderson's employer, John Clay, manager of the nearby, huge Quarter Circle 71 Ranch, admitted in his famous book, *My Life on the Range,* that George Henderson was an indirect party to the lynching which would take place. The discovery of Ellen's newly-branded livestock certainly could have led someone to draw a very wrong conclusion. However, there remains the possibility that this "discovery" was a set-up, perpetrated to create a cause for the events that followed. This, by the way, was the morning immediately following the Reverend Frank Moore's overnight stay and religious debate with Al Bothwell.

Some writers have incriminated this dreadful man, George Henderson, as one of the lynchers. He was the foreman and stock detective of the Quarter Circle 71 Ranch about twelve miles away. However, Henderson was not involved in the actual lynching, probably on orders from his boss. But Henderson was certainly a part of the roundup previous to the lynching and was almost certainly the party who announced that Ellen had stolen and branded some of her neighbor's mavericks. But to avoid direct involvement in matters soon to transpire, he must then have propitiously run off to Cheyenne, fifty miles away by horseback and another one-hundred-fifty by train, to join his employer who many felt and still feel was also somehow implicated indirectly in this matter. Henderson had earlier been a Pinkerton detective and a skull-cracking strike breaker in the Molly McGuire coal miner uprising in Pennsylvania and was Clay's hired goon at this time. However, we can count him out as a direct participant in these events because he was in Cheyenne. He may have been involved in the indirect way alluded to by his employer, together with some involvement in additional activities in Cheyenne shortly after the lynching.

Anyway, that news of Ellen's alleged illegal branding spread to Bothwell, and he discovered a long sought-after opportunity—an excuse to rid the countryside of Ellen Watson and Jim Averell. Bothwell sent for his neighbors to meet him for an urgent pow-wow in his main hay meadow. This is the same Horse Creek meadow on which Ellen and Jim had filed their last homestead claims. Before long the six neighboring cattlemen who were involved in the roundup had gathered in Bothwell's pasture and entered into an animated discussion. Listening in were several understandably curious cowboys from the same roundup. One was the Butler brothers' foreman, Joe Sharp.[2]

Early reports said that there were seven stockmen involved in the events. Some have claimed as many as ten or even twenty, but there were only six. The confusion arises due to testimony made by a close friend of Ellen's and Jim's, Frank Buchanan, who was a witness to most of the events which follow. In sworn testimony he initially named five cattlemen and spoke of another sixth man whose name he couldn't remember, but before long he recalled the sixth name as Robert Galbraith.

The six ranchers who gathered were M. Ernest McLean, Robert "Captain" M. Galbraith, John Henry Durbin, Robert Conner, Tom Sun and the self-appointed ringleader, Albert John Bothwell. A number of non-participants also attentively listened in on this discussion. Tom Sun showed up in his new, white-topped buggy which had both front and back seats. It was reported by local residents that Bothwell introduced John Barleycorn into the gathering that morning, and certainly alcohol would likely have had an effect upon the outcome.

Certainly Bothwell's neighbor friends must have already heard about his difficulties with the two homesteading nesters. They must have heard his bitter complaints about Jim and Ellen. It was reported in sworn testimony that Bothwell had visited Ellen's place and offered to lend her the money to prove up early on her claim if she would then sell it to him. Perhaps holding out for a better price, Ellen repeatedly told him she wouldn't need his help to complete her proof. Bothwell's ranch buildings were less than a mile from Ellen's cabin and pasture and because of his proximity to Ellen's place, it seems impossible that he could have missed noticing her little herd nor could he have been ignorant of how she acquired it since she would have had to wrangle it right in front of his ranch house to reach her pasture. According to Ruth Beebe, Sam Johnson, the Durbin precinct voting judge and foreman of the Bar 11 Ranch on Pete Creek, certainly knew about Ellen's herd. Some of his cattle must have broken through Ellen's fence and mixed in with her herd because he had to cut his cattle back out from hers and, like a gentleman, he repaired her fence.

Back at the hastily called meeting, Bothwell accused Averell and Watson of rustling and branding cattle. Someone must have suggested that they ride over to Watson's place to see the evidence for themselves. Two of Bothwell's cowboys who claimed to have listened in on the stockmen's plans that morning were Will and Rob Hays who went to their graves swearing that, after hearing Bothwell's plan, Tom Sun and one other unnamed rancher "opposed the plans with vigor."[3] Unfortunately those objections apparently fell on deaf and perhaps intoxicated ears.

They mounted up and rode over to Ellen's homestead for a first-hand look, with Tom Sun reluctantly tagging along in his tandem-seated buggy. Sam Johnson initially started out with the bunch but apparently decided against it and dropped out and returned to the roundup—perhaps he'd come to doubt Bothwell's story because of his previous experience with Ellen and her little herd. When they arrived, the six cattlemen saw just what Bothwell knew they would see. It was now somewhat after noon.

Ellen was away from her place. She had left her cabin earlier in the company of her fourteen-year-old ward and helper, John L. DeCorey, to saunter down into the river bottom where Horse Creek emptied into the Sweetwater. She went to visit a friendly Shoshone Indian encampment where she had heard they might have some fancy beadwork to sell. She had earlier bought some pretty Indian saddle blankets and various other things with which to dress up and decorate her little cabin.[4]

Ellen purchased a pair of exquisitely beaded moccasins and proudly wore them during the lighthearted walk home with DeCorey across Bothwell's hayfield. The moccasins were particularly fine specimens of sinew-sewn deerskin, with tiny multi-colored beads sewn tightly together in a unique design. Except for the ankle pieces which were turned down to expose the beautiful beadwork inside and, of course, the soles, they were smothered in tiny beads, mostly white,

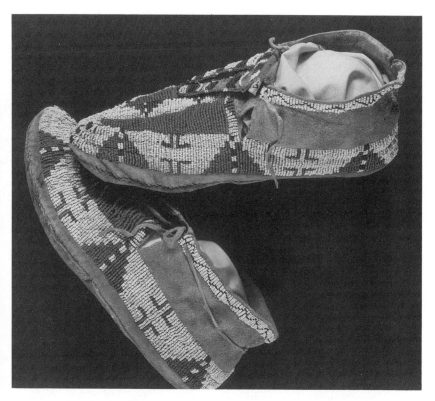

Ellen Watson had just purchased these deerskin moccasins from a nearby Indian encampment when the cattlemen arrived and abducted her. (Wyoming State Museum.)

with large triangular splashes of green and some broad brown lines and bright red triangular accents.[5] Ellen and John DeCorey must have felt particularly euphoric that early afternoon, what with Ellen's new moccasins and her little cattle herd safely branded and grazing away in their pasture.

When the cattlemen arrived at Ellen's house and found her gone, they sent Ernie McLean out scouting to see where she might have gone. He stealthily rode down toward the river bottom, discovered Ellen and DeCorey at a distance, and galloped back with the news. Without waiting, however, the suspicious cattlemen began examining her pasture. They found her cattle with the fresh new brands, and all their worst suspicions were immediately, but, of course, erroneously, confirmed.

So, it now seemed clear that these two nesters were rustling livestock. They now believed exactly what Bothwell wanted them to believe.[6] Impulsive, hot-blooded John Durbin lost his Irish temper and in an exploding rage, began kicking the staples out of Ellen's fence posts and yanking the barbed wire down. Little eleven-year-old Eugene Crowder, on hearing the noisy commotion, rushed out of Ellen's cabin and asked them what they were doing. The cattlemen shouted at Gene to shut up and get back in the house or suffer the consequences and little Gene ran back into the house.

When Ellen approached near enough, she saw Tom Sun in his buggy, with two saddle horses tied to the back of it, and the rest of the men over by her house tearing down her pasture fence and running her cattle out. She and DeCorey broke into a run and breathlessly reached her cabin screaming angrily at the intruders. The men immediately surrounded her. They told DeCorey to get in the house with Gene Crowder and for him not to show his face outside again. Bothwell then coarsely shouted at Ellen to get up into the buggy. Ellen must have been incredibly frightened. She must have been shaking like an aspen leaf. While the tears burst forth, she shouted at them to get off her property. The men told her what they had just seen with their very own eyes.

During the wild confusion of the escaping cattle and the cursing men, Ellen tried desperately to explain that her cattle were not stolen, and that she had been pasturing them for nearly a year. She tried to explain that she purchased the cattle and had a bill of sale. She must also have said that Bothwell and others had known about the calves for a long time. But they all guffawed and told her to go straight to the devil, unless she could produce either the seller or the bill of sale.

Five of the ranchers obviously believed the calves were from their local roundup. Bothwell surely never disclosed anything to the contrary. Ellen must have tried frantically to explain that the seller was a traveler on the Oregon Trail and that she had witnesses. She surely named the witnesses but they weren't nearby to back her up. She promised to produce the bill of sale and explained it was in her bank in Rawlins. No one believed her story except smug Bothwell, who knew perfectly well it was true, and so the men just guffawed nastily in her face again.[7]

About this time, Ellen's youngest ward, brave little Gene Crowder, suddenly exploded out of the house and bolted into Ellen's pasture where his pony was tied to a fence post with a halter. He raced over with all his might, jumped onto the pony bareback, and tried to ride right over the stockmen and out through the break in the fence to warn Jim over at the store. But Bothwell lunged directly into the path of the galloping pony, grabbed the halter, spun the frightened animal around to a dusty stop and yanked Gene off the pony with his other hand. He roared at him to get the hell over by Durbin and help him move the calves off. Scared out of his wits, little Gene obeyed. He cast a frightened glance over at his foster mother. Bothwell gave him a rough shove toward Durbin.

Then Bothwell yelled at Ellen to get up in the back seat of the buggy. Ellen asked them where they were taking her. Somebody shouted they were going to take her to Rawlins and put her on the next train out of the country. She pleaded with them to let her put on some proper clothes, but Bothwell growled that "where she was going she wouldn't need any fancy clothes."[8] There was no question what Bothwell wanted the outcome of this matter to be. Ellen again tried desperately to get them to let her change her clothes, but Bothwell howled at her that if she didn't get up in the back of the buggy immediately that he would tie her on behind and "drag her to death"—more evidence of his intentions.

Impatiently Bothwell grabbed Ellen and shoved her roughly up into the back seat of the buggy behind Tom Sun, and the men swung back up onto their horses. The procession turned around and rode over toward Averell's road ranch. They found Jim just inside his second gate driving his wagon toward Casper to get supplies for his little store. He had loaded a bunch of empty, dark brown, narrow-necked beer bottles into the back of his wagon to be refilled at the new brewery in the fledgling town of Casper at the terminus of the new Fremont, Elkhorn and Missouri Valley railroad.[9] Jim glanced around and spotted Ellen in the buggy with her pallid cheeks covered with dusty tears. His blood must have pounded up into his throat. It was now probably 2:30 or 3 P.M.

Struggling to hide his feelings, Jim asked the expressionless men what they wanted. Bothwell assumed the role of mouthpiece and blurted out that they had a warrant for his arrest. Jim asked to see the warrant. Bothwell and Conner stepped back slightly and swung up their rifles. They said the rifles would be just about "warrant enough."

At this point there was nothing Jim could say or do but give in. He was caught off guard and unarmed. The cattlemen told him to get in the back of the buggy with his woman. He complied. The other men swung back up onto their horses, and the ominous procession started out again.

To avoid riding right in front of Averell's store and alerting anyone who might be there, they turned north up the east side of Averell Mountain and around its north end and then headed southwest across the sagebrush toward the Sweetwater River and Independence Rock.

Still watching from Ellen's cabin, as soon as the procession was out of sight and with courageous disregard for their own lives, DeCorey and Crowder bolted out of Ellen's house, gathered up her little herd, drove it back into her pasture, temporarily cobbled up the fence and then raced on foot headlong across the mile-and-a-half or so from Ellen's house to Averell's store. When they arrived, they were gasping for breath and barely able to stand up.

Luckily, two good friends were there. One was Jim's nephew, twenty-year-old Ralph Cole, who had just arrived April 10 from Eureka, Wisconsin. Ralph's mother, Sarah Cole, who was Averell's sister, had sent the young man at Jim's invitation to spend some time with his uncle at his Wyoming ranch. Jim had left him in charge of the store while he drove to Casper. Ironically, Ralph had waved a last goodbye to his uncle only minutes ago.

The other person at the ranch was B. Frank Buchanan, a tall, dark-complexioned young man[10] in his early twenties who was a close friend of both Ellen and Jim. When Buchanan and Cole saw the wild-eyed anxiety in Gene Crowder's and John DeCorey's faces, they loudly demanded to know what was wrong. Between gasps, the two boys blurted out the story.

Ralph Cole glanced cautiously out the windows and door to see if anyone was lurking around, and then he leaped outside. He raced down the road to where he could see Jim's team untied in the roadway, yanked off the team's harness, threw it in the back of Jim's wagon with all the boxes and bottles, and turned the horses loose. He then foolishly raced north over to Bothwell's ranch to see if any ranch hands were still around to help. They seemed all to be out on the roundup, so Ralph turned around and raced back to the store. No one was there, so there was nothing to do but settle down and wait.

There were two other documented, but tight-lipped witnesses to the abduction, whom history seems to have forgotten entirely. They were H.B. Fetz, editor of the *Sweetwater Chief*, and his assistant J.N. Speer, who had recently run unsuccessfully for Sweetwater precinct voting judge. They actually witnessed the whole frightening abduction with field glasses from the rooftop of their new frame newspaper building in Bothwell. They had earlier been alerted by two unnamed cattlemen.[11] They watched the angry procession file right by, or very near, the newspaper office on its way to examine Ellen's calves, and they watched them parade by again later when the abductors passed around the north end of Averell Mountain and turned south toward Independence Rock.

Neither editor volunteered to give that firsthand testimony about the abduction at the grand jury hearing later in Rawlins. They must have decided it was healthier to remain tacit, rather than view a Winchester down the barrel. Both these men will reappear in this story, but in a surprisingly different way. Unfortunately, no known copies of their newspaper with their editorials on this matter survive, or we might have been able to learn still more.

The fact that these two men were actual witnesses to the abduction did not become known until the *Carbon County Journal* of November 2 printed the story, long after the grand jury had dismissed the case. The following is what Jim's friend, editor John Friend, said in that issue of the paper:

> There were witnesses who saw Averell and Ella taken by the accused, and as they were last seen in the hands of these parties, it is reasonable to suppose that the story told by Buchanan was at least true in substance. How did the proprietors of the "Chief" know the lynching was to take place and went to the roof of their office to watch the arrest? Shortly after the departure of two of the men

accused of the crime from the office of the "Chief", where they rested for a couple of hours, the proprietors took up their position on the roof and with the aid of field glasses, watched the taking of the victims until the view was obstructed by the granite rocks. After descending from the roof, they told some cowboys who dropped in that "Jim Averell and Ella Watson were hung". This was admitted to Coroner Bennett by Mr. Speer, who, when pressed to tell where he got his information, replied that there were some things connected with the case which he did not care to talk about.

The very fact that Speer knew that Ellen and Jim had been "hung" without having seen the actual event himself may suggest that the two cattlemen who earlier rested at the newspaper office prior to the lynching must have discussed such an eventuality. That is further evidence that the lynching may have been premeditated. Somebody sure "spilt the beans." Otherwise how could assistant-editor Speer have known before the fact that Ellen and Jim were "hung?"

Back at Jim's store, Frank Buchanan, after learning from the boys of Ellen's and Jim's abduction, instantly grabbed his cartridge belt and six-shooter, threw it around his waist, buckled it up, and charged out the front door of the store. He jammed the dangling bit in his surprised horse's mouth, tightened up the cinch, swung up on the horse, wheeled it around and raced down the south side of Averell Mountain, the opposite side from the one the stockmen took, to intercept and keep a close vigil over his friends.

After galloping crazily across the sagebrush for about a mile he finally spotted them off in the distance. He raced for the concealment of the rocks and reined his horse in. He could see that the buggy was still surrounded by the stockmen, and he could even hear them arguing loudly. Jim and Ellen were still trying to convince the men of their innocence. The men and the buggy just kept on bumping roughly along over the tall sagebrush and greasewood while the quarreling continued.

When the party reached the Sweetwater River, it plunged in off the shallow bank with a splash, buggy and all, and started up the gravel riverbed for two miles. At this point, Buchanan, by hiding behind whatever he could, was able to get close enough to overhear parts of their conversation. The men were threatening to yank Jim and Ellen out of the buggy and drown them in the river. Ellen quickly pointed out that there wasn't enough water in the river "to give a land hog a decent bath." Then the men became sullen and continued on southwest up the riverbed toward and around what is today called the Sentinel Rocks, where a few scattered springs flow west down and out into the Sweetwater River during the spring and summer.[12]

Apparently there was still another witness to this dreadful business, but he quietly chose to withhold his information. Ironically he later became a state's witness at the second coroner's inquest still without revealing what he knew. If his story is true, he could have changed history. He was a cowboy by the name of Dan Fitger, who, with his brothers, his wife and young daughters, came into the Sweetwater Valley from Nevada. He became interested in local politics and soon became a voting precinct judge for the Durbin precinct and later became a Natrona County assessor. Fitger's daughter Helen, later Mrs. Clayton Danks, revealed to Ruth Beebe years later that her father confessed to his family that he was a witness to the abduction and lynching while he was plowing up a new hay meadow for an experimental alfalfa planting on Schoonmaker's "Gate" Ranch just north of, and a little downstream from, Devil's Gate. From this vantage point, Fitger said he clearly saw Tom Sun's white-topped, tandem-seated buggy and attentively observed the progress of the lynching party down in the river bottom. At first he surely must have wondered why his neighbors were down in the water and gravel of the riverbed, of all places, and not up on the Oregon Trail where everybody usually travelled. He must also have wondered why Frank Buchanan was skulking along alone over in the shadows of the Sentinel Rocks such a long way off from the rest of the bunch.

Although a case could perhaps be made for premeditated murder, it seems more likely that, except for Bothwell, the cattlemen never planned to murder their captives. On the other hand, they surely must have been doing their double damnedest to frighten Ellen and Jim into quitting the valley. However Bothwell was such an erratic, unpredictable personality, that almost anything was possible. With him around, anything could go hay-wire and even a tiny spark could easily set fire to the whole incendiary program. Small operator Ernie McLean was probably just trying to prove he belonged along with the big boys.

There is one place in this whole area along the Sweetwater River, and one place only, where there is a lonely stand of tall cottonwood trees. It is where the Sweetwater River turns northeastward through a cleft between a long, wide two hundred-fifty foot high tumble of huge, grey granite rocks on the south side and an enormous, lone-standing, fifty-foot-tall granite rock on the other. From this defile the river then flowed down near Jim's road ranch across a grassy plain to its confluence with the North Platte River. If there really had been a premeditated plan to lynch this couple, here would have been the logical place to do it. However the lynchers seem to have driven right on through the trees as if they weren't there.

In looking back at this episode, it appears that Bothwell's conniving had carried the matter this far. He had conned his neighbors into their present compromised situation. Men of that era, ilk, and status were incredibly self-willed. Once the enormous emotional weight of that collective, determined mentality had been pried loose and shoved downhill, such momentum could only result in a violent crash onto the shuddering valley floor below. And we know that Albert J. Bothwell had reason to see the matter through to its dreadful conclusion.

But what actually transpired from this point on? The somber procession rode along for about five miles, perhaps consuming a couple of hours without hanging anybody, or drowning anybody, or shooting anybody, or hitting anybody, or for that matter, without doing much of anything, except intimidating Ellen and Jim. Whether the group was collectively angry and excited enough to carry out a probable death threat at this point is anybody's guess. But you can be sure of one thing. They were used to having their own way, their blood was running high, they were growing increasingly impatient, and, if seriously pressed for a conclusion to the whole matter, they were potentially able to do anything they damned well wanted to do!

Jim and Ellen must have realized, and rightly so, that these men, if shoved between a rock and a hard place, could ultimately and collectively explode. But would they commit mayhem without considering the consequences? Besides, it would be nearly impossible to gather six more unlikely partners together with such a single-minded purpose.

It seems likely, however, that Bothwell had just such an idea all along. But how about the others? Ellen and Jim were neither individually nor jointly a threat to them. Besides, it would have been foolhardy not to remember Averell's friends in high Democratic Party circles. Consider especially the preposterous idea of lynching a woman! So let's examine these men closely and individually.

Tom Sun, although hard-headed, didn't seem like the kind who would set out to be involved in something like a lynching. He had a wife and kids at home. And not long before, he had interceded to save Ben Carter, a notorious rustler, from certain lynching. Tom actually protected and sheltered Carter in his own house, even putting his life on the line for this man. He wouldn't turn him over to the law until the sheriff had given Tom his personal guarantee of Ben's safety until trial. He would seem to be the last to go along with such a crazy idea. [Ben Carter was legally hanged in the territorial penitentiary at Laramie for his multiple crimes including murder.][13]

Then there was Bob Galbraith. He had a wife and several youngsters at home. He was also a pillar of the Methodist Church in Rawlins[14] and was an up-and-coming ambitious politician. His name was sometimes mentioned as a future gubernatorial candidate. This would certainly be extremely poor publicity for election to any public office.[15]

John Durbin was clearly hot-headed and volatile, but would he actually murder someone—a woman, a man, a couple—in cold blood? Besides, he was worth millions. What did he have to gain? Why would he risk everything, including his wife, family and reputation, for one impulsive, reckless moment? Irish temper—?

And what in the world would Ernie McLean have to gain from such a wild course of action? He wasn't really a cattle baron anyway; he was primarily a dairy man. Nobody would try to rustle his shorthorn calves; they were too easy to spot. He was hardly a candidate for aiding and abetting homicide. He didn't seem like a violent, impulsive kind of man. But he sure did want to be one of the boys.

Sure, Bob Conner was a friend to rustlers. So was John Durbin.[16] But who wasn't then? And Conner was quiet and mild-mannered. Would he actually have carried out a death threat? However, he didn't have a family to consider.[17] But would he risk everything else?

In fact, when the chips are down and you look closely at the group as individuals, they seem about as unlikely a lynch mob as could have been assembled. All except Bothwell. He's an unpredictable quantity. Of all those men, he is virtually the only one with anything to gain—land, money, and above all, ego.

By now the party had been traveling a very long time and must have been getting impatient to conclude this matter. We will probably never know what triggered the final terrifying event. Maybe Ellen or Jim said or did something abrasive that ignited the powder keg. Maybe the whole thing *was* premeditated. Anyway something volatile happened. The procession suddenly changed its southerly direction toward Rawlins and veered sharply eastward, splashing up over the shallow but precipitous bank and out of the river,[18] and headed directly toward the nearest rocky canyon up in the Sentinel Rocks called Spring Creek Gulch where lots of tall pitch-pine and juniper trees grew.[19]

After riding and bouncing across the sagebrush for about three hundred yards, the men halted, swung down off their horses and tied them to some young, dark green junipers. They roughly yanked the terrified, protesting couple out of the buggy and, half-dragging and half-shoving their prisoners, the ashen-faced cattlemen slipped and stumbled along in their high-heeled riding boots up over the smooth boulders of a strange, eerie-looking canyon. There were many tall pitch pine trees. Almost all of them were at least twenty to thirty feet high, and they were interspersed with shorter junipers.[20]

It is probable that Ellen and Jim were very frightened for it now appeared as though the stockmen might actually carry out their threats. The men suddenly shoved their captives toward a wide, multi-branched pine tree about twenty feet tall. My God! Could they be serious?

All the while, Frank Buchanan had been stealthily trailing these cattlemen. When he saw them veer out of the river, tether their horses and start up the narrow canyon, he knew something was up. Frank spurred his horse around to the south end of the rocks, swung down, frantically tied his horse to some sagebrush and began scrambling headlong up over the smooth boulders. Damn, he slipped around and made too much noise. Frank threw himself down and yanked his boots off.[21] In his stocking feet, he could make better time and with less chance of noise. He must have been gasping for air and stumbling up over the huge rocks on all fours in his rush to get up where he could find the cattlemen. His hands and feet must have been getting damned sore, too. All at once he could hear voices not far away.

He scrambled around a grey granite boulder, and there they were about fifty yards away! Frank wiped the perspiration from his burning eyes and tried to see what they were doing. He saw that Bothwell had thrown the loose end of his lariat over a limb and tied it to the tree and already had the noose over Jim's head. My God, they didn't really mean to hang him, did they? Jim kept shouting hoarsely that neither he nor Ellen had rustled anybody's calves, and they were not leaving the valley. But nobody seemed to be listening. Nobody seemed to care what he said. Things were way beyond that now.

Over the dry, scuffling noises and frantic confusion, Jim tried to fight his way loose of Bothwell's lasso. The men must have been breathing heavily and cursing. Bothwell looked at

Jim with towering arrogance and told him that if he wanted to show everyone how brave he was he ought to be "game and jump off." [22]

All this time Ernie McLean was trying unsuccessfully to put his lariat over Ellen's head, but she kept dodging to avoid the noose. Perhaps to gain some precious extra moments, she begged for a chance to utter a prayer, but she was gruffly told she could deliver it in person.

Frank suddenly realized they were really going to lynch Ellen. Ellen? Not Ellen, too! For a while, by dodging around, she kept McLean from getting the noose over her head. Finally he succeeded.

In desperation Frank Buchanan jerked out his six-shooter and started to fire bullet after bullet at the would be lynchers. John Durbin grabbed at his hip and fell to the ground. Thank God, Frank thought! Maybe he could put an end to this.

The cattlemen scrambled wildly for their rifles and returned fire at Frank. He was too far away to do much good with just his six-shooter. Then his six-shooter hammer started clicking. The pistol was out of bullets! He clawed down into his cartridge belt and fingered out six more shells, broke open his pistol, jammed them into the empty cylinder, slammed it shut and began firing again. He heard the bullets from the stockmen's rifles buzzing and hissing all around him. He saw the men force Ellen and Jim to climb onto a boulder.

Finally Frank caught himself clicking away uselessly again. He had fired two cylinders full of bullets. It must have occurred to him that he had better damned well get down out of there or get himself killed, too.

Then suddenly it happened! Maybe even because of Buchanan's shooting. Frank spun around as he heard Ellen scream and saw Bothwell lunge forward and shove Jim off the boulder he was standing on. He saw the tree shiver under

Jim's weight. But Jim hadn't fallen over a foot or two. He was writhing and jerking and kicking wildly and trying to pull himself up on the rope. That was when Frank noticed that they hadn't even tied Jim's arms or legs.

Then suddenly it happened again! Ellen screamed as McLean leaped heavily forward and shoved her, too, off the boulder on which both Ellen and Jim had been standing. The tree trembled and then both Ellen and Jim were suspended, writhing and kicking! Ellen, like Jim, hadn't dropped very far at all, nor had the men tied her hands or feet. She could probably nearly touch the ground from time to time with the toes of her moccasins. The dust flew. Frank saw that Jim and Ellen were tied to the same limb! It bent down under their combined weight. But the limb didn't break! The two home-steaders were banging up against one another and were hitting and gouging and kicking unmercifully and spinning one another around. It must have been the most horrible and gruesome sight Frank Buchanan had ever seen. The two homesteaders were gurgling and grabbing one another, while they tried again and again to pull themselves up on those thin lariats. But it was no use. Neither Ellen nor Jim had fallen far enough to break their necks. They were strangling—slowly suffocating! In Ellen's struggles, she must have kicked off her pretty beaded moccasins.[23]

All at once the noisy shooting and shouting stopped. The cattlemen dumbly stared at what they had done. Certainly no one would have been able to utter a sound. The men stood transfixed like shale gravestones watching the foaming blood begin to ooze from the noses and lips of the grotesquely struggling pair grappling for life at the end of cowboys' lassoes. Silent echoes fell so heavily over the eerie, heaped-up granite rocks that the muffled gurgling noises of the dying couple sounded like the snarling of angry wolves.

This picture of the hanging tree was taken by Mr. and Mrs. Frank C. Jameson a few days after the lynching. The photograph appeared in Mokler's History of Natrona County.

Those men must have been pursued by that indelible picture of an innocent, garroted man and woman bouncing and twirling around like voiceless marionettes in their last macabre death dance—marionettes wearing misshapened masks of bulging, sightless eyes, and protruding, swollen tongues, fighting wildly for one last breath at the end of cowboy lariats. Then, gradually the dancing subsided. The twisted bodies relaxed and, at last, the final, terminal twitching ended. Then it was over, finished, nothing. Bothwell had won. Virtually everyone else had lost.

Although the tree is now dead, the shape of its branches and the geological formations in the background easily identify it as the hanging tree. (Author.)

It was clear that Frank Buchanan could do nothing further. He crammed his empty revolver back into his belt, grabbed his boots and scrambled headlong back down over the slippery rocks. When he reached the bottom, he shoved his feet back into his boots and untied his horse, then he mounted and spurred his weary horse back toward Jim's road ranch and away from that dreadful place of death. But he knew he now had to ride northwest to Casper to tell the sheriff what had happened. He was sure he was the only innocent witness to the lynching. He knew he must stop first at Jim's store to tell

Ralph Cole and the two boys the dreadful news. He probably galloped far enough away so that he was out of immediate danger and slowed his poor, exhausted pony down to a walk, slumped forward over the swell of the saddle and shut his smarting red eyes. The horse knew the way back.

13. THE AFTERMATH

It must have been about five or six o'clock on that hot summer afternoon, as the shadows were getting longer when Frank appeared back at the store. Gene Crowder had hurried back to Ellen's place to finish fixing the fence, and Ralph Cole was at the store by himself. Shouting one frantic question after another, Ralph rushed out to meet Frank. He saw that Frank's horse was lathered up and shivering from exhaustion. Ralph looked at Frank's face and swollen, red eyes and knew the news was bad. Ralph angrily yanked his saddle and blanket off the hitching rail, heaved them up onto the back of his horse and cinched the saddle tight. Then he grabbed the bridle and jammed the bit impatiently between his horse's teeth, shoved the headpiece over its ears, and buckled up the throat latch.

Without turning back to look at Frank, Ralph reached up, grabbed the saddle horn with both hands and swung heavily up into the saddle. As his jittery horse stood waiting, Ralph kicked the animal forward into a gallop and headed south down the military road toward the Seminoe Mountains[1] and the busy little community of Sand Creek where there were several homes, a saloon, a post office, Justice of the Peace Art Roberts and Constable Gates.[2]

As Ralph disappeared behind the Sentinel Rocks, Buchanan nudged his horse northeastward up the Military

Road to report the terrible news to the sheriff. No need now to be in any hurry. He must have felt completely and utterly wasted. He reached up and pulled his sweaty hat down over his face, hunkered down again over his saddlehorn and slowly walked his poor lathered-up horse toward Casper.

No one knows how the six stockmen dispersed from the scene. We do know they rode off without taking the bodies down from the unlikely gallows. A hundred years later, the whole matter seems like such an unnecessary immolation, but after the dust settled, and the silent pall of absolute, irreversible death fell over that place, the stockmen themselves must have questioned the sanity of what they had just done. Certainly there would have been little to say to one another. They must have stumbled awkwardly over and around those smooth, wind-worn rocks in an effort to be the first to reach the horses and escape the dreadful scene. Certainly no one looked back over his shoulder at the two bodies they abandoned to the elements, to the buzzards and to the inevitable insects.

Only a few stories survive about the immediate aftermath of that terrible tragedy.[3] One was told by Dan Fitger's daughter, Helen Danks, who heard it from the Charles Countryman children. When Countryman, who owned the Bar H6 Ranch in the shadow of Split Rock, woke up the next morning, he dressed, walked to the front of the house, threw open the screen door and stepped outside onto the porch into the cool, fresh morning air. To his astonishment, he discovered someone sitting hunched over on the porch steps sobbing. When Charlie saw the person, he asked who he was and what he wanted. The figure slowly rose to its feet, turned around and looked straight at Charlie with swollen, red eyes, and then between wrenching sobs, he almost incoherently blathered out what had happened. It was Ernie McLean.

By this time Mrs. Countryman and the six children had crowded into the doorway and were listening in shocked horror and disbelief. Ernie said he just had to tell somebody to get it off his chest. Without even a single conciliatory word of sympathy toward his neighbor, Charlie quietly told him he didn't want to hear anything more about it, ordered him off his ranch, and told him that he never wanted to see him again. As Ernie's ears burned with humiliation, he turned dully around, stepped heavily down the steps, and rode silently away from the Countryman ranch forever.

The second story involves John Crowder—the sometimes freighter from Whiskey Gap, the widower-father of nine children. John Crowder had bought a horse and wagon from a neighboring rancher/freighter named Irving Hays from the north side of Whiskey Gap[4] and was on his way to Casper. He was camped out along the Oregon Trail very near where the lynching took place. Early in the morning a cowboy rode up and warned him about what had happened there the previous afternoon. Upon hearing the terrible news, Crowder promptly unhitched the horse, struggled up onto its back and galloped away leaving the wagon standing there in the sagebrush flats where it remained unmolested for three years before Crowder suddenly returned briefly and drove it off. After that, John Crowder was never seen or heard from again. Was he Gene's father? Did he drop everything to make plans to get little Gene out of the country as soon as possible to avoid the possible consequences of Gene's witnessing the abduction? Perhaps little Gene Crowder was not murdered as some said. It makes one wonder what really happened to Ellen's young ward, but more on this later.

The last story affords us an unusual glimpse at Al Bothwell. The morning following the lynching the ranchers and their roundup cowboys were gathered on horseback in a large circle on Schoonmaker's old "Gate" Ranch [now part of the Dumbell Ranch] just north of Tom Sun's Hub and Spoke Ranch on the Sweetwater River. Cowboys were receiving roundup orders for the day from the ranchers, when brave little Gene Crowder rode up with tears in his eyes and screamed in front of everyone that Ellen and Jim had been lynched and shouted the names of all six of the cattlemen involved. Joe Sharp simply didn't believe it, but as he was mounted right next to Bothwell, he whirled around in his saddle and asked "Why, you didn't hang them, did you, Bothwell?" Bothwell never answered him or even looked up but just kept looking down at the ground. Everyone else was struck mute. The total silence became absolutely deafening and suddenly the realization of what had happened the previous afternoon hit everyone like a clap of thunder.[5]

As an interesting aside, John Durbin's cowboys were instructed for a long time after the lynching not to gallop their horses when coming into camp as they had always done in the past because it might create the image there that the approaching men were being chased by unfriendly parties, perhaps bent on revenge. So the cowboys were ordered to walk their horses into camp unless there really was a problem. The atmosphere in the Sweetwater Valley changed to one of general mistrust; men who had never carried a gun decided to arm themselves.

14. The Coroner's Posse

Frank Buchanan must have spent most of the night riding northeast along the Oregon Trail. About three in the morning, Buchanan arrived at "Tex" Healy's log cabin at the head of Fish Creek on the Oregon Trail about twenty-five miles southwest from Casper. He dropped down off his horse, stumbled over to Tex's cabin and thudded on the door. Tex climbed out of bed, slipped into his trousers and opened the door.

When he saw Frank's hollow eyes, he must have thought he was drunk. Frank gushed out the whole story. When Tex realized what had happened, he finished dressing and told Buchanan not to go any farther, that he, himself, would finish the trip to Casper to advise the sheriff. Healy rushed out, caught his own horse and rode the remaining twenty-five miles to Casper, where Tex informed startled deputy sheriff, Philip Watson [no relation to Ellen]. It was now a little before Sunday noon.[1]

As soon as Deputy Watson heard the story, he rounded up and deputized several willing, eager and able-bodied men.[2] He was aware that the coroner should be in attendance to hold a proper inquest over the bodies. He unsuccessfully searched everywhere for Coroner Dr. A. P. Haynes, who will figure prominently in the story later. Unable to locate Haynes, he deputized Dr. Joseph Benson, in his stead, to serve as Acting Coroner. Dr. Benson, who was a civil war veteran, also supplemented his income as a dentist.

As an aside, a couple of years later, during one of his not infrequent incarcerations for drunkenness in Casper's one-room city jail, the same Dr. Benson, whose real name was Joseph P. Riley, stupidly built a fire trying to burn a hole in the wall through which to escape. Unfortunately, the fire got away from him, and he was caught in the fire (nearby citizens unsuccessfully tried to shoot the heavy lock off). While the fire was still raging away, his badly burned body was extricated with a long-handled rake, but he was dead.

But back to our story at the Tex Healy Ranch. Frank Buchanan awakened, caught his horse, and rode back to Averell's road ranch. He discovered Cole, DeCorey and Crowder already at work making caskets out of rough pine lumber for Ellen and Jim.[3]

In Casper the next morning the coroner's posse was anxious to get going, and they started out for the Sweetwater post office about fifty-five miles away. It was about two on Monday morning when the Sheriff's posse finally arrived at the Averell's road ranch and awakened the boys.[4] The posse was exhausted and begged Watson to wait till daylight to get the bodies, but Watson ordered that they go out at once to get them. Frank Buchanan led them by the light of the moon and, after about an hour, they reached the awful scene. They had brought along a couple of kerosene lanterns from Jim's house. One of them struck a wooden match one-handedly on the end this thumbnails and lit the lanterns.

What an eerie procession it must have been to the place of death. As the men struggled up over the rocks to the grisly hanging tree, it could clearly be seen—in the white light of the moon and the flickering yellow light of the lanterns—that the couple were still hanging there, still touching one another even in death. There were signs of a bitter struggle. Jim and Ellen had now been hanging there for two and a half days in the sweltering July heat. Their faces were swollen almost beyond recognition and their dried eyes were bulging. Their tongues had turned black and were as hard as elk jerky and were protruding from their mouths. Buzzing blow flies almost smothered the ghastly faces. It was the most macabre, shuddery thing any of these men had ever seen. Ellen and Jim were gently cut down and carried back to Averell's ranch where Justice of the Peace B. F. Emery, a Casper attorney, solemnly swore in those present and held an official coroner's inquest over their bodies. After hearing the testimony of Buchanan and Crowder, it was officially judged that the deceased were hanged until dead by Albert Bothwell, Robert Conner, Tom Sun, Earnest McLean, Robert Galbraith and John Durbin.[5] A large single hole was then dug slightly southeast of Jim and Ellen's road ranch house, and the men silently placed the homesteaders into the rough hewn boxes which Cole, Buchanan, DeCorey and young Crowder had prepared. Then, they nailed the lids shut forever on irrevocable, eternal darkness.

There was about a foot of water in the bottom of the gaping hole due to its proximity to Horse Creek and the Sweetwater River on both sides, so the men probably dug down only about five feet before reaching water. One of the men probably gave a brief, extemporaneous prayer commending the homesteaders to their Maker, and the men carried the two caskets to the wet grave. With red and sunken eyes, Ralph Cole insisted on carrying one end of his uncle's casket, and he helped lower it into the hole.[6]

As for little Gene Crowder, the sheltered world that he had known with his Ella had suddenly come crashing down around him. He must have been inconsolable as he watched the men lower those two boxes, the very ones he had helped build, into that soaking wet hole. The soft, chunking sounds of the spades was heard as they were jammed into the damp, sandy earth, followed by the hollow sound of the earth hitting the two wooden caskets as several of the men filled the hole. No one said a word as the last dirt was heaped over those sodden graves.

Someone rounded up two oak wagon wheels and placed them side by side over the fresh graves.[7] Although the wood today has rotted away, the remaining old iron hubs and iron tires, now broken and encrusted with a century of heavy, flaking rust, still survive there.

Their melancholy duties over, Sheriff Watson gave orders to the posse and, one after another, they silently swung into their saddles and rode off together in the direction of Tom Sun's ranch in the company of Buchanan and Healy.[8] They knew what they had to do. Ralph, John, and little Gene stared blankly after them for a while. A sliver of the morning sun had just begun to make the faintest golden corona in the eastern sky. Emotionally exhausted, the three companions sorrowfully turned away from the soft, humped-up earth and shuffled back to Jim's house without a word and closed the door. Sleep must not have come for a very long time.

15. THE LIE

The telegraph wires began to click away with news of the lynching, but, as yet, no one had many facts. George Henderson, stock detective and foreman of the huge Quarter Circle 71 Ranch under Split Rock and neighbor of the lynchers,[1] who was in Cheyenne, received a short, ten-word telegram from someone in Rawlins. No one has discovered what that telegram said, but we can guess, because Henderson went immediately to the offices of the *Cheyenne Daily Leader*.

That newspaper had the largest circulation in the territory and was controlled by the Wyoming Stock Growers Association. Whatever the paper wrote represented the sentiments of the majority of the big cattle ranchers across the territory. Ed Towse was handed the formidable task of justifying the lynching of a man and a *woman*. How could anyone justify that? Women had been lynched only twice before in the whole history of the West, one in Nebraska and the other in Texas, and each of those women had murdered a man. This man and woman had done nothing to warrant a capital sentence. In any event, lynching women was not acceptable. But Towse's directions must have been unmistakably clear: Justify it!

Time was of the essence. As soon as the other newspapers in the territory heard about the lynchings, all hell would break loose. There would surely be incendiary outrage, which could result in a necktie party in honor of the lynchers. It would be a miracle if this matter didn't explode into a wild-eyed range war. Towse must have decided that he and his paper had to scoop everyone else and somehow the report must twist the events to the cattlemen's advantage. One thing was already to their advantage. The *Cheyenne Daily Leader* was a daily rag and most of the other newspapers in the state were weekly. But Towse knew few facts about the lynching—except what Henderson or possibly his boss, John Clay, could tell him.

If Towse could muddy the waters enough and quickly enough, he could cloud everyone's mind. He had to try to get the story out before any other newspaper. Then, whoever copied Towse's story would be playing right into the hands of the stockmen. Whoever told a different story later would simply have less credibility. The bad seeds were quickly sewn. And things went forward as predicted.

To be the "firstest with the mostest" became all important to the *Cheyenne Leader*. Towse and Henderson needed to fabricate an unbelievably believable story recounting how two vicious homesteaders victimized the cattlemen. The two men must have stayed up most of the night writing it.

Towse's first report was presented word for word in Chapter One of this book. Perhaps before we progress further into the story, the reader might reexamine that article in the light of what has now been learned. It gains an entirely new perspective, and it also clearly illustrates how reporter Towse wove his incredible, journalistic witchcraft.

Now we are going to take an interesting new tack. We'll reprint word-for-word what was actually written in the sizzling editorial debate that exploded all across Wyoming and we'll exhibit the actual newspaper articles from a wide cross-section of newspapers around the territory, not only to illustrate public reaction, but to follow the exciting events that will cascade precipitously over one another.

The first article after Towse's original masterpiece was from the competitive paper, the *Cheyenne Sun,* also controlled by rich cattle interests, and it came out later the same day. The story was written by Edward A. Slack, the editor, who was six-feet-one inches tall, weighed more than 230 pounds and was branded by competition editors as "The Cheyenne Avoirdupois," "Adipose Archie" or "the obese and oily Col. Slack." He immediately took up the cudgel and did exactly what Ed Towse expected he would do. He did not realize how badly he had been duped by Towse and jumped on the band-wagon with both feet. In his eagerness he even trumped up and piled on some very colorful additional information.

In Slack's article, he probably inadvertently confused Ellen Watson with a real-live notorious trollop by the name of Kate Maxwell, well known around the little town of Bessemer about ten miles south of Casper. Much earlier, Kate Maxwell had been editorialized in the Wyoming press as "Cattle Kate." She did rob a Faro gambler, did associate with and cater to rustlers, did shoot and kill a man, and did run a dance parlor, whorehouse and gambling den in that town. However, she was not Ellen Watson.

Never, at any time, before this July 23 article in the *Cheyenne Sun,* had anyone ever accused Ellen Watson of being a prostitute, of running a bawdy house, or of being the original Cattle Kate. But the catchy name stuck, and Towse gleefully pounced on the misidentification with all fours the very next day and continued to use the name Cattle Kate in his newspaper. But the damage had already been done and has continued for a whole century until Ellen Watson has become more frequently known as Cattle Kate than by her real name. The information for Slack's article was allegedly sent by telegraph from Douglas on the previous day. It must have been information delivered to Sheriff Watson by Tex Healy and then rushed to Douglas, the nearest telegraph station fifty miles west of Casper.

By this time Slack had surely interviewed George Henderson, too, and it is further strongly possible that he even conversed over the Union Pacific's telegraph lines with someone in Rawlins. That someone probably was John Durbin who sneaked off to Sand Creek after the lynching, bandaged the hip-wound inflicted by Buchanan and galloped off to Rawlins where he caught the next train to his baronial home in Cheyenne to avoid arrest. In fact, it is not impossible that Slack may have interviewed Durbin in person if Durbin's train arrived in Cheyenne early enough.

Towse's seminal article, followed immediately by Slack's, was a virtual one-two punch—one, a punch straight to the solar plexus followed by an uppercut to the chin. The following is Slack's article in the *Cheyenne Daily Sun* later the same day of Towse's original article, July 23, 1889.

Two Notorious Characters Hanged for Cattle Stealing.
Jim Averell and His Partner, Ella Watson,
Meet Their Fate at the Hands of
Outraged Stock Growers.

Special to the Sun. Douglas, Wyo. July 22nd.

Early yesterday morning a cowboy named Buchanan reached the ranch of E. J. Healy, forty miles west of Casper, and reported the lynching of Jim Averell and Ella Watson, Saturday afternoon by stockmen. Averell kept a "hog" ranch at a point where the Rawlins and Lander stage road crosses the Sweetwater.

Slack obviously didn't know Wyoming geography very well. The stage line crossed the Sweetwater fifty or sixty miles west and upstream from Averell's place and only a few miles from the Rongis Stage Station, named after the owner, Eli Signor, whose last name was spelled backwards. Slack continues:

Ella Watson was a prostitute who lived with him and is the person who recently figured in dispatches as Cattle Kate *[There it is!]* [2] who held up a Faro dealer at Bessemer and robbed him of the bank roll. Both, it is claimed, have borne the reputation of being cattle rustlers and are believed to have been in league with Jack Cooper, a notorious cattle thief who died with his boots on in that vicinity a few months ago.

Buchanan said Averell started for Casper Saturday, accompanied by the woman and that they were taken from the wagon by a party armed at gun point on the Sweetwater, not far from the town of Bothwell and hanged from the summit of a cliff fronting the river. Buchanan, who was a friend of Averell, came upon the lynchers just after the woman had been swung up and as they were in the act of hanging Averell. He fired at the lynchers, who returned the fire with interest and pursued him, but he had a good horse and managed to escape.

He claims to have identified several men, among them four of the most prominent stockmen in Sweetwater valley. Healy reached Casper last night and swore out warrants for the arrest of these men, and Deputy Sheriff Watson and a posse left at once for the scene of the tragedy.

The lynching is the outgrowth of a bitter feeling between big stockmen and those charged with cattle rustling. Every attempt on the part of the stockmen to convict thieves in the courts of that county for years has failed no matter how strong the evidence might be against them [This allegation is patently false],[3] and stockmen have long threatened to take the law into their own hands. This fact, together with the further one that Averell had had more or less trouble with every stockman in the section, probably accounts for the violent death of himself and the woman Watson.

Jim Averell has been keeping a low dive for several years[4] and between the receipts of his bar and his women, and stealing stock he has accumulated some property. While on one of his drunks not long ago, he so abused one of the women that she tried to escape. Averell caught her and tore her clothes from her body, but she got away and ran from the place. Unable to catch her otherwise, he got in a wagon and drove in pursuit. [The idea of a man in a horse-drawn wagon chasing a nude woman across the sagebrush because he couldn't otherwise catch her creates an interesting visual image, but it is preposterous.] Upon capturing the woman he tied her to the wagon and left her outside during the whole night. Averell evinced his right and title to be called a dangerous citizen by using his gun on several occasions and in one instance he killed his man.

Jim Averell was not always thus. Few men in the west had better opportunities. He comes from an excellent family and received instructions in one of the best educational institutions of the east.⁵ A minister who recently delivered a course of lectures in the Episcopal church in Cheyenne that electrified his hearers, referred to the fact, while here, that he had an old classmate in Wyoming—one James Averell.

The story of the man's descent into the vile avocation which he pursued when justice overtook him is not a marvelous one. It is the old tale. A few words will suffice, a passion for gambling, for liquors and for lewd women carried him on to destruction.

In an attempt to outdo even himself, and to keep the iron hot, Towse again hit the printers' ink with total abandon. On the next day, July 24, he picked up the ball from Editor Slack and continued to confuse Ellen Watson with Kate Maxwell from Bessemer Bend:

> Cattle Kate Maxwell, the woman lynched with Postmaster Averell, has been a prominent figure since her advent in the Sweetwater country three years ago. She had been a Chicago variety actress and was brought from that place by Maxwell upon the occasion of one of his trips to the market with cattle. She simply revolutionized ranch life. Fond of horses, she imported a number of racers. With the attendants came bull dogs which were pitted against coyotes and prairie wolves. A couple of her jockeys were fleet of foot and they were matched against Indian sprinters, defeating the red man with ease.
>
> Sharp Nose, a rapacious Arapahoe chief, cudgeled his brain to devise ways for winning the white squaw's money, but was unsuccessful. Her

thoroughbreds ran away from his best ponies. At one meeting which lasted several days, the wily chief and his warriors were fleeced of every thing except their mounts and guns. They showed fight, but were driven from the place with the loss of several braves.

About this time Maxwell's place was taken over by his foreman. It is said that Kate poisoned her husband. The ranch now became a thieves' resort, and all the neighbors were sufferers. A big spree followed the recovery of the money from the skin gamblers at Bessemer. Things went from bad to worse; the foreman came to his senses and left; the retainers deserted, stealing her horses; the cattle were scattered; a colored boy made away with Kate's diamonds. She shot him and recovered the jewels, but they soon followed her other property. When the queen[6] and Averell joined issues, Kate was but a poor tramp of the worst type.

Towse deliberately has continued to confuse Ellen Watson with a Kate Maxwell, the dance hall virago from Chicago, and constructs a scandalous scenario based on deliberate lies and half truths. Writers and historians from then on didn't know whether to call her Kate Maxwell, Ella Maxwell, Ella Watson or Kate Watson, or any of the other contrived appellations, like "Queen of the Sweetwater" which have been tacked on in more recent years. One of the more preposterous charges was made by Harry Henderson, originally from Rawlins and later from Cheyenne, who was quoted by a Cheyenne paper as having said in a recent luncheon speech that Cattle Kate passed out green stamps. Will it never end?

After the coroner's inquest at the Sweetwater post office, one of the men from Deputy Watson's posse, Arthur Post, returned to Casper and as soon as possible galloped to Douglas, the nearest telegraph office, where he immediately disclosed what had happened in the Sweetwater to Merris Barrow, editor of *Bill Barlow's Budget* in Douglas.[7] Barrow then relayed the facts to Edward Slack, editor of the *Cheyenne Daily Sun,* and Editor Slack, realizing how terribly wrong his first article was and how duped he had been by Ed Towse, immediately performed a 180-degree flip-flop and apologetically corrected his first article. He tried to undo his errors by publishing the following headline article in the *Cheyenne Daily Sun* on the next day, July 25. He wrote:

THE TRUE STORY
Of The Lynching Of James Averell And Ella Watson
Graphic Details Of The Affair Given By Eye Witnesses
The Coroner's Verdict Implicates Some Very Prominent Men
A Sheriff's Posse Arrests Sun, Bothwell And Others.

> The dime novel literature telegraphed from Cheyenne Monday night regarding the lynching of James Averell and Ella Watson Saturday last is the veriest bosh.

The next part of the article corrects the previous misinformation and sets forth the actual facts leading up to the lynching as we now know them and proceeds to give its readers the first details of what actually occurred after the coroner's inquest and burial:

> Sheriff Watson and party then proceeded to the ranch of Tom Sun, who admitted he was one of the lynchers and readily gave the names of the others. He stated further that one of the shots fired by

Buchanan at the lynchers, when they were in the act
of stringing Averell up, struck John Durbin in the
hip, inflicting a wound. The wounded man had been
taken to Sand Creek [which was right next door to
Durbin's massive Lazy UT "Buzzard" Ranch]. Sun
said he did not know whether Durbin was badly
hurt or not.

Taking Sun into Custody the party next proceeded to the ranch of A.J. Bothwell, who also
readily admitted that he had assisted at the hanging.
He told Buchanan and Healy that both would go
over the range in the same way if they did not leave
the country, and on being told he was under arrest
and would be taken to Rawlins he warned the
sheriff to take a good look at every tree he came to
on his way back to Casper for he would be likely to
find six or eight more cattle rustlers hanging by the
neck. The two men who furnished these facts left
the party there and returned to Casper. Watson
probably had no trouble in arresting the balance of
the lynchers and should have reached Rawlins with
them some time today.

The following day, on July 26, Towse's *Cheyenne Daily
Leader* reported:

A Rawlins telegram says that all the men were
arrested by Sheriff Hadsell of Carbon County and
given a preliminary hearing yesterday afternoon.
[It was actually early morning.] Bail was fixed at
$5,000 each and surety promptly furnished.

We finally learn that Deputy Sheriff Phil Watson had
delivered his five prisoners safely to Sheriff Hadsell in
Rawlins. John Durbin had returned to his elegant home in

Frank Hadsell, sheriff of Carbon County, received the cattlemen from Deputy Phil Watson. (Carbon County Historical Museum.)

Cheyenne to lick his gun wound and avoid arrest. Justice, for reasons still not clear, was actually circumvented in Rawlins in the wee hours of the morning because Casper's Justice of the Peace, Judge Emery, who held the coroner's inquest over the bodies, set up an extralegal court in a horse stable and allowed the lynchers to post $5,000 bail each, which, in capital offenses, was utterly improper. Worse than that, the lynchers were allowed to put up each other's bail. Then the men trotted back to their ranches as if nothing had happened.

Nor is this the last time we will see justice thwarted. Political power and big money speak softly and carry a terribly big stick. The next day's Rawlins paper reported that Deputy Watson and Judge Emery had returned to Casper.

Still on the same day we observe that the *Cheyenne Sun* had apparently had its knuckles rapped by powerful cattle interests and must have been told in no uncertain terms *not* to continue to side with the homesteaders, because Editor Slack immediately did another complete 180-degree about-face and returned to the offensive again pushing the attack against Ellen and Jim. So Slack editorialized:

> The honest ranchmen and stock growers were met only by threats and fresh depredations.[8] Averell constantly threatened death to those who interfered with him and the wretched woman he kept was equally desperate and uncontrollable. Buchanan was known to be one of the gang. Bothwell, Sun, Durbin and other prominent settlers had received intimations that their lives would be taken.[9] Neither the property or the lives of these men were safe at any time. The worthless wretches who carried on these depredations completely controlled and terrorized the whole region and the conditions of life there became unendurable. It was not and is not a conflict between large stockmen and poor ranchmen, but a question of life and death between honest men and cut-throat thieves. The heroic treatment must prevail and the gentlemen who have resorted to it are entitled to the support and sympathy of all good citizens.

It is interesting to note the editorial charge that Jim and Ellen had threatened the lives of the lynchers. If Ellen and Jim had actually threatened the lives of the stockmen, it would have been a reason, but certainly no justification, for the lynching. It is interesting to learn, too, that, after Durbin escaped to his home in Cheyenne, Democratic District Judge Corn, who was a fine, impartial judge, later to become a justice of the Supreme Court of Wyoming, tracked him down and promptly issued a summons for him to accompany Sheriff Hadsell back to Rawlins where he then appeared before Assistant Carbon County Prosecutor H. H. Howard.

On July 27, just a week after the lynching, Reporter Towse wrote again in the *Cheyenne Daily Leader* under the heading:

LET JUSTICE BE DONE

The lynching of the man and woman on the Sweetwater may be deplorable. All resorts to lynch law are deplorable in a country governed by laws, but when the law shows itself powerless and inactive, when justice is lame and halting, when there is failure to convict on down-right proof, it is not in the nature of enterprising western men to sit idly by and have their cattle stolen and slaughtered under their very noses.

Apparently what Towse said is that it is justifiable to commit murder if the law can't prevent thieves from stealing. That was not then, is not now, nor will it ever be justification for strangling someone to death. But Towse must receive an "A" for effort, if not for logic. Then he continued and tripped himself up with the next statement, inadvertently condemning the very people he tried to defend. He said:

Lynch law is rarely justifiable though we have known cases where it was. The trouble with it is that like justice it is blind and gives way to the mad passions of men which it is always better to keep within bounds.

James A. Bennett, coroner and justice of the peace, refused to disinter the remains of Averell and Watson during the second coroner's inquest, thereby leaving the first inquest intact. (Carbon County Historical Museum.)

The next development should have been expected. Money and political position talks. The acting Carbon County Prosecuting Attorney, H. H. Howard, filling in for Prosecutor David Craig, who was sojourning in Ireland, obviously had been threatened or bought out, or both, and climbed in bed with the stockmen. He improperly found Deputy Watson's coroner's inquest illegal and then ordered a replacement coroner's inquest made up of jurors who were nowhere near the lynching. However, Coroner James A. Bennett was clever enough to choose jurymen whom he knew were sympathetic to Jim and Ellen such as William Granger, whose wife helped take care of Sophia Averell during her dying days and Dan Fitger who later revealed he was a witness to the abduction during his job on the Gate Ranch.

On July 23 Howard sent Coroner Bennett, who was also a justice of the peace, to the gravesite to hold a new inquest over the graves. Bennett was not in sympathy with the cattle kings, especially when it involved his friend, Jim Averell, and he was very much upset by this obvious subterfuge. Bennett was the mortician who prepared the bodies of Averell's first wife and baby for shipment back to Wisconsin. But as an elected public servant he did what he was told to do.[10] It is during this second inquest that we learn that Tex Healy and a cowboy named Charles Buck, who lived about four miles northeast of Tex on Poison Spring Creek, dug the actual grave and that nephew Ralph Cole actually helped carry his uncle's casket into the grave.

If the cattlemen had been able to discredit the first inquest and supplant it with this second inquest, there would have been no legally documented testimony from witnesses to the lynching or abduction. Jim's friend, Coroner Bennett saw to it that the second jury didn't exhume the remains, saying that they were "in no condition to be disinterred." That was a subtle, clever maneuver on his part, since that made the second inquest invalid so it could not legally supercede the original which named the lynchers. However, Bennett went still further and gathered two new sworn depositions, one by Charles Buck and one by Ralph Cole, which incriminate the lynchers even further. Buchanan and Crowder would certainly also have testified at this later inquest, but they couldn't. They were in Casper hiding.

AT AN INQUISITION

Holden at _Averill Ranch_, in _Carbon_
County, on the _Twenty third_ day of _July_ A. D. 18 _89_
before me, _J. A. Bennett_, Coroner of said County,
upon the body of _James Averll and Ella Watson_
lying dead, by the Jurors whose names are hereto subscribed, the said Jurors upon their
Oath do say —

We came over to Averill Ranch arriving here on the night of the 22nd of July we organized and found according to testimony given. The bodies of James Averll & Ella Watson were burned at Averll Ranch and were not fit to be exhumed. From the evidence given we the Jurors summoned by J. A. Bennett Coroner of Carbon Co Wyo find from the evidence given that James Averll and Ella Watson came to there death by hanging by parties unknown to us.

In Testimony Whereof, _The said Jurors have hereunto set their hands the day and year_
aforesaid.

JURORS.

A. R. Gates.
H. L. Mead
George Birmingham
L. L. Hitshew
William Granger
Jeff Day

The second coroner's inquest ruled the bodies not fit to be exhumed and therefore did not legally supercede the first. (Wyoming State Museum.)

On the same day as the previous article, July 27, the *Cheyenne Sun* snidely wrote:

> It turns out that the coroner's inquest [the first one conducted by Justice of the Peace Emery together with Deputy Sheriff Watson] held upon the remains of Averill and Watson was not, strictly speaking, an inquest. The Coroner of Carbon county has since held an inquest, and the verdict was that the parties came to their death by violence by persons unknown to the jury. This is more like it.

Still on the same day, July 27, the *Salt Lake Tribune* in Utah lectured:

> The men of Wyoming will not be proud of the fact that a woman—albeit unsexed and totally depraved—has been hanged within their territory. That is about the poorest purpose a woman can be put to! The woman may have been all that she was pictured. If that was true, it was a clear case that her proper place was a madhouse, and certainly there were methods by which she might have been made to leave the region without hanging her. This is so certain that we do not believe the men who strangled her are just the class of men that decent people would like to make their homes among. There is many a tragedy on the frontier: there is much that is rough and wild, but there is generally, withal, a crude chivalry which protects the most abandoned of women. This is a tough business in Wyoming.

The *Denver Republican* in Colorado, chided on that same day, July 27:

About the only question to be settled in the Wyoming lynching case seems to be whether there is law enough in the territory to punish a man for murder committed as a member of a mob of lynchers. At least two of the lynching party admit that they were connected with the crime. This is enough to secure their conviction unless public sentiment endorses and excuses the lynching of cattle thieves.

Edward Slack of the *Cheyenne Sun,* also on the same day, noted:

There will arrive in Cheyenne today on a cattle train, fifty-three head of mavericks, shipped from Rawlins. These mavericks will probably be unloaded at the stockyards, where they will be seen with great interest as they have a peculiar history, a portion of them being the mavericks taken from Ella Watson's pasture and all of them being the mavericks taken from rustlers in Sweetwater country. They will show the different brands of the rustlers of that section, and in view of recent occurrences, will doubtless be visited by many of our stockmen and citizens.

However, the cattle did not arrive until July 30.[11] The evidence was evidently not incriminating, though, because it is never mentioned again. The matter was quietly dropped. Slack reports only a total of fifty-three head in the whole shipment, some of which were not Ellen's, verifying that Ellen's herd was not large, certainly not the two hundred head alluded to by other news articles.[12] The *Leader* admitted that part of the fifty-three head came from rustlers somewhere else in that area. Nothing further about this matter ever appeared in the *Leader,* however. But such an important piece of evidence against the homesteaders, especially if there were incriminating brands or evidence of the use of a running iron would hardly have been overlooked by the editors, not in Cheyenne. Besides all they would have found was Ellen's legal "LU" brand which was purchased from John Crowder and also officially registered in the Rawlins courthouse, as well as the later brands inflicted by Bothwell and Durbin.

Also on July 27, Bothwell, Durbin and Galbraith, with a peculiarly sanguine disregard for having participated in the shocking gibbeting of two homesteaders, casually moved out the very first annual Wyoming shipment of cattle on the Union Pacific Railroad, of which Galbraith alone represented eight carloads.[13]

On July 31, Merris C. Barrow, editor and owner of *Bill Barlow's Budget* of Douglas, Wyoming, editorialized with tongue in cheek and with biting irony:

> Healy, his brother, the cowboy Buchanan, and
> the boy who lived with Averell and Ella Watson,
> have fled to Casper for protection.

The boy they speak of must have been Gene Crowder; John DeCorey had already left on July 23, headed for Steamboat Springs. And by the by, does this mean that Buchanan is Healy's brother? No one ever mentioned that before. Or could it mean that a third person, Healy's brother, went along for protection to Casper? That is more likely. Barrow goes on to say:

> There is now no evidence against the accused
> men except that of Buchanan, and it is reported
> that he has skipped the country. The accused par-
> ties deny having confessed to the hanging or any
> complicity with the matter in any way or shape.

That settles it probably! Averell and Watson committed suicide, probably! Buchanan will disappear, probably, and that will end the matter— probably!

Although the accused parties initially admitted their involvement in the lynching, they had apparently changed their tune with the advent of legal counsel.

On August 1, the *Bessemer Journal* published an editorial in which the editor confessed to having been duped earlier by Towse. He said he now felt compelled to reveal the truth. His apology was under the heading:

THE HANGING
Avril It Is Said, Was Innocent and
Ella Watson Could Prove Where She Got Her Cattle.
Many Stories Were Told Before
The Facts Could Be Ascertained

Last week the Journal made a hasty announcement of the Sweetwater hanging based upon a report which reached us on Monday following the lynching. [Illegible] various rumors were afloat, and it was a hard matter to get the facts. It seems that the trouble which led to the crime was not cattle stealing, but grew out of land difficulties. We have heard parties say they would wager their last dollar that Jim Avril did not own a hoof and never put the branding iron on a calf in his life, as for Watson, it is said that she told the mob that if they would take her to Rawlins she would prove to them that she came by every head honestly and could show a bill of sale for each "critter" she owned or branded. Jim Avril had lived in the Sweetwater country for years, and is said by those

John Friend was the editor of the Carbon County Journal *and a social and military friend of Jim Averell.* (Carbon County Historical Museum.)

who know him, to have been a "big hearted fellow" always willing to help the poor and unfortunate. As for Ella Watson, her career was not that of a cattle thief....

On August 2 Averell's friend, Jim Casebeer, editor and owner of the *Casper Weekly Mail* published the following:

Did I know Jim Averell? Well, I should say I did—knowed him as a pretty decent fellow, too, and for that matter I think you will find that personal feelings have as much to do with this whole matter as cattle stealing.

The same day the *Rock Springs Independent* wrote:

> It is hoped that this plot upon the escutcheon of
> Wyoming will be wiped out by a speedy punish-
> ment of the lynchers, and that the courts will see
> that full justice be done.

Another news article by Jim's and Ellen's friend, John
Friend, of the Rawlins *Carbon County Journal* admonishes:

> The lynching is attracting a great deal of atten-
> tion in the city, and the highly colored accounts
> sent out by Cheyenne correspondents and pub-
> lished in Cheyenne papers, in which Averell is
> spoken of as a particularly tough citizen are
> severely censured. Averell was well and favorably
> known to this city, and has always been spoken of
> as a peaceable, law abiding citizen. He was Justice
> of the Peace in the precinct in which he resided.

The *Casper Weekly Mail*, under the steady-handed editorial arm of James A. Casebeer, wrote again on August 2
what was probably the best summary of editorial thinking
written during the post-lynching months. It seems to reflect
the general public sentiment across Wyoming. The editor
pulled no punches in laying responsibility for false and
misleading articles on the Cheyenne papers, and boldly put
the matter out on the table for everyone to see. He wrote:

> The hanging of James Averell and Ella Watson on
> the Sweetwater is still engaging considerable
> attention, and the fact that a farce was enacted at
> Rawlins in the shape of a preliminary examination
> causes thinking people to wonder whether any
> effort at all will be made to bring the murderers to
> justice. Men accused, and with convincing evi-
> dence, of a cold blooded and heartless murder,

admitted to bail in the sum of $5,000 each, and to cap the climax of this mock justice, allowed to sign each others bonds. No one but the accused was called upon to sign a document for the appearance and answering of these men to the charge of a heinous crime. And then, shades of departing justice! allow men to give bail for an unbailable offense.

Is a human life held at no value whatever? Are forty mavericks—allowing full credence to the accusation against the victims—to be put in the balance on the one side and be made to weigh more that two human lives on the other? Can it be, in this age of enlightenment, in the God-favored territory, soon to become a state, that the worst of all crimes can be committed and the perpetrators go free? It is surprising that such leading papers as the Stock Journal, Cheyenne Sun and Leader should even hint that the crime is excusable. Shame to such teachers of public morals. And the more shame that they should try to draw public sentiment into this channel of thinking before the time of trial in October.

The *Stock Journal* mentioned above was published by Asa Mercer who would later write the infamous *Banditti of the Plains,* that scathing condemnation of the cattlemen's invasion of Johnson County in 1892 to wipe out rustlers. This invasion was responsible for the murders of Nate Champion and his companion, Nick Ray at the Norton "K C" Ranch at present-day Kaycee, Wyoming. The wealthy cattle interests that had previously helped sustain his paper finally withdrew their advertising and forced the bankruptcy of Asa Mercer and his newspaper.

Casper editor Casebeer stated in another article:

It is argued that cattle thieves could not be convicted, and doubtless in many cases this was true. But that is not here nor there in the case. James Averell was not a cattle thief and if this business is sifted to the bottom, it will be found that his death was caused by far different reasons. He opposed the gobbling up of the public domain by individuals or corporations. He had no fear of, nor did he show any favors to a rich man. He held that a bona fide settler had a right to enter an enclosure, fraudulently held or covered up by a large land owner.[14] He favored the settling up of the rich valley of the Sweetwater with small ranches and the making of homes for hundreds of families, instead of having it owned and controlled by one or two English land lords.[15]

They talk about Averell stealing cattle. It is all bosh and buncombe. The writer was personally acquainted with him and knows that he expected there would be serious trouble over land affairs in the valley. As to the woman, she was never accused of using rope and branding iron by anyone near her. Whatever the outcome of the whole matter will be, is yet hard to predict, but all fair-minded people of the territory surely favor a thorough investigation. The protection of home, life and liberty demand it, and unless money and influence are brought to bear in the cases, a legal hanging may be in order within the next twelve months.

Also on August 2, another editorial by Barrow, the tongue-in-cheek editor of Douglas's newspaper *Barlow's Budget,* taunts George R. Caldwell, editor of the Lander paper, who, originally believed the Cheyenne rags and sided with the cattlemen. Barrow chided:

> Brother Caldwell: "That Lander Liar," [this was his well known nickname] must look to his laurels, else Ed. Towse will soon be an applicant for his crown. A man and woman were the principals in a necktie festival held up on the Sweetwater the other day. A man in Cheyenne received a ten word telegram two days afterward announcing the fact, and upon these ten words Towse built an air castle eight sticks in height, crowned with a scare head. It was the finest bit of dime-novel literature ever produced in these parts, reads like the third chapter of "Pop-Eyed Sam, the Sweetwater Swipe," or something like that. Hardly a word of truth in it, of course—the creation of Eddie's brain entire—and yet nine out of ten of his editorial colleagues copied it instead of the true account of the affair which appeared in The Sun.[16]

He referred, of course, to Ed Slack's second news article in the *Cheyenne Sun* where he did a 180-degree flip-flop and sided with the homesteaders.[17]

On August 3 John Friend of the *Carbon County Journal* in Rawlins shot from the hip and showed how editorial sentiment had quickly solidified against Cheyenne:

> The Cheyenne papers are the only ones in the territory that condone the Sweetwater lynching!

The article then went on to say something about editor Fetz and the *Sweetwater Chief* at Bothwell. Since no copies of the *Chief* seem to have survived and because both editors did actually witness the abduction, it is interesting to see what the Rawlins paper says about Fetz's *Sweetwater Chief's* editorial on the subject. It is one of only three known comments on the *Sweetwater Chief's* editorials following the lynching. Here is the first from the *Carbon County Journal* on August 3:

> The Bothwell Chief is very mild on the recent Sweetwater strangling, and, being on the ground, shows a lamentable lack of enterprise in not giving a full account of the affair. But then, as the police justice of the embryo city and its only female inhabitant were the victims, the editor perhaps thought he would be next, should he give the snap away, and wisely knew nothing.

Although it is chronologically premature here, another reference to the *Chief's* editorials was from the *Casper Weekly Mail* on August 16, almost two weeks later:

> The Sweetwater Chief still gets its news of the lynching from abroad.

Apparently it was still copying the *Dublin Times* articles of two weeks previous, which copied Ed Towse's first and second articles.[18] Fetz and Speer were still looking straight down the muzzle of Bothwell's 10-gauge shot gun! No wonder they soon loaded up their presses and moved to Rawlins.

Also on August 3 the *Carbon County Journal* had this to say about Jim Averell:

> Jim Averell was one of the biggest-hearted men in the country. No one ever went hungry from his door, and his house was always open for all. He was formerly Postmaster and held the office of Justice of the Peace. He was obliging, sociable and always a friend to the poor man. It is reported that he lived with this woman Watson at one time and was not married to her, but if this is sufficient

cause for mob law, what a glorious field Wyoming presents for hanging parties. Ellen Watson took up a ranch on Horse Creek a few years since and has improved it in a very creditable manner.[19] Her reputation has not been that of a cattle rustler, but of a common prostitute. [It is evident that this particular editor evidently gave credence to Towse's fabrications or to rumors.] There will doubtless be a trial. But what the outcome will be is hard to predict. It is hoped that law will be recognized and justice dealt out regardless of wealth or position.

As a state, Wyoming was excoriated in an news article on August 8 from Denver, Colorado's *Rocky Mountain News:*

The reputation of Wyoming will suffer for the murder by several rich cattlemen of a man and woman accused of having unlawfully branded some calves. This affair will attract wide attention and will unjustly reflect on the people of a large section of the country. The far west has not been fairly understood in the past and the erroneous impression that prevails undoubtedly operates in many ways to our prejudice. This Wyoming outrage is not a representative act. It is exceptional...! These self appointed judges and executioners represent a class who constitute a formidable barrier to the settlement of various points in the west. They are hostile to the settler and his family and lose no opportunity to discourage him by instigating annoyances and outrages. Only in exceptional cases have they any right to more than small bodies of land, except such as been gained by crooked methods. The honor of Wyoming is concerned in an impartial enforcement of the law in this disreputable affair.

On August 15, Editor Caldwell, the Lander Liar, of the *Fremont Clipper* of Lander, who was earlier berated by editor Barrow of *Bill Barlow's Budget* in Douglas for Caldwell's initial sympathy with the cattlemen, finally saw the error of his ways and lashed out against the Cheyenne editors with this editorial comment:

> Some people, and we regret to say, some papers, condone the hanging of this helpless woman and her paramour on the grounds that the laws cannot be enforced. All such know that they are giving utterance to false statements and do it simply to give a coloring of legality to a most hideous crime, simply because the guilty parties are men of "standing" in the communities where they live.

The *Casper Weekly Mail* on August 16 said defiantly:

> The victims of the late hanging party have not yet proven to be thieves, but on the contrary, there is positive and convincing evidence that neither Averell not the woman ever stole or assisted in stealing any cattle. Let it be distinctly understood that nine tenths of the people of Carbon County know that these parties were hung for another reason than that charged against them.

On another page of the same paper on the same day in an article credited to the *Laramie Boomerang*, the editor reprinted the following.

> A reporter to the Boomerang gets the following from a Sweetwater ranchman, which coincides

with the opinion expressed by nearly every man in that part of the country: Instead of being anything like the mythical "Kate", she was her exact opposite. She was neither bold nor daring. She could not ride horseback, neither could she throw a rope.

On the same day Ed Towse struck back with the following statement in the *Cheyenne Leader* where he whined:

> Quite a number of the territorial papers are making more or less fuss over the late Sweetwater lynching. Those apologists for cattle thieves should content their souls in peace, a condition in which they will be much better off than the thieves themselves, who will also have to be content with piece—a piece of a good stout rope!

The *Buffalo Echo* wrote the following on the same day:

> [Those] who exhibited their resentment of the so-called intrusions of these parties upon their unowned and unearned domain are wealthy and prominent in business circles. They have made the boast that their money would clear them in the courts when the time came for them to answer to the charges of murder which will certainly be brought against them. Who can imagine more flagrant violation and defiance of the law? How long will it take to remove the foul blot upon the territory's fair escutcheon which this shameless outrage has propagated.

On August 23, Douglas's paper, *Bill Barlow's Budget,* the paper of humorist M.C. Barrow, again wrote indignantly but prophetically:

> Of course the hanging of James Averill and Ella Watson was nothing but murder—and a murder of

the cold blooded, premeditated order, also. Averill was not a rustler, and while the woman Watson did have stock in her possession, it is a fact that she, herself, did not steal, or illegally brand, a single steer. She bought them. But what is to be gained from this incessant cry of murder? The men who hung this man and woman will never be punished therefor. They have too much money and too many friends who—believing that the victims were rustlers—endorsed their action. The fact is that land troubles, instead of cattle rustling, was what caused the tragedy; but if the men who did the hanging are to go unpunished, as they will, what's the use of wasting paper and ink?

Not long after, on August 28, the *Lusk Herald* pointedly asked this question:

When will the territorial papers get through "scrapping" over the lynching of James Averill and Ella Watson in Sweetwater Country? It looks to us as if they were trying the case outside of the courts, without having either a judge or jury!

Suddenly unexpected news appeared in the *Casper Weekly Mail* of August 30, about a month after the lynching, relative to Jim Averell's young nephew who came out from Wisconsin to visit his uncle less than a year before:

Ralph Cole, who has been sick for some time at the Averell ranch, died the first of last week and was buried near Bothwell!

This shocking development was luckily documented in a coroner's inquest at which editors Fetz and Speer of the Sweetwater Chief testified under oath.[20] It was suspected then, and it is still suspected today, that, although Ralph Cole's

H.B. Fetz, editor of the Sweetwater Chief, *was a witness to the abduction and also cared for Ralph Cole when he was ill.* (Carbon County Historical Museum)

sickness certainly was Mountain Fever accompanied by lower back pain and spasms, according to contemporary historical pathologists a hundred years later, the real culprit may very well have been orally-administered strychnine. It may very well have been added to the whiskey donated by lyncher Bob Conner, in small, almost undetectable doses. Or perhaps it was added to the medicine prescribed by Doctor A.H. Haynes, the local coroner from Casper, which was then administered unwittingly by the *Sweetwater Chief's* assistant editor Speer according to the doctor's orders. Thus Speer could have been unaware of his role as an accomplice when he helped Ralph take his medicine, as we will soon see. But perhaps he wasn't unaware at all.

Although such an allegation cannot be proven, it is possible that even Dr. Haynes, himself, may have been an accomplice in this matter. He was hired by Bob Conner who said not to worry, that he would take care of everything. Maybe Conner did. Since Bob Conner sent whiskey to Ralph, and since Conner, like Bothwell, said he felt no remorse regarding the murder of the two homesteaders, it seems logical to assume that he would have felt no pangs of remorse in administering a little poison to save his own neck.

The previous year a serious epidemic of Mountain Fever had spread throughout the West, and there was some residual carry-over into 1889. Although Mountain Fever was occasionally fatal, it was not so in the majority of cases. Could it be that Conner was simply guaranteeing Ralph's demise, insofar as Ralph would certainly have been a militantly hostile witness for the prosecution?

It is also to be remembered that under United States law, if the accuser does not, or cannot, testify in the trial affording cross-examination by defense, the accuser's testimony is inadmissible as evidence, even if it were officially sworn to and documented. The accused is entitled to face his accuser and cross-examine him. Most of the known witnesses to this lynching or abduction disappeared mysteriously or soon died (except for Ellen's young ranch-hand, fourteen-year-old John DeCorey, who was still apparently under heavy guard at Steamboat Springs, Colorado, and two sudden, last-minute, surprise witnesses for the prosecution).

The first surprise witness was John S. Cranor, a twenty-three-year-old bachelor homesteader from Split Rock, who apparently participated in the roundup and overheard the lynchers' plans in Bothwell's hay meadow or was perhaps a witness to the abduction or both. Just what John S. Cranor testified to is still unknown.

The second surprise witness was Bothwell's own foreman, John L. Sapp, whom Bothwell fired after their bitter argument over the lynching and who was perhaps another witness to both the lynchers' meeting or abduction.

Editors Fetz and Speer also witnessed the abduction, and Speer also was part of that unique conversation in the newspaper office with two of the lynchers prior to the hay meadow meeting. The editors were apparently so badly intimidated that they did not reveal that knowledge until after the grand jury hearing. And then finally there was Dan Fitger, if he told his daughter the truth about seeing the events.

It is ironic to discover that Assistant Editor Speer was originally from Red Cloud, Nebraska, where Ellen filed for divorce when she moved from Lebanon, Kansas. Whether they had met one another in Red Cloud is unknown, although, as we will learn, Ellen's father did not recognize him when he later ran into Speer at the *Sweetwater Chief* office in Bothwell.

Let's examine further Ralph Cole's death and determine why Bob Conner appears so guilty relative to Ralph's death. Luckily Ralph's last few days alive are documented in the official coroner's inquest held after his death.

The following is the "Evidence and Verdict of the Coroner's Inquest" held in the death of Ralph Cole on September 9, 1889, about two months after the lynching.[21] Two of the jurors were listed as B. Frank Buchanan and Ed Joseph "Tex" Healy, who must have been there, but curiously did not actually sign.

The first testimony at the inquest was given by H.B. Fetz and is as follows:

I was acquainted with Ralph E. Cole since about the middle of April 1889. The first I knew of his sickness, was about the 15th of August 1889. Stayed at my residence until he died on the 24th day of August 1889. Mr. Spears and I nursed him through his sickness up until the 18th day of August 1889. I did not consider him very sick until Sunday evening when he was taken with a pain in the small of his back. On Monday morning the 19th day of August 1889 the Doctor was sent for.

I started from here to get some one to go after him. I got Johny McCabe to go to Casper after the Doctor. The doctor arrived here on Tuesday morning the 20th day of August 1889. The Dr. remained here until Wednesday morning. The Visitors were John McCabe, [Dan] R. Fitger, Fred Turner, Peterson of Bessemer, also J.H. Omstead visited him. Mr. Conner was here on Sunday evening. I was out and in the room and helped to take care of him.

Question: Was Conner in the Room?

Answer: Not to my knowledge.

Question: Was the Round up boys here?

Answer: They were.

Question: Were you acquainted with any of them?

Answer: I don't know that any of them visited him.

Question: Was any of the men here that was interested in the lynching?

Answer: Mr. Conner was the only one that was here. He [Ralph] died at my Residence on the 24th day of August 1889. .

Question: Do you know anything of his effects?

Answer: Some of his things are here and some of them are at the Averell ranch.

Question: Can you tell any of the conversation?

Answer: "[Ralph Cole said] Don't believe there is any more danger of dying today than there was yesterday." From the very first of the sickness he seemed to feel he would not get well.

Signed: H. B. Fetz

The testimony of J. N. Speer followed:

I was personally acquainted with Ralph E. Cole deceased. He came here Thurs. evening about dusk a horse back. I asked him in to stay. [He said], "I've been sick for a few days and have just came from a doctor who is with some troops who advised me not to stay alone as I was liable to have a spell of sickness. The doc. gave me some medicine to take and said I had the Mt. Fever or that it would run into it." He and I slept together Thus. Fri. and Sat. nights. He complained of no pain but was very restless Sat. night, and complained of pain in small of back.

In the morning as he made no complaint I applied no remedy. In the evening about 7 P.M. he complained of severe pain in small of back and said "Really my back has been hurting me all day." A few minutes afterwards he seemed to go into a convulsion or spasm which lasted perhaps 3 minutes and then he would have relief about the same length of time, and spasm being repeated, only much longer. He complained only of his back when spasm was not on. I was alone at the time, Mr. Fetz being gone after medicine. Fetz returned with whiskey and the spasms continued until he had had 25 more or less. At times it was difficult to hold him in bed.

On Fetz's return we applied hot applications and brought relief about 2:30 A.M. Monday. We sent for doctor on Monday. Doc. arrived on Tuesday 7 A.M. He left on Wednesday at 10 A.M. Ralph seemed better and very much encouraged. I gave him his medicine regularly as directed that doctor Haynes left for him. I could see no particular change until Friday. His fever seemed broken and he sweat profusely until he died. On Saturday he [had] no pain apparently except in his groin which became swollen. He died on 11 P.M. Sat., Aug. 24, 1889 and was buried on Mon. the 26 on the townsite of Bothwell.

On Sunday evening the 18 of Aug. word was brought me that Ralph thought that he was dying and wanted me to come over. Mr. Conner & John McCabe were there with me. I came over and on my return said I did not think him dangerous at that time. Conner said he ought to have a doctor and when you think that he needs one let me know and I'll send for one from Casper. Mr. Conner, McCabe and Mr. Fetz went up to Conner's Ranch after whiskey. I gave him small doses of the whiskey. He said he thought it gave him strength.

[Notice that Ralph Cole is receiving regular doses of whiskey as treatment. The whiskey came from Bob Conner through Fetz to Speer and it was not part of a doctor's orders.]

While in convulsions his arms & legs were entirely paralyzed but he regained the use of them after his pain left. After he would have a spasm he would say "Well, I did not go that time." He authorized me to write to his parents to say to them that he had had no pain—that he was thoroughly reconciled to death and thought it better to die now than to linger longer, that they would understand why he made that statement.

He said that my only anxiety is on acc't of the indebtedness of my uncle to my father. On Sunday evening the 18th Aug. 1889 at intervals he frequently asked me to write to his parents. After his convulsions were over he asked me not to write. On the Sat. following about 4 A.M. I began a letter at his dictation which was not finished but was forwarded to his father at Eureka, Wisconsin. One expression in this letter was as follows: "I think that I'll be alright again in a few days".

On Saturday I wrote a letter to Dr. Haynes and sent by messenger to Casper for medicine. Ralph was dead before he returned. He said my father furnished my uncle James Averell $300.00 (Three Hundred dollars) to prove up on desert claim with.[22] I induced my father to furnish the money which is the cause of me worrying so. Cole said that the Dr. told him that Conner would stand good for the doctor bill.

His uncle James Averell owed him and said that I could find an acc't on the table at said James Averell's Ranch. He had $7.08 when he came here. The time the Round up was in this vicinity I think Sam Johnson [23] was here and if he was not here that day, he has been here since. I do not know whether he stated that doctor told him or whether he said the boys told him that Conner would stand good for the Doctor's expenses.

      Signed: J. N. Speer
      J.A. Bennett—Coroner.

The last part of the inquest was the coroner's list of Ralph Cole's possessions.[24] They were certainly austere:

"One pen holder, one money purse, one pocket knife, one shot gun, one pair of shoes, one coat & vest, one pair pants, one hat, three quilts, one suit of underclothing, $7.08 in cash."

Lastly, there was a personal note for $46.15 from Jim Averell to Ralph's parents. The reader will recall Ralph's concern about the money Averell owed his father just before his death. That's it. That's everything. It is abundantly clear that Ralph had no money for frivolities.

It is also interesting to note that Sam Johnson, Averell's friend, from the Bar Eleven ranch, which bordered Averell's first homestead on Cherry Creek, where Jim's wife Sophia miscarried, came to check on Ralph's well-being.

16. A Father's Agony

The Rawlins' *Carbon County Journal* of August 31 reported that Thomas Watson, Ellen's father, arrived in Rawlins, from Kansas several days previous. He immediately contacted George W. Durant, court appointed administrator of Ellen's estate, in the offices of attorney George C. Smith. The next day Watson and Durant caught the stage north to Sand Creek. There was no regular stage run of any kind through the Sweetwater Valley to Casper until October 1889, but a Concord stage mail route had recently been initiated and ran north as far as Ferris Post Office at Sand Creek, about twenty miles south from the town of Bothwell. When Tom Watson and George Durant got off the stage at Sand Creek, they then must have borrowed or rented horses for the rest of the trip north to Bothwell. It would have been highly unlikely that they actually walked the rest of the way.

Durant didn't divulge Tom Watson's real name or identity, so he traveled incognito. Upon their arrival, they set about auctioning off Ellen's and Jim's belongings. While at the Averell road ranch, they were accompanied by Stewart Joe Sharp, and Bothwell's foreman, J.L. Sapp, who showed Watson the graves of his daughter and Jim Averell. Ruth Beebe, Joe Sharp's youngest daughter, very well recalls her father telling about that sorrowful moment:

247

When they arrived at the gravesite, Ellen's father slowly let himself down off his horse and stood silently looking down with his eyes fixed on the large, soft mound of dirt and, for a very long time, he just kept on staring down at his daughter's grave. He then turned to my father [Joe Sharp] and chokingly said: "I wish my little girl had listened to her mother. She told her not to leave home. If she had listened to her mother, she wouldn't be buried here today." Then he suddenly lost all composure and began sobbing uncontrollably. His poor little girl, his first-born baby, lay murdered under all that soft, fresh dirt.

In an interview with the *Rock Springs Independent,* Ellen's father, Tom Watson said in his thick Scottish brogue:

I am 52 years of age, and have a wife and nine children living. She [Ellen] was with us for the last time nearly two months, June and July, a year ago. We were always in regular correspondence with her. In answer to my questions as to how she made a living on her ranch, she said she worked part of the time for Averill and she had saved considerable money while working out before she located her claim.

I read the first account of the hanging of my daughter in the Omaha Bee. I wrote to the postmaster at Sweetwater for particulars.

Ironically Watson had unwittingly written to Al Bothwell, who had just supplanted Averell as postmaster with the political change from the Democratic administration under Cleveland to Republican under Harrison. Watson continued:

I received no answer from him, but had a letter from young Cole, to whom Bothwell, the postmaster

turned over my letter. Cole is now dead, and Bothwell is accused of being one of the gang who murdered my child. In his letter Cole referred me to
George W. Durant, the administrator appointed in
the estate.[1] I opened communication with Durant,
and as a consequence I arrived in Rawlins on the
26th of August.

On the following day I accompanied Durant to
Ella's ranch and served as clerk at the sale of her
property. In that country I travelled under an
assumed name and no one knew I was the father of
Ella, the murdered girl.

The auction of Ellen's property, under the official sanction
of George Durant as administrator, with Ellen's father as sales
clerk, listed her property as:

2 Cows and calves, 1 cow, 1 two year old steer,
4 yearlings,[2] 1 pony, 1 mare and colt, 15 chickens,
1 cook stove and furniture, 1 heating stove, 4
doors, 5 windows, 1 bedstead and bedding, dishes
and kitchen utensils, 1 grind stone, 1 hoe, 1 rake, 1
clock, 1 sewing machine, 1 dining table, 1 starred
quilt, 6 chairs, 1 side-saddle, 1 hanging lamp, set
of knives and forks, 1 set of bracelets, 1 breast pin
& ear bobs, 2 finger rings, 1 chain, 1 trunk & contents, 1 log house on claim, wire fence on claim,
about 200 feet of flooring.

That's it. That's everything. Sounds pretty domestic.
Hardly seems like a whorehouse. It is evident that Ellen made
her own clothes, and perhaps even made some extra change
by sewing or repairing the clothing of others. In those days
most women made their own clothes.With chickens, cows,
and a garden, she probably needed little store-bought food.

While in the Sweetwater country, as administrator for the estate of James Averell, with Thomas Watson again officially sworn in as sales clerk, George Durant listed Jim Averell's possessions as:

Two checks, (Charter Oak) cook stove and furniture, two heating stoves, silver (plated) caster (salt & pepper holders), two bedsteads with bedding (6 quilts, 4 mattresses, 6 wool blankets), one Regulator clock, one (Parker) shot gun, one cartridge belt, (one pistol) [brass pistol shell casings discovered at the road ranch site indicate it was probably .44 caliber], one Winchester rifle [.44 caliber brass rifle casings also found on location], dishes [pieces of delft-type china with delicate, pretty brown and white designs were also found at the site of road ranch store], (utensils & tableware), lamps and all household goods, one set Fairbanks scales, one and one half bottles of beer, 16 beer mugs, 12 glasses and one lemon squeezer, three bottles extract, 13 pails of axle grease, three boxes blacking, one sack of timothy (grass seed), 3 sacks of dried fruit, one can of coal oil, 9 ducks, twelve chickens, chains and grindstone, two picks, two saws, 2 axes, one trowel, 1 spade, one (McCormick) mowing machine, one (breaking) plow, one set of carpenter's tools, (one set of blacksmith's tools), mining tools and fuse, nails, hoe and shovels, surveyor's compass and chain, twine, lamp chimneys, stencils, one packet rice, one patch of potatoes, desk, two nose bags, one harrow, one (horse) hay rake, one shovel plow, six spools of wire, two horse collars and double harness, man's saddle, one three truck (3 inch) Bain wagon [this was a trade name for the six-by-twelve foot wagon which Jim was driving to Casper when he was abducted], one sorrel horse branded Andiron, one bay horse branded Andiron, one horse branded Reverse J T J, and two mares branded Reverse J T J, one (log) dwelling/house (eighteen-by-twelve foot with addition seventeen-by-fourteen foot), 1,000 lbs. flour, 1,000 lbs. oats, one buggy, one saloon building, one ice house, and one stable on desert claim homestead.

[The things in parentheses are additional items or more completely described items found on chattel mortgage papers. The mortgages were to J.W. Hugus and Company or John C. Dyer, a saloon keeper and money lender in Rawlins where Averell initially bought keg beer on credit for his little store.]

If Jim sold hard liquor at his road house, someone had already made off with it since there was only beer inventoried. It is quite possible that he had no hard liquor. It is interesting to note that many of the mortgaged items go back to his first marriage on the Cherry Creek homestead.

Jim had collected a lot of items over the years, but they surely don't resemble what one would expect to find in a house of ill repute. It is, however, exactly what you would find on a hard-working granger's homestead. It seems evident that Jim was doing exactly what he advocated in his crusading letter to the *Casper Weekly Mail*. He was trying to farm, run a store and serve meals and beer on the side. He was evidently an extremely busy fresh produce farmer. No wonder he needed Ellen and Ralph Cole to help him. When did the man ever find time to sleep?

The fact that so much of the above property was mortgaged indicates that Jim certainly hadn't made a killing in any legal or illegal enterprise. It appears as though he was struggling along trying to improve both his Desert Land Act claims. Nothing in his possessions vaguely smacks of cattle stealing or illicit business of any kind. The sale of his possessions didn't even cover his financial obligations.

It has previously been alleged that Ellen's cabin was hauled to Bothwell's Ranch and turned into an ice-house. Not so according to Stanford Sanford, grandson of the Sanford family who bought the ranch from Bothwell. Sanford said that it was Averell's ice-house, mentioned above in the inventory, that was moved in as an ice-house. After the ranch was sold to the Sanford family, they skidded the ice-house northeast across Bothwell's favorite hay meadow with a tandem team of draft horses and added it to Bothwell's existing complex of ranch buildings on top of Jim Averell's last homestead claim. Averell's road ranch would have needed ice all year round to cool the beer. Jim obviously had to keep the beer from souring in the spring, summer and fall, and from freezing in the winter. And he needed the ice house to refrigerate the fresh produce he grew for sale to the public. In addition to the dozens of other chores in the winter, Jim must have kept busy cutting, loading, hauling, stacking and covering the ice with hay for next year's ice supply. Jim was clearly not afraid of hard work.

Now let's return to the interview with Ellen's father, Thomas. He continues:

> She had sixty acres under a three-wire fence strung on strong cedar posts. The fence on the east and west sides was torn down and Bothwell's cattle were running over everything and everywhere.
>
> At the time she was forcibly taken from her home and hanged she was building a new log house and some of the doors and windows were already

in. It is situated at least 1 3/4 miles [northeast] from Averill's store. Ella lived alone,[3] with no one about her premises except a young boy, Decorey, 14 years of age, to whom she was paying wages. She had about forty head of young stock running in her pasture,[4] which the devils who took her life drove away. I am told the Wyoming Stock Growers Association got them after the lynchers had committed their bloody work.[5]

After Durant went away I remained in Averill's ranch all day Sunday alone. In the afternoon I rode to the very spot where my Ella was strangled to death, and saw the limb of the tree over which the rope was thrown.

Actually the cattle were stolen by Durbin and Bothwell after the lynching. George W. Durant, as administrator of the Ellen L. Watson Estate, sued both Durbin and Bothwell to recover the combined value of the cattle, the destruction of property, court costs and legal fees in the amount of $1,100 as compensation to her estate. We have been unable to discover the outcome of the action, but if Ellen's bad luck continued as before, Durant was probably unsuccessful.

In the following letter written back home and printed in the local newspaper in Lebanon, Kansas, Thomas Watson said he used his daughter's pony for the ride to the hanging tree. He wrote:

The bark is abraded and plainly shows the mark of their fiendish work. Underneath the limb a little to one side stands a rock, from which they no doubt were shoved off after the ropes were adjusted around their necks. The tree stands at the head of a rocky canyon about two miles from Ella's ranch.

John L. Sapp who was Bothwell's foreman, on learning what had taken place raised a vigorous howl against such unjust and unlawful procedure, which of course, precipitated a quarrel with Bothwell. This quarrel resulted in Sapp's dismissal from Bothwell's employ.

Another cowboy who quarreled with Bothwell over the lynching was Joe Sharp, the Butler brothers' foreman, who was also working at the roundup and who also confronted Bothwell at his ranch with questions directly after the murders. Not long after the lynching Joe Sharp purchased Averell's first homestead, the V Bar Ranch on Cherry Creek, from the Butler brothers when they both moved back to Philadelphia for good. Joe then went into ranching for himself. As a postscript, Ruth Beebe recalled that one of the Butler brothers, which one is unknown, after moving back to Philadelphia, took a pistol, planted himself in front of a full length mirror and blew his brains out. No explanation can be found.[6]

Ellen's father continued in the Rock Springs newspaper interview:

> I visited Bothwell's ranch but failed to find him at home. I also called at the headquarters of the Sweetwater Chief, a sheet published where there are two houses and a vacant townsight. I met Fetz, the presumed editor, and Speer, the supposed associate editor. With the latter I entered into conversation. After some hesitation and evasion he pointed his finger to the very spot where the lynching was done, and when I informed him I had just come from there his curiosity became aroused and he drew himself within his shell. Both his looks and his actions excited suspicion within

me, but further probing on my part could elicit no
response about the hanging. He informed me that
Cole had died from the effects of an operation that
had been performed for the mumps. After my
interview with Speer I returned to Rawlins.

As far as can be determined, this is the only mention of an
operation for mumps. Very curious. Sounds contrived.

On September 6, an article in the *Platte Valley Lyre* of
Saratoga, Wyoming, expounded:

County Surveyor Sterrett, who returned this
week from the scene of the brutal outrage, informs
us that the feeling is very intense against the perpetrators of the double murder in that neighbor-
hood,[7] and that the determination of bringing the
offenders against law and order to justice, is gaining daily in strength. James Averell seems to have
borne the reputation of a quiet man and good
neighbor. The only fault that can apparently on
good ground be found with Kate, is that "she
loved not wisely, but too well." We are glad that a
subscription list has been started for the purpose
of aiding the prosecution of these votaries of
Judge Lynch.[8]

In a different development, on September 10, Sheriff
John Williams of Converse County and the Crook County
sheriff arrived in Casper on a special train and served a warrant for the arrest of Phil Watson (now the Sundance Town
Marshal) and Jess Lockwood on charges of horse stealing.
Ten days later they returned to Sundance and served a similar
warrant on Tex Healy. The three men were arraigned in Sundance. Watson's and Lockwood's bonds were set at $2000

each and Healy's at $1500. Watson, age 30, was convicted of grand larceny and sentenced to six years in the brickyard at the penitentiary at Joliet, Illinois. He was placed at Joliet because the Territorial Prison in Laramie had been closed and the new Wyoming State Penitentiary in Rawlins was not yet open. After serving four years and three months, Watson was released on executive pardon by Governor Amos W. Barber and moved to Montana. Jess Lockwood, age 22, received a sentence of four years, but was released after three years and two months, apparently on good behavior. Healy, after posting bail, forfeited his bond and skipped the country for a while, after which he calmly returned to his ranch on Fish Creek and no further efforts were made to prosecute him.

Phil Watson's conviction on charges of horse stealing, however, did not invalidate the original coroner's inquest over which he presided which identified the lynchers by name and contained the testimony of Buchanan, Crowder, DeCorey and Ralph Cole and where both Watson and Tex Healy also testified.The lynchers, their attorneys, and powerful friends had strong reasons to want that testimony negated. In fact, before long the Rawlins officials did just that. They declared the first coroner's jury invalid and insisted that the second coroner's jury was the only legal one. This was not only illegal, but was also blatant chicanery.

Meanwhile, from the *Cheyenne Sun* of September 11 came an entirely unexpected development:

> A brother of Jim Averell, whose home is in Tacoma, Washington Territory,[9] appeared upon the scene as the avenger of his brother's death. He came quietly into the country, and without making known his business went to the Sweetwater region to pursue his investigations.
>
> He succeeded in securing five witnesses.[10]

The Cheyenne Daily Leader *was housed in the elegant Cheyenne Opera House building.* (UW American Heritage Center.)

Buchanan, it seems, had not left the country as reported, but was in the employ of the Niobrara Transportation Company as a mule puncher. The feeling runs so high that the witnesses in passing through the country along their old haunts keep themselves well armed with Winchesters[11] and are ever on the alert.

The person they spoke of is a younger half brother of Jim Averell whose name was R.W. (Willie) Cahill who was a laborer and boarded in a single room at 1955 Jefferson Avenue in Tacoma, Washington, and later moved to Spokane. It is also true that everyone did, indeed, go heavily armed for an extended period of time. It was in fact for several decades, according to old timers and the newspapers.[12]

Also on September 11, in the *Cheyenne Daily Leader,* this article attracted a lot of attention.

WAS AVERILL'S NEPHEW POISONED?

> Coroner Bennett has just returned from Bothwell. The remains of Averill's nephew, who died suddenly last week, were exhumed. They found his eyes protruding out on his cheeks. There are strong suspicions of poisoning.

Then, in the same paper we read:

> Buchanan, the principal witness who saw the hanging by the mob, and is the one who shot at the lynchers, was brought in and is protected here from harm, to appear before the grand jury next month.

What? Buchanan had been brought to Cheyenne? For protection? By whom? Frank Buchanan had been moved to the very hot-bed of his enemies with a whole month and a half still to go before the grand jury hearing. How was such a maneuver ever allowed by the Carbon County officials? What an incredible mistake!

In the *Casper Weekly Mail* of September 13 the following news story appeared:

> The body of Ralph Cole has been placed in the hands of eminent physicians to be examined as to the cause of death.

Something else now floats to the surface and is very strange indeed. On September 15, the *Carbon County Journal* in Rawlins published a letter to the editor, signed only as "Citizen." The letter said:

> Some officers[13] started north to procure witnesses for the grand jury which meets in October. Ain't it very strange that things are allowed to run so loose in the country? It is a well known fact that our sheriff has in his possession a letter from a sheriff in an adjoining state notifying him that there was a man

there who witnessed the strangling of Miss Watson and Averill, and, if our sheriff wanted him, he could be brought inside of four days.

The deputy prosecuting attorney [Howard] was shown the letter by the sheriff to know what to do and for advice. The County Attorney says: "I think it a d—n lie!"

It looks strange that a sheriff should send a letter from another state to our sheriff when he could not certainly have any interest in the matter; only to help to see the dead have justice. Another strange part! The men who are alleged to have done the lynching were brought to town in the evening. The following morning, somewhere about 6 A.M., a justice of the peace from Casper [Emery],[14] was called to hold an examination. We have two justices of the peace in the city. The report is that the examination took place in Rankin's stable. Only four citizens here knew anything about it. [15]

The letter referred to above was probably a letter from the sheriff of Steamboat Springs, Colorado, advising of the presence there of young John DeCorey. That letter has never been found and was probably destroyed.

The October grand jury referred to is the preliminary hearing called by Judge Corn of the third judicial district in Rawlins. The newspaper article also referred to the preliminary hearing that was held soon after the murders and was held early in the morning by Deputy Prosecutor Howard when the lynchers were first brought into Rawlins by Deputy Sheriff Phil Watson and Casper Justice of the Peace Emery when they were put under bail of $5,000 each.

The letter to the editor from the citizen went on to complain further:

> Our county attorney takes on himself to fix the
> grade of crime at manslaughter so as to make it a
> bailable offense, he said, to save the county expense.

So now it becomes clear how the lynchers were released
on $5,000 bail. The judge called it manslaughter, not murder.
Judge Emery must have been duped, bribed, or coerced by
Prosecutor Howard, who was also there, to pass down the
decision of manslaughter. Is that collusion or what? The letter
to the editor continued further:

> Remember, not a single witness for the prosecu-
> tion was present, when the officers knew who they
> were. Do such things look right when we are sup-
> posed to be governed by law?

But Deputy County Attorney, H. H. Howard, however, did
indeed later try to excuse Casper Justice of the Peace Emery's
action with the old, threadbare excuse of "fiscal responsibility." The County was saved an unnecessary expense.

Next we find the following interesting tidbit in the
Laramie Boomerang of September 15:

> Coroner Bennett of Carbon county caused the
> remains [of Ralph Cole] to be exhumed and the
> stomach to be taken out, a jury for the purpose of
> holding an inquest having been first impaneled. In
> the presence of the jury, Dr. Haynes of Casper
> placed the stomach in a glass jar and sealed it. The
> inquest was then adjourned to meet at Rawlins,
> October 15. The stomach will in the meanwhile be
> sent to a competent chemist for analysis.

Dr. Haynes, who attended Ralph Cole, and may even be
implicated in the poisoning, has unbelievably been allowed to
cut out Ralph Cole's stomach and then to seal those remains

in a jar. It increasingly appears that Dr. Haynes may possibly be an accomplice in Ralph's death. Back in those frontier days, with the primitive clinical procedures that were then known, it seems almost impossible that tiny amounts of strychnine could have been detected. We have more chemicals and medicines under the sink in the bathroom and kitchen today than doctors had then.

Nothing ever came of the postmortem. The "competent chemist," whoever that was, purportedly said he found no trace of poison. Since others with incriminating testimony in this case seemed to die, remain mute, or change their tunes, it would be naive not to wonder if Dr. Haynes or this chemist might also have been bribed or threatened. However, that may not have been necessary because it is unlikely that strychnine in small doses could have been detected by the chemist. Nothing was left as evidence in this matter. But the symptoms and circumstances of Ralph's death had the smell of collusion about them, which, of course, was why the coroner's inquest was called in the first place.

Four days later on September 19, a new letter to the editor appeared in the *Cheyenne Leader*:

AVERILL'S HALF BROTHER
He Has Something To Say
About The Recent Lynching.

To the editor of the Leader.
Rawlins, Wyo. Sept 16

Dear Sir: There is some dime novel friend in Cheyenne who has been ridiculing the character of James Averill. Why don't he let up, or be a man and come out and sign his name? Nothing but a coward will impose insults on both dead and living, and not give them a chance to defend themselves. Could that dime novel cur look one of Jim Averill's friends fair in the eyes, let alone express his sentiments to one of them? Is there any satisfaction the dirty coward wants? I expect he is waiting to get a chance to help lynch some one so as to satisfy his dime novel lust. Whenever he does meet a relation of James Averill, he will meet a man whose hands ain't red with the blood of an innocent fellow man and a man who, like James Averill, was always ready to share his dollars with those in trouble and never stoop so low as to uphold murderers in this beautiful land of the free, where the law is made by the people and for the people. Now those whom this fits can fight back and will find a man who ain't afraid to sign his name to the public.

Respectfully,
    R.W. Cahill—Half brother of James Averill.

The letter certainly made its point. Jim's half-brother was livid about the scandalous lies in the *Cheyenne Daily Leader* about his brother. He didn't know that the person he was railing against was Ed Towse, and Towse would no more sign his name to those news articles than walk a tight wire across Niagara Falls. The latter would have been far less hazardous to his health. This, by the way, is Cahill's only known utterance.

From the *Rock Springs Independent* we read two days later on September 21:

James [should be Thomas] Watson, father of Ella Watson, who was lynched on the Sweetwater a couple of months ago, is in town and will work here until the trial of the supposed lynchers takes place at Rawlins. He is a common farmer and laborer from Kansas. He tells us that his daughter had a husband in Kansas, but left him because they could not get along together, and that he knows nothing of her character or career since she has been in Wyoming.

It was sorrowful for this author to learn recently that the lies and editorial subterfuge finally convinced Ellen's distraught father that she was actually guilty of prostitution and rustling. As a final indignity inflicted upon Ellen Watson and her family, upon his return home to Kansas, Ella's father autocratically declared that no member of the family was ever to utter Ellen's name again so long as they should live. Anything belonging to Ellen was destroyed. How sorrowful that Ellen's own mother and father and all her sisters and brothers actually believed Ellen was a trollop and a rustler. But as a result of Thomas Watson's admonition, the family obediently abided unswervingly by his wishes for over one hundred years. Many of the remaining family members are still unaware of the true story. The Cheyenne editorials were effective, indeed!

Thomas Watson took up residence in Rock Springs, a mining town on the Union Pacific Railroad about one hundred miles west of Rawlins. He probably chose Rock Springs for security reasons. Many Rawlins politicians had climbed in bed with the lynchers, and Watson had been advised that staying around Rawlins might be hazardous to his health.

Also on September 21, we find Ralph Cole's obituary, which was originally published in Eureka, Wisconsin, reprinted in the *Carbon County Journal.* Most ritualistic lodge material has been deleted for brevity:

Died-Sweetwater, Wyo., August 25, 1889,
Ralph Cole, of Eureka, Wis., aged 21 years.
Ralph was the oldest son of A. R. and Anna [should be Sarah] Cole. He left Eureka for Wyoming

last April to spend some time with his uncle, James Averell, who was a ranchman at Sweetwater. On July 20 Averell was taken from his ranch by a posse of his enemies and hung.

The sad news was a terrible shock to his family and friends, and Ralph had many friends and no enemies. He was such a boy as one makes the acquaintance of, perhaps but once in a life time. His life and character was as pure as the snow from heaven. He was an honored member of Rushford Dio. of Sons and Daughters of Temperance.

Resolved, that we, the members of the Rushford Dio. No. 228, Sons and Daughters of Temperance, deeply sympathize with the family in their affliction, and in the hereafter may we all meet our brother in that grand fraternity where God is the grand patriarch "who doeth all things well." [16]

On October 12, Owen Wister, the famous author of *The Virginian,* while at a stage stop on the road northwest from Rawlins to Fort Washakie, wrote this about his Union Pacific Railroad train ride the day before. His companion was probably John Durbin, since he was the only one of the lynchers who regularly commuted back and forth from Rawlins to Cheyenne:

Sat yesterday in smoking car with one of the gentlemen indicted for lynching the man and woman. He seemed a good solid citizen and I hope he'll get off. Sheriff Donell [he meant Hadsell] said "All good folks say it was a good job; it's only the wayward classes that complain".

Now we know for certain where Sheriff Frank Hadsell's sentiments were.

17. THE LOST CAUSE

On October 16, 1889, the following appeared in the *Cheyenne Daily Leader*:

The grand jury, to which the Averill-Watson lynching case will be presented, was empaneled this afternoon. I.C. [Issac] Miller, the sheep grower, is foreman. Messrs. J.H. Mullison, W.B. Hugus, [John] Milliken, [Alfred] Crane, [John] Mahoney, [C.W.] Burdick, [H.A.] Andrews, [W.L.] Evans, [T.J.] Dickinson, [James] Candlish, [Charles] Hardin, [Harry] Haines, [John C.] Dyer, [F.M.] Baker and [George] Mitchell comprise the jury.

Judge Corn[1] charged them in regard to the lynching of Averill and the Watson woman, that it had come to the ears of the court through various channels, rumors and newspaper publications that certain parties are charged with hanging a man and woman in this county, that your attention is impartially called to this matter, and that you are sworn to prosecute none through ill will or malice and to leave none unmolested through fear or favor.

After the judge's charge, the jury were sent out under a bailiff, when court adjourned until this

265

morning. The city is crowded with people, and great interest manifested in the result of the jury's deliberations. The jurymen are all reputable citizens, men of standing in the county. Corlett, Lacey and Riner, with J.R. Dixon are defending and D.H. [David] Craig,[2] together with Assistant Attorneys [H.H.] Howard and D.A. [David] Preston,[3] are prosecuting.

A challenge to the entire panel was interposed by the defense and overruled, and a challenge against William Jungquist, being excused, I.C. Miller was chosen to fill the panel.

This omnipotent array of legal might in defense of the cattlemen is unquestionably one of the most prestigious and politically powerful in the entire history of Wyoming. The Wyoming Stock Grower's Association rolled in virtually all its firepower. The attorneys, except for Dixon, had previously been employed in the defense of the Association and its members, but not all at once. Dixon was evidently added to lend still greater local influence and credibility.

David Preston's term as county prosecutor was about to expire, and he had inadvisably and prematurely moved northwest from Rawlins to Lander in Fremont County where he set up a new home and practice. He returned to Rawlins only under duress when he was asked to assist David Craig in prosecuting the lynchers. It appears, however, that the lion's share of the preparation for the trial and its prosecution was carried out in frantic haste by David Craig with very little help from either of his assistants, who had earlier had all the time in the world while Prosecutor Craig was still in Ireland, London and Paris.

Craig was also possessed of a thick Scottish brogue which was not generally perceived to be an especially desirable

Judge Samuel T. Corn presided over the grand jury proceedings in the Watson-Averell case. The grand jury met in Rawlins in October following the lynchings. (Wyoming State Museum.)

asset. He was, however, the only one of the attorneys militantly loyal to the prosecution from the beginning to the end. He proved himself to be one of the unsung heroes in this story, even in the face of fantastic political pressure to the contrary.

Craig had recently completely severed his association with his law partner, now probate judge Fenimore Chatterton, because Craig suspected, with what he considered adequate justification, that Chatterton was involved in illegal chicanery favoring the cattlemen while Craig was sojourning in Ireland.[4]

Chatterton then instantly became an up-and-coming, fair-haired boy in the Republican party and was later elected Secretary of State, and still later, upon the premature vacancy of the governor's office, became Wyoming's acting governor, while, on the other hand, loyal Craig had his political job snatched from him.

Parenthetically, Chatterton, in his autobiographical book, *Yesterday's Wyoming*, wrote that he had stayed overnight with "the Averills" at their comfortable Sweetwater road ranch on a trip to Casper in August 1888 to try to suppress the votes of Democratic railroad workers there. As an up-and-coming Republican politician, Chatterton would never have been caught dead in a house of prostitution and would certainly never have admitted to such an overnight stay if "the Averills" had possessed even the slightest reputation of impropriety. So we have still further evidence that neither Jim nor Ellen were engaged in the business of prostitution. It is interesting to note, however, that in the same chapter, he referred to Jim Averell as if he had never seen him before, even though Jim was his employee at the sutler's store at Fort Fred Steele for nearly six months after Jim's discharge from the Ninth Infantry. It seems unlikely that Chatterton was unable to remember someone with whom he worked side-by-side for a half a year. Chatterton was doing his best to distance himself from even the tiniest suggestion of disrespectability.

It is interesting to learn that Averell's friend, William Junquist, was removed from the jury after William Daley swore, that around August 1, 1889, he overheard Junquist declare that he thought Jim Averell was a better man than anyone of the lynchers ever was and that he would cheerfully give one hundred dollars toward the prosecution of the lynchers. Jungquist then swore that Daley was a liar and published a full denial in Rawlins' *Carbon County Journal* on October 26.[5] At this

David H. Craig, the prosecuting attorney, pursued the case against the lynchers with vigor. (Carbon County Historical Museum.)

point very little seemed to be going well for the prosecution.

But, in the same issue of the same paper, the "coup de grace" was fired directly into the face of the prosecution's case. The paper screamed:

Frank Buchanan, chief witness for the prosecution in the Averill/Watson lynching case has forfeited his bond of $500[6] and fled the country. An attachment has been issued for his arrest and an officer dispatched in search. He is supposed to have been bribed to leave. Buchanan was here last week and left for a visit to Dana, this county, [a water-stop on the Union Pacific, thirty-five miles east of Rawlins] promising the return for court. No indictments have yet been presented in court against any of the parties accused of the lynching.

Well, there it is! That's it! The prosecution's case was demolished! Without Buchanan's testimony there was nothing but circumstantial evidence and hearsay left. The supporting evidence of the other witnesses would certainly have been the prosecution's clincher. But without Buchanan, everything else was meaningless.

It is inconceivable that Buchanan would not testify as a militantly hostile witness for the prosecution. But it must also be remembered that before his excursion to Dana, the last sight of Frank Buchanan in advance of the grand jury hearing was in Cheyenne in the intimidating company of his enemies, and he was spotted in a buggy riding with a new attorney.[7] Billy Walker, in his book, *The Longest Rope*, alleged that Buchanan accepted an enormous bribe and was whisked off to the British Isles where he spent the rest of his days in comfort. How Walker knew such a thing, if he really did know, nobody knows. It is not at all difficult, however, to imagine what the deadly alternative offer must have been.

But considering Buchanan's almost super-human effort to deter the lynching, even to the point of risking his own life, it is difficult to believe he accepted a bribe. It is much easier and more logical to believe he was removed from the scene by the cattle barons. But money talks and if Buchanan did accept a bribe, it most certainly must have been enormous. However, it really doesn't make any difference whether he was dry-gulched, dropped dead, ran away, or took a bribe, he was definitely gone, and with him went the entire case against the cattlemen.

Fenimore Chatterton was unduly sympathetic to the lynchers in the eyes of his law partner David Craig. The partnership broke up, at least in part, over this matter. (Carbon County Historical Museum.)

An additional piece of information discovered was a disjunctive, penciled-in, frayed and rain-damaged notebook from the years 1890-1920, some of which is illegible. The notebook was discovered in the Kansas City attic of an elderly widow named Hartwell during construction of a new wing on her home. It was written by W. R. Hunt, a reporter for the *Chicago Inter Ocean* at the time of the lynching. Mrs.

Hartwell's sister was purportedly a friend of the reporter. The document somehow fell into the hands of Malcolm Moncreiff of Big Horn, Wyoming, who published it probably in the 1920s in a periodical entitled *The Sweetwater Rustler*. Ironically Moncreiff was himself a wealthy businessman and rancher but was evidently also a friend of the homesteaders.

Hunt wrote in a style which is typical of the era, and it also exposes his somewhat melodramatic tendencies as a writer. He wrote that he fought with his editor over publishing an unsubstantiated telegram wired to them from Ed Towse of the *Cheyenne Leader*, but more important that Towse was also "acting as the official writer—in-pay of the Wyoming Stock Growers Association."

If we accept what Hunt wrote, he quit his job with the paper after the argument with his publisher, and sensing a possible scoop started out on March 12, 1890, by rail for Cheyenne where he arrived on March 15 and personally interviewed Ed Towse at the newspaper office of the *Cheyenne Daily Leader*. Unfortunately his journal does not enlighten us as to what transpired. He then travelled north 160 miles to Casper

On March 28, he wrote from Casper that he tried "with difficulty" to find witnesses there. The "people are reluctant to talk, seem frightened," he wrote and made a particular point of correcting the spelling of Averill to Averell and then named the six lynchers with the comment that they were "all landowners, not a single cowboy among them." His journal entries continued:

> April 12. Still no sign of witnesses, but have spoken with others who knew Jim Averell and Ellen (also known as Ella) Watson. [Hunt then makes a point of mentioning that] Kate Maxwell was another woman altogether, notorious at Bessemer City. Sold her services

to the Army stationed out here. Still alive. Surely the news reports we received deliberately obfuscate the identities of these two....

It is evident that Hunt felt he was onto a scoop that might make him famous overnight. He continued:

> May 15. Breakthrough...Met today Sarah Giles, knows one of the witnesses, Frank Buchanan. Says he will be in town in two weeks' time. She knew E. Watson well, claims she had a legitimate bill of sale for the 25 cattle in her pasture, from an outfit in Nebraska... more about Albert Bothwell. Said he was the leader of the lynch gang...driven by great ambition...known for impatience, cruelty to men and animals.

> June 2. Jim Averell's brother here from Spokane...a man bent on vengeance.

If Averell's half-brother was, indeed, still in Wyoming, he did not give up as easily as had been previously thought. Hunt's journal later stated:

> June 25. Discovered today that Frank Buchanan was here for two days and is now gone! I left instructions with Miss Giles that she was to contact me as soon as he arrived, but he slipped away! ...Miss Giles indicated he would go to a trapper's cabin in the so called Pedro Mountains, some forty miles west....

A novice to the terrain, Hunt clearly meant the adjacent Rattlesnake Mountains which was where Healy's cabin was located. Hunt, together with "Will" Cahill, Averell's half-brother, then set out together to find Buchanan.

> July 1. Discovered Buchanan [at] sunset yesterday, afoot in rough country, partly delirious. Someone

had shot at him, killed his horse...Buchanan un-
harmed...Brought him here to Tex Healy's place.
Healy, a hermit trapper...most remote location...
eerie place, windy plateau with a good spring and a
few trees. Buchanan silent all day, unwilling to talk
to us...very hard to penetrate.

Hunt's diary indicated that although Buchanan was still
alive, he was terrified, disillusioned, in fear for his life and,
even though the grand jury hearing absolved the lynchers
several months ago, his enemies were still doggedly pursuing
him and trying to do him in. Buchanan still had lethal testimony which could reopen the case against the lynchers and
they knew it. He was in grave danger.

July 4. Healy's cabin. Today at last he spoke...
prompted by the name Kate Maxwell! Patience at
last proves up...he begins to tell us about his summer at Sweetwater...the man (boy really) who
revealed himself today is of exceedingly few
words, exceptional reticence, probably due to suspicion...whittles nearly all the time with an intensity
of concentration that belies his calm exterior.

Buchanan was obviously in bad emotional shape and
simply didn't know who to trust.

July 6. Healy's cabin. George Henderson arrived
today, looking for Frank Buchanan, who has vanished. Henderson said nothing he just moved on.

It requires little imagination to guess why Henderson
arrived there looking for Buchanan. It was probably Henderson who shot at him and killed his horse in the first place.
Averell's brother departed for his home that day. With
Buchanan gone, Hunt also left and traveled south to Rawlins.

On August 12, from Rawlins, Hunt wrote:

> This town mostly favorable to Jim Averell and
> Ella Watson, abounds with bitterness about their
> fate. Ellen Watson met Jim Averell here some
> years ago while she worked as a cook in a board-
> ing house, not a bordello...both are remembered
> fondly, even idealized, they have become martyrs
> of a sort to a cause of conflict brewing in the terri-
> tory between big-time stockmen and homestead-
> ers...rooted more in class struggle and concerning
> land and water. Cattle thieving appears to be, in
> part, an excuse for murdering settlers who take
> over choice bottom land and good water.

Hunt then discovered something else about Al Bothwell,
because he wrote:

> The wolves...word is that he has surrounded the
> old post office and mercantile at Sweetwater with
> fences and has turned his wolves loose in there...
> Bothwell now controls the lands that formerly
> belonged to those he lynched! ...nobody will go
> near the place, it seems, too dangerous for man or
> beast.

Then startlingly he added:

> George Henderson...killed last week...Shot in the
> head as he was taking home food for his family....

In reflecting upon Buchanan's agonizing struggle to survive, it is hard to believe that Carbon County officials allowed
Buchanan, of all people—the principal witness, the linchpin
for the prosecution—to be brought to anywhere, but especially Cheyenne without court ordered official protection, into
the very epicenter of the lyncher's influence. Then they

allegedly allowed him to traipse off by himself to the tiny water-tower-stop of Dana on the Union Pacific Railroad, twenty-five or thirty miles east of Rawlins in the desert. It certainly appears it was an out-and-out invitation by Carbon County authorities to have Buchanan finished off. The officials did nothing to assure the future safety and appearance in court of the only virtually indispensable witness for the prosecution. It was open and flagrant complicity. Carbon County citizens rose up in defiance and immediately screamed about it in the press and howled about it on street corners and church pulpits. But as far as the legally uninformed general public was concerned, it appeared to be too late to do anything. The case had already been dismissed and nobody apparently knew Buchanan was still alive, but had found it impossible to show up for the grand jury hearing except at the cost of his own life.

According to Hunt's account, Buchanan clearly was not bought off, nor did he run from the country, but incredibly he survived his would-be assassins up until and beyond the time of the grand jury proceedings.

A few years later a human skeleton of about the right height and build was found about nine miles north of Rawlins far out in the sage brush. It was popularly believed to be Frank Buchanan. A special bandanna about the neck and the special way in which it was knotted was said to have verified it. Did they finally get him? We will probably never know for sure.

Dr. Charles B. Penrose, friend and confidant of the cattle barons, was the attending physician accompanying the notorious invaders during Wyoming's 1892 Johnson County Cattle War. He added some information on Buchanan's whereabouts. He must have been privy to a conversation between some cattle barons, likely at Major Frank Walcott's ranch on Deer Creek east of Casper. He wrote in his book about the Johnson county invasion, *The Rustler Business:*

It was said that a man named Buchanan, who was stopping overnight at the ranch, and who was the only witness, had to be put out of the way so that he might not testify.

Asa Mercer, then owner and editor of the pro cattle baron Cheyenne newspaper, *Northwestern Stock Journal,* was also a close friend and confidant of the powerful stockmen before he later turned against them. He also presented evidence that Buchanan was dry-gulched. He seems, however, to have confused the names of Ralph Cole, Averell's young nephew, (who, it will be remembered, died of Mountain Fever or poison, or both) with Frank Buchanan. In *Banditti of the Plains,* Mercer's scathing book derogating the cattle barons, Mercer wrote:

...he was overtaken by George Henderson, who shot him, and the body of the victim burned to ashes...he was hunted like a wild beast....

The evidence becomes increasingly more convincing. Mercer had somehow learned about Buchanan's fate. That, coupled with the confession of Dr. Penrose and the discovery of Buchanan's suspected skeleton nine miles north of Rawlins, all seem to point toward his murder, probably at the hands of George Henderson. That would seriously implicate Henderson's employer, John Clay, and the Wyoming Stock Growers Association, as well as the six lynchers and the Carbon County political hierarchy in a massive political conspiracy to exonerate the murderers. And that is indeed what seems to have happened, but we will probably never know for sure. Money, however, can do almost anything if there's enough of it, and there was certainly plenty to go around in this case. In any event we can be pretty certain of one thing. Henderson was hired by someone to be hot on the heels of Buchanan.

And perhaps Henderson was then shot to eliminate the possibility of his confessing or naming his employers.

An important point is that to secure an indictment against the six cattle barons, at this or any grand jury hearing, it was necessary to have not just a simple majority, but the unanimous agreement of all twelve jurors against the cattlemen. Without Buchanan's eye-witness testimony, such a unanimous decision against any of the six lynchers was next to impossible. Remember, however, that *Sweetwater Chief* editors H. B. Fetz and J. N. Speer could perhaps have changed history with their testimony, as they were actual witnesses to the abduction and obviously knew a good deal more than they would admit. Ranch hand Dan Fitger also had the same opportunity, as he probably witnessed not only the abduction, but also heard and saw the fight between Buchanan and the lynchers, as well as the actual lynching. However since these men decided not to risk the likely lethal consequences of challenging the wealth and political power of the establishment and opted to remain tacit and alive, they smothered the last possible evidence against the lynchers. Therefore the final action by the court was inevitable. The actual wording of Judge Corn's dismissal of the charges was simple and to the point:

> Not a true bill. The grand jury at the present
> term of this court, having failed to find a true bill
> of indictment against the above named defendants,
> or either of them, it is ordered by the court that the
> above named defendants and each of them and
> their bonds be discharged.

Samuel T. Corn, Judge.

The amount of adrenaline that surged through the courtroom at the moment of the judge's spoken decision must have been incredible.

TERRITORY OF WYOMING,
COUNTY OF CARBON.
ss.

In the District Court of the Third Judicial District:

At a term of the District Court begun and held at Rawlins, within and for the County of Carbon, on the _Fourteenth_ day of _October_ in the year of our Lord one thousand eight hundred and eighty _nine_, the Jurors of the Grand Jury of the County of Carbon, good and lawful men, then and there returned, tried, empanneled, sworn and charged according to law, to enquire within and for the body of the County of Carbon, at the term aforesaid, upon their oaths aforesaid, in the name and by the authority of the Territory of Wyoming,

Do Present and Find that _Albert J. Bothwell, Earnest McLean, Robert B. Connors, Tom Sun, Robert M. Galbraith and John Durbin_ late of the County aforesaid, on the _Twentieth_ day of _July_ in the year of our Lord one thousand eight hundred and eighty _nine — (1889) with force and arms within and_ at the County and Territory aforesaid, _not having the fear of God before their eyes, but being moved and seduced by the instigation of the devil in and upon one Ella Watson in the peace of the Territory of Wyoming then and then being unlawfully feloneously wilfully purposely maliciously deliberately premeditatedly and of their malice aforethought did make an assault with intent her the said Ella Watson then and there unlawfully feloneously wilfully purposely maliciously deliberately premeditatedly and of their malice aforethought to kill and murder, and that the said Albert J. Bothwell, Earnest McLean, Robert B. Connors, Tom Sun, Robert M. Galbraith and John Durbin a certain rope around and about the neck of her the said Ella Watson then and there unlawfully feloneously wilfully purposely maliciously deliberately premeditatedly and of their malice aforethought did fix tie and fasten with intent her the said Ella Watson then and there unlawfully feloneously wilfully purposely maliciously deliberately premeditatedly and of their malice aforethought to kill and murder, and that they the said Albert J. Bothwell, Earnest McLean, Robert B. Connors, Tom Sun, Robert M. Galbraith and John Durbin_

The murder indictment against the ranchers was ruled not a true bill after witnesses mysteriously died and disappeared. (Wyoming State Museum.)

Although the case was now concluded, many citizens were convinced that justice and equity had been circumvented and became loudly critical about everything, even the grand jury proceedings, and the selection of the grand jurors. It was widely believed that only jurors sympathetic to the cattle barons had been chosen to sit on the panel. In fact it is true that only men of high social and pecuniary prominence were seated.

However, these men did not look forward to serving on the grand jury any more than anyone else. Margaret Wilson, the daughter of George Mitchell who was one of the grand jurors and was also the first mayor of Casper, repeated this story about her father during a recent interview:

My father and another man rode from Casper to Rawlins for the grand jury proceedings. When they reached the courtroom, Dad was standing outside the courtroom waiting to be called in. He was talking with some other men he knew. A young fellow he didn't know was standing a bit away, leaning against the wall. Dad told his acquaintances that he didn't want to serve on this grand jury. He said he was busy and that the hearing might take several days. He said he thought that no matter what the verdict was, there'd be controversy. He said he was going to get off jury duty. One of the men asked how he planned to do that. Dad said, "Oh, I'll get off all right. I'll just make up some cock and bull story."

When my father finally got called into the jury room, he knew the judge looked familiar. Then he remembered where he had seen the young man, and he knew he was in for it. The judge was the fellow who'd been leaning against the wall.

The judge greeted my father by saying, "Well, George Mitchell, let's hear your cock and bull story."

Whatever excuse George Mitchell had concocted wasn't good enough; he was seated on the grand jury. However, without Buchanan's testimony, the proceedings didn't take long.

Loyal coroner Jim Bennett, became so incensed at the intentional bungling and mishandling of the whole affair, that he wrote what must have been a scorching letter to Governor Francis E. Warren, known friend of the powerful cattlemen, whose reputation was not utterly unsullied, accusing Warren of complicity. The actual letter has been lost or destroyed or at least cannot now be uncovered.[8] In his answering letter, however, the Governor categorically denied such complicity, but such anger illustrates the public indignation and outrage at the grand jury's decision. Wyoming citizens wanted blood.

The prosecution's case against the lynchers continued to unravel because on October 18 the following information regarding the inquest into Ralph Cole's death appeared in the *Cheyenne Daily Sun*:

> A few days ago, a Chicago chemist [whose name was not disclosed, and perhaps never really existed] made his report to the effect that there was no poison or trace of anything unusual in the stomach. The coroner's inquest thereafter reconvened and returned a verdict that the "Deceased came to his death through natural causes."

How many hands had the stomach gone through before it even reached Chicago, if indeed it were actually sent there?

Finally on October 25, over three exhausting months after the lynching, the following short piece triumphantly screamed forth from Reporter Towse's mouthpiece, the *Cheyenne Daily Leader*:

NO ONE INDICTED!

The grand jury finished their labors today, and were finally discharged without indicting any of the Watson-Averill lynchers. Their failure to indict is attributable to the lack of evidence necessary to sustain the charges. This is caused by Buchanan's sensational disappearance. He claimed to have witnessed the lynching and to have identified everyone present. The attorneys for the territory, Messrs. Craig and Howard seemed to have done all in their power to secure the necessary evidence and the facts were fully presented to the jury as far as they were obtainable, but without avail. The result is that the defendants still labor under the accusation without taking any steps to clear themselves.

Although not really of any importance after the jury was dismissed, the whole article, especially the first and last sentences, may indicate that in his secret heart of hearts even Ed Towse, himself, wondered if the cattlemen were free from carrying the mantle of guilt. Perhaps that is just wishful thinking on the author's part. But then again, perhaps it is not.

Chief Prosecutor David Craig, with very little time to prepare the case, seems to have done everything possible, but, for whatever reason, recalcitrant Deputy Prosecutor Howard appears to have done everything he could think of to impede justice and disgruntled Deputy Prosecutor Preston seems not to have done much to help.

But what about Gene Crowder who also recognized the abductors? Where was he? Gene Crowder mysteriously disappeared several days after the lynching and was reported hiding with Buchanan in Casper. Could it be that he really did escape with the man who may have been his father, John M. Crowder?[9] It was said by Alfred Mokler, in his *History of Natrona County* written in 1923, that Gene was taken in custody by the cattlemen and suddenly died of Brights Disease. Brights Disease is not usually a childhood disease. It is a kidney disease usually associated with later years. The story is not impossible, of course, but since the cattlemen probably did him in, couldn't they have come up with a better alibi than that? Infantile paralysis, Rocky Mountain Spotted Fever or even Bubonic Plague would have been more believable. Of course, Mountain Fever had already taken Ralph Cole. It was also mentioned by Reporter Hunt, in his notebook, that rumor had it that Crowder had been fed to Bothwell's wolves.

In looking back, Deputy Prosecutor Howard, who was in charge during Prosecutor Craig's absence, waited a long two weeks after the lynchings before sending anyone to locate either Buchanan or Crowder with a subpoena. Constable Lineburger, who was himself falsely accused of rustling and then exonerated, was assigned to bring Crowder and Buchanan in. He would certainly have done so if he had been able, for he was firmly on the side of the homesteaders, but he was able to find only Buchanan. Gene Crowder seems to have vanished from the face of the earth.

And what of John DeCorey? What happened to him after the hearing? If he returned to Steamboat Springs, which seems probable, it cannot be verified. John Decorey, not unexpectedly, appears to have quietly vanished.[10]

According to the 1890 census, John Cranor, who was one of the surprise witnesses for the prosecution at the grand jury hearing, was still homesteading as a stock raiser in Sweetwater county on the Sweetwater River. Perhaps his testimony was not that incriminating. Perhaps there was no need for him to disappear once the case had been dismissed.

Rumors abounded concerning the wolves Al Bothwell kept on his ranch, including one that some of the witnesses to the lynching became wolf-chow. Here Jack Bothwell playfully wrestles with the animals. (David Collection, Casper College Library.)

Last but not least, it seems none of the cattle barons in the Sweetwater country would hire Bothwell's dismissed foreman, John L. Sapp, and he finally gave up trying and moved his wife and three children to Rawlins where he was described in 1910 as doing "odd jobs."

18. POSTLUDE

At this point in the story, let's look at the ultimate fate of the six members of the lynching party. What became of them?

Ernest McLean

Hardly anything can be found about Ernie McLean. We do know, however, that in the face of heavy public ridicule, he sold his ranch and moved back to wherever he came from. It is generally believed he was from the Chicago area. He sold his purebred Durham milk cows to the Bar V's new ranch owner Joe Sharp. Joe's daughter, Ruth Beebe, remembers how she, her mother and her older sister, Mary, made butter of the rich cream from those purebred milk cows from the West Coast. To help make ends meet the Sharps sold their dairy products to the road ranches along the stagecoach routes. After leaving the valley, McLean seems to have dropped from sight forever.

Robert Galbraith

Robert M. "Captain" Galbraith, also suffered personal indignities and threats to himself and family and did not stay in the Sweetwater Valley very long after the lynching. Increasing criticism forced him to sell his large holdings, give up his ambitions for a political career, and together with his wife and family, move back East. He made a fortune upon the sale of his ranch, and with the proceeds, he became a prominent banker in Little Rock, Arkansas. He and his wife celebrated their fiftieth wedding anniversary in September 1920. Upon her death at seventy-four, his wife was returned by rail to her birthplace in Illinois and was buried in the Wilson plot next to her parents. Curiously Galbraith seems not to have accompanied his wife's body home to her final resting place or even attended the funeral. At the time of his wife's death, they resided at 502 West Fifth, in Pine Bluffs, Arkansas. "Captain" Bob outlived his wife by many years. He died in 1939 still in Pine Bluffs at the advanced age of ninety-five. Galbraith's children and grandchildren still reside in the nearby environs.

John Durbin

Durbin's enormous wealth wasn't able to buy him protection from relentless public humiliation, and he was forced to give up his official position as a Wyoming cattle inspector. Still under the stigma of his participation in the lynching, he found it necessary to sell his Wyoming holdings in 1891, less than two years after the murders. He then moved his family to Denver, Colorado, where he found social prominence and artificial monetary anonymity from his past. He used his knowledge of the packing industry and his fortune from the sale of his land and cattle interests to invest in a huge string of slaughterhouses in the principal cities of the West.

His Denver obituary said in part:

> At the height of his power, he had government contracts showered upon him for furnishing supplies to the Indian agencies. Immense profits from this source were added to his other heavy receipts and helped to amass the many millions he owned in his

best days. In his later years, he gambled too often with fate and the amazingly fortunate outcome of his earlier livestock ventures failed him. He lost. But not all. Enough remains so that those who are left behind will ever live in luxury, although, in comparison with his former tremendous financial power, he died a poor man. Millions as he grew older, melted away like snow under a burning sun. The Midas gift to turn to gold all that he touched, was taken from him.

It was said that at one time his estate would have been counted in the tens of millions of dollars—and that was using 1880s currency standards. He was associated for many years in stock raising with Francis E. Warren and Joseph Carey, who each served Wyoming as governor and later as senator. When still in Wyoming his cattle and sheep empire could be counted in the multiple millions of head of livestock.

His newspaper obituary continued:

> Durbin was an active member of the Plymouth Congregational Church. The funeral will be held at 2 P.M. [April 16, 1907] from the residence at 2701 East Colfax, with interment later at Fairmount.[1]

He lived over seventeen years after he was involved in the lynching and died at the age of sixty-four.

Robert Conner[2]

Bob Conner also did not waste time before selling out his huge ranch holdings and moving back East to his childhood home in Mauch Chunk, Pennsylvania, where he lived out the balance of his life in quiet affluence. He, too, became a multi-millionaire upon the sale of his Wyoming ranch. In Mauch Chunk [now renamed Jim Thorpe] his past has been kept utterly secret. Today few in Mauch Chuck know, nor are his benefactors aware, that he was implicated in land stealing, cattle rustling, lynching of a young homesteader and wife, and the suspected poisoning of Ralph Cole. Here in his flowery obituary, somewhat condensed in the interest of brevity, notice the minute, almost insignificant mention of Wyoming:

Robert B. Conner died suddenly of heart failure in his rooms at the American Hotel at 7:30 last night, September 13, 1921. He was discovered by Byron W. Esser. Mr. Conner and he have been great friends for years. Almost invariably they spent the evening together following a stroll to the Central news stand for the latest evening papers. Mr. Esser found his friend in a chair struggling for breath and life almost gone. Only a short time previously he was about the hotel and had arranged to spend the evening at the home of his niece Mrs. J. A. Remmel. He expired in a reclining chair reading a newspaper. For a time he resided on his ranch in Wyoming and afterward took up residence with his mother, wife of the late General William Lilly in Mauch Chunk.

Mr. Conner was of a quiet, retiring, unassuming disposition. He loved to do good for those in need and his charity was unbounded. During the world war he was very active in the projects to aid the cause. He was especially interested in the Red Cross Society and gave liberally to every drive. Quietly he did the same for the Salvation Army. There was never a good cause that he didn't aid morally and financially. Personally he was of a sociable nature and endeared himself to legions of people because of his fine qualities. He was, however not prominently identified with many business enterprises here; was very modest and retired in conversation.

The world will never know the many beneficiaries of Bob Conner.

The funeral was held at 2 o'clock this afternoon from the residence of his niece on Broadway with services by Rev. W. C. Roberts. During the funeral, business in town suspended. After the service the cortege proceeded to the Mauch Chunk Cemetery where the body was reverently placed in the Lilly vault. He was 72.

Broadway mentioned in the obituary was and still is referred to as Millionaire's Row by local residents.

After first making only modest financial provision for his favorite relatives, Robert Conner left a good sum of money for the benefit of the poor and indigent, which is in trust with the Mauch Chunk Trust Company. It seems that Robert Conner's experiences in Wyoming may have left him a different man.

Tom Sun

Even in the face of a seemingly quiet, but never-ending, public criticism behind his back, Tom Sun stood his ground and doggedly stuck it out in the Sweetwater Valley. His health finally failed him, and he passed away in Denver, Colorado, in 1909 at the age of 65.

Tom's children and grandchildren have continued to expand the size of his original land holdings and have succeeded in putting together one of the largest and most prestigious ranches in Wyoming. They are respected leaders in their community and in the state.

Today his gracious and hospitable grandson, Bernard, and his charming wife, Noeline (née Esponda), and their children, still live and work on the site of the first ranch holdings. They raise some of the very finest Hereford beef anywhere in the world, and are most fortunate, indeed, to live in the shadow of spectacular and historic Devil's Gate and Independence Rock, two of the world's unique natural treasures.

Albert Bothwell

Bothwell is a different case. He did not immediately leave the valley, but stayed on for two and a half decades until the sale of his ranch was completed in 1916. He made regular and frequent visits to his second family in Los Angeles, California. While still in Wyoming, he lived almost as a hermit and was in constant fear of reprisal. His one close friend was Tom Sun. Bothwell continually professed to having no regrets regarding his involvement in the lynching, but when confronted with questions about his part in the hanging, he became sullen and tacit. He must have developed a shell of solid, impenetrable granite like the bare, mountainous rocks which surrounded him in the Sweetwater country. But there were cracks, as we shall discover.

The Reverend Frank Moore, the young Congregational missionary, who struggled endlessly to organize new congregations and Sunday schools around Wyoming and the Sweetwater country, said this about Bothwell on August 11, 1889, three weeks after the lynching affair:

> I had a long talk with Mr. Bothwell on the evidence of Christianity the day I went up the Sweetwater, [in fact it was the very evening before the lynching] and heard from him his idea of religion. In the lynching business he carried out the spirit of such teaching, I suppose. Wyoming, I fear, will not soon get over the influence of such deeds.[3]

With Bothwell's quasi-deification of the Charles Darwin theory of evolution and the survival of the fittest, he must have been 180-degrees at variance with fundamentalist missionary Frank Moore.

Almost immediately after extralegally acquiring Ellen's and Jim's homesteads, he abandoned the town of Bothwell and skidded all his ranch buildings, which were about a mile away over by the northwest corner of Steamboat Rock, together with most of Averell's log buildings at Jim's road ranch, to a location directly over the top of Averell's final Desert Land Act claim on Horse Creek. The buildings were then situated only about a sixteenth of a mile south of Ellen's still standing one-room log cabin. Those ranch outbuildings and corrals still stand today as staunchly as they did a hundred years ago. It was as if Bothwell continuously needed to keep heaping insults on Ellen and Jim.

It is also incredible to learn that, in the same year as the lynching, both Albert Bothwell and Tom Sun were made members of the Wyoming Stock Growers Association Executive Committee and "Cap'n" Galbraith was elected to the legislature, just as if the lynchings had never happened. Bothwell and Sun both remained members of that executive committee into the next century till as late as 1902. John Durbin served one year on the committee with his two neighbors in 1894.

After the lynching many citizens armed themselves, and Bothwell further went to the trouble to build a twenty-by-thirty foot woven sheep-wire enclosure against the west side of his ranch house where he kept four vicious, grey, white-eyed prairie wolves whom he named Greeley, Polly, Lap, and Judge. Bothwell took them as puppies from a den near the base of Ferris Mountain on his most southerly Arkansas Creek property. They loudly announced the approach of anybody and anything. They served as super watchdogs, but were quite docile to members of the family. Bothwell's son Jack even played with them inside the pen at feeding time.[4] Bothwell became unnaturally fond of them, treating them almost as members of the family. Stanford Sanford, a grandson of Stewart Sanford, the original purchaser of the Bothwell ranch, said during an interview in 1988, that they were still on the ranch in 1917, but that as soon as the ranch sale was finalized and Bothwell moved away, they were summarily shot.

In spite of or perhaps because of, everything, Tom Sun and Al Bothwell remained fast friends for twenty-eight years after the lynching until the sale of Bothwell's ranch when he moved permanently back to California. While still a resident of Wyoming, during his not infrequent social trips on horseback to Tom Sun's ranch, Bothwell selected a different out-of-the-way route in order to avoid establishing a well-traveled trail. He was always armed and even slept with a pistol under his pillow, according to descendent local residents.

Bothwell had earlier sold much of his ranch to the federal government just before the building of Pathfinder Dam, whose reservoir now covers that portion of the original ranch. In 1906, upon its completion, the Pathfinder Dam was the highest dam in the world. The balance of the ranch, which is still very large, was sold to the Sanford family in 1916, although the final outcome of a federal case clouding final title was not completely resolved until 1919. As is typical, Bothwell's shady dealings also caused the trusting Sanford family enormous legal difficulties. Bothwell had not received clear title to many sections of his ranch before he sold it to the Sanfords.

The following fascinating document was written by Judge William R. Kelly of Greeley, Colorado,[5] who was the Sanford family's legal counsel during litigation in a fencing case in 1919 involving the United States of America versus Albert J. Bothwell and Stewart Sanford, et al, in Federal District Court in Cheyenne. It was exactly thirty years after the lynching. Nothing substantive has been deleted from the full statement, although an earlier part of the judge's story, which is not important to this story has been dispensed with.

Judge Kelly wrote as follows:

The hanging of "Cattle Kate," thirty years earlier, was sprung in the fencing case against Albert J. Bothwell. With him, Stewart Sanford, as Bothwell's ranch successor, was a co-defendant. Then Cattle Kate got into it!

Stewart Sanford had signed a contract, written in pen by Bothwell, at the Alcova Ranch in August 1916, to buy the Bothwell ranch. It could run 2,000 cattle, and looked like a good buy.

Bothwell's title defects delayed Sanfords in taking possession until April 1917. They learned then, of a federal suit being readied. The federal agents claimed there was illegal enclosure of thousands of acres of government land by a Bothwell system of fences to keep out other's cattle and sheep.

Sanfords began to learn, after they had bought the ranch, that Bothwell was known for controversy and had been active in a shocking lynching, the hanging of "Cattle Kate" and Jim Averell.

Bothwell had represented to Sanford, when he showed the ranch in 1916, that his record titles were good to 3,000 acres as deeded land, beside many thousands of acres of state land purchase contracts of leases. Sanford, used to taking men at their word, trusted him and signed the Bothwell pen written contract.

That signing there, fifty miles from Casper, without submitting it for legal advice, or matters of titles, was to cause Sanford much anxiety and delay.

Title deficiencies of Bothwell had to be cleared for Sanford to finance the purchase. Sanford required their correction. Bothwell first threatened law suits against Sanford, execrated attorneys in general, and Sanfords in particular.

Among Bothwell's titles which had to be cleared of record, were one to land which had been the Ella Watson homestead, another encumbrance of platted streets and alleys of the defunct Town of Bothwell, which had been promoted by him.

Sanfords had no more than gone into possession of the ranch in April 1917, than they found themselves entangled as co-defendants with Bothwell, in the impending case of United States against Bothwell and Sanford. The suit demanded removal of fences and over forty thousand dollars rent, upon a complaint of illegal enclosure of government lands.

Bothwell was a seasoned litigant with the government. Now the government claimed he had by fences, created a practical monopoly on about 30,000 acres of public lands. He was a "never surrender" designer of that fence system. He insisted on upholding them as they were.

Sanford's policy was not to hunt a fight, nor to try to appropriate to themselves, by maintaining the continuity of fences, exclusive use of the thousands of acres of public lands pasture within somewhat natural barriers.

Sanfords promptly, in 1917, began to make opening for access by others in the fences complained of. They continued this removal policy in early 1918, before the suit was filed. WWI was delaying them some.

In May 1916, the United States filed the suit in Wyoming United States District Court against Bothwell and Sanfords. Sanfords had to defend themselves separately. The writer served as their attorney.

The public lands so alleged to be illegally "enclosed" by Bothwell ranch fences lay within natural barriers joining deeded lands of the ranches which met at the two sides of the Sweetwater River, the north tracts were on Horse Creek near its mouth on the Sweetwater.

Bothwell had successively broken with his previous attorneys in the course of his litigations.[6] For this trial he had William E. Mullen, as his defense attorney. Mullen was a former Attorney General of Wyoming. On getting ready for the trial, to post the attorneys for the defense on what could, or could not be brought out, and by whom, a meeting of counsel and witnesses was held in attorney Mullen's office in the Harry Hynds Building at Cheyenne, in September, 1919, an afternoon two days before the trial began. The witnesses were mainly riders and neighboring ranch owners. Some were long notable in Wyoming affairs.

Sanfords were there, Stewart, the greying veteran, and Archie. [Among other witnesses present at this meeting were former Governor Carey, and former Governor Brooks all of whom had had land in the Sweetwater country.] The vigorous rancher, Albert J. Bothwell, was not present. That meeting had the good fellowship, at the outset, of a sort of reunion of ranch neighbors. That is, until "Cattle Kate" floated in as a cloud over the company.

John Mahoney, a sheep rancher, was a key witness. His testimony had the valuable element that, by him, we could prove that he had trailed two bands of sheep through that Arkansas pasture from the south, across the Sweetwater and out at the north, although it was not "sheep country."

The year of such grazing was important to identify. Mullen asked him to fix the year. "Well," answered Mahoney, "it was the year after they hung "Cattle Kate."

Mahoney's answer was a grim reminder which at once brought embarrassed shifting among those men present. Several suggested that "We ought to keep the 'Cattle Kate' affair out of this. Bothwell would not like it!" Mahoney was asked to calculate back. He concluded the year was 1890. "When you are on the stand and I ask you what year it was, just say 1890." "That's better," breathed Mullen. Others also were relieved.

But the specter of "Cattle Kate," lynched by the Bothwell crew, was thenceforth over those present. It was a sobering pall.

When the subject was introduced in those days in a group of old cattlemen it was usually received with silence. The speaker would soon sense that in such company, its mention was a social error.

A young woman had been hanged without trial. It was an act, not of a frenzied mob, not done at night time, but by a few, six men. It was done on a hot, July Saturday afternoon in 1889, in broad daylight. The hangmen were big cattlemen. Bothwell had incited that they get rid of "Cattle Kate."

The woman was a homesteader. She had no one present, to listen to her defense. Other cattle ranch histories have omitted, or sought to justify the act.

So, back to the federal court room in Cheyenne, September, 1919:

Bothwell, as principal defendant, still strong bodied, white hair, erect, of masterful Roman nose and commanding carriage, sat at the counsel table behind his lawyer, William E. Mullen. The writer sat next behind Bothwell, and in front of Stewart Sanford.

Attorney Mullen had defendant's witness, John Mahoney, on the stand. Those present at the preceding meeting of witnesses showed a little uneasiness. Mahoney recited his trailing of two bands of sheep across the Arkansas pasture from south to north and back again one summer. Then was asked to identify the year. Mahoney, in response, brought out the "Cattle Kate" hanging. The witness again told that it was the year after her hanging, that one sheep herder then was afraid to go through, and more recitals, bringing in "Cattle Kate."

A silence that was emphatic fell upon the court room. Judge, witnesses, all, were benumbed in an awkward pause. Bothwell's frame shuddered, gave a jerk, as if a high voltage current had been shot through it. Maybe he was reenacting the strangling of Ella Watson on the rope end. District Judge Riner[7] announced a recess. The released audience drifted into the corridor, but the men could think of nothing with which to begin a conversation.

"Cattle Kate" was back to all, in the Cheyenne Court room. Albert J. Bothwell, now in his seventies, stunned by that public resurrection, slumped. He was no longer the imperious ranch proprietor and public land possessor who, in his strength, had set out to get rid of "Cattle Kate." Bothwell, that 1889

July afternoon, thirty years earlier, had threatened to use a rope on her as he would have on a cow. He had helped haul her the five miles from her cabin to the gulch on Spring Creek and there saw done his purpose to hang the begging woman. He saw her body there kicking, dangling from the scraggly pine. She would not get a homestead patent.

The fencing case trial went on in subdued tones. The outcome of the trial was a judgement denying injunction against the fences, as to both Sanford and Bothwell.

Bothwell had got Ella Watson's homestead land and had resold it, with the rest of his assembled big cattle ranch. He was now a prosperous retired man of substance, who now craved the esteem of his fellows, but they shunned him there in court. Thirty years had made his conscience acute.

After all, had Albert J. Bothwell, now the old man, really got rid of "Cattle Kate?"

You can't help thinking about that shudder!

> Signed: William R. Kelly
> Greeley, Colorado
> July 12, 1962

Strangely a newspaper obituary for Albert Bothwell cannot be found, which is in itself mysterious. In piecing together his later life and death, these facts have been discovered:

Until 1916, Bothwell divided his life between the Sweetwater Valley and his second family and home back in Los Angeles. After the sale of his ranch to Stewart Sanford, Bothwell moved permanently back to Los Angeles and purchased a home at 614 South Carondeleg where he spent the balance of his life.

Bothwell was preceded in death by his youngest son, John Randoph Bothwell, whom Bothwell called Jack. The son and his mother's sister were killed together in an automobile accident in the mountains of Arizona near Seligman on January 4, 1926. Jack was 29. Upon learning of their deaths, and within a couple of days, someone purchased six contiguous funeral plots in the Inglewood Cemetery. The son and his aunt were laid to rest on January 11. Bothwell, his sister-in-law and one daughter occupy the three far left plots and John ("Jack") the far right. The plots reserved for the twins oddly are unoccupied.

Bothwell did not long survive the death of his son, because after two weeks in intensive care Bothwell died at 5:40 A.M. on March 1, 1928 of Brights Disease [as purportedly did poor, little Gene Crowder] and chronic heart problems, which he had endured for several years. He had been under the care of Dr. W. D. Sansum in the Santa Barbara Cottage Hospital. His interment was four days later on March 5.

There is a story which persists with the old-timers in the Sweetwater Valley that Al Bothwell died utterly insane, a madman. That allegation is supported by the notebook kept by W. R. Hunt, the *Chicago Inter Ocean* reporter—the frayed notebook discovered in the attic in Kansas City.[8] Hunt wrote in 1920 that he visited Bothwell upon Bothwell's admission to a Los Angeles institution in November 1918, ten years before his death and only a short time after he completed the sale of his Wyoming ranch to the Sanfords. Hunt reported that Bothwell had been admitted for the treatment of "undisclosed physical and mental illnesses." Hunt further stated:

> Bothwell was a sight to behold...bereft of all vestige of human dignity, a grotesque image, a frail, pathetic body, possessed of a monstrous passion....

Hunt then referred to "the madness of this one old man" who uttered only a "few recognizable words such as 'that whore' and that 'thief' in all his incessant mumblings."

Still later Hunt referred to Bothwell's being "consumed in the madness of the struggle [in] which he lived entirely alone."

19. Epilogue

Ellen's one-room log cabin cannot be found where it once was. It was sold at auction to Joe Sharp. Later, however, when Bothwell sold the remainder of his huge ranch to the Sanford family, the cabin was still in place on Horse Creek. Perhaps Joe Sharp turned around and sold it back to Bothwell. Perhaps, Sharp simply abandoned it. Bothwell so thoroughly intimidated all future homesteaders by the incomprehensible lynching, that no one else henceforth dared challenge Bothwell's control of any of the surrounding land, and particularly Ellen's homestead which is the very thing Bothwell fiendishly desired.

After the sale of the Bothwell Ranch to the Sanfords a quarter of a century later, the building was used for many years as a one-room school house. Mary Sharp, the elder of the two daughters of Joe Sharp and Ruth Beebe's sister, taught the Sanford children in the building. After the children were pretty much raised, the Sanfords put skids under the building and, with two teams of draft horses, skidded it over into the eventual Averell/Bothwell/Sanford complex of ranch buildings, placing it directly behind Bothwell's dwelling.

It was used not as an ice-house, as previous writers have suggested, but, according to Stanford Sanford who had attended school in the building, it then housed the ranch's new, "modern" Lolley light plant, which generated electricity for the ranch buildings. Sometime, probably in the middle twenties, Ellen's house caught fire and burned to the ground.

Averell's ice-house was not log, but a unique two-room frame building. It had double walls with a four-to-six-inch space between filled with dirt and was admirably suited to its insulating function. It was moved to the Sanford complex, and some have confused it with Ellen's homestead cabin. Averell's ice house finally became too unstable, and the Sanfords tore it down about 1921.

It is also interesting to discover what Al Bothwell's actual ranch house was like. It originally had three rooms and was situated at the northwest edge of the aspiring town of Bothwell, adjacent to Steamboat Rock. The walls were made entirely of logs, and the roof, like many of the early Wyoming ranch houses, was made of poles and sod. After Bothwell moved it over on top of Averell's final homestead filing, the house was expanded by abutting several other log houses up against it. These added buildings were probably the Averell dwelling and store, which would have been the closest log buildings in the area except for Ellen's cabin. The Sanfords occupied Bothwell's expanded ranch house for several decades, but tore down the wolf pen.

Because of an inadequate foundation, the heavy log construction, and weighty sod roof, the dwelling sank almost a foot into the ground over the years, and it became necessary for most people to stoop down in order to get through the doors. The building was finally torn down some years back and a much newer ranch home now occupies the original Bothwell homesite. Most of Bothwell's other log outbuildings and corrals still stand today, and are still in use by the current Pathfinder Ranch managers, Haney and Ruth Stevenson and their family. They have been most gracious and patient in

Ruth Beebe, at 90, and the author at Beebe's ranch home at Whiskey Gap, Wyoming. The clock in the background belonged to Jim and Sophia Averell. (Author.)

answering questions, pointing out various sites and helping to fill in a few blank areas of the story.

Finally, it is the author's sincere hope that future research will continue on this matter and that new evidence will regularly be unearthed to throw even more, or even different, light on the still dark corners of this tragic story, and perhaps to correct some inadvertent mistakes made within these pages. It is certainly not impossible that eager enthusiasm may perhaps have led the author to draw some logical, but nevertheless inaccurate, conclusions. I sincerely hope not. I have tried to avoid such pitfalls. However, since some pieces of this complicated jigsaw puzzle still lie undiscovered and unresolved, it is possible I may have made mistakes. But at least now, most of the illusive pieces are fitted into place, and we have a clearer and more complete picture of this atrocity in the opening of the American West.

The boxes full of obscure information dredged up in the course of this fascinating and exhilarating search for the truth cannot help but correct much of what has been unmasked as historical nonsense. This notorious and significant historical tragedy must now be viewed in a fresh, new light, and from an altogether different perspective. If that really proves to be the case, this book has surely been worth the trouble.

In reluctantly closing these pages, the author feels compelled to mention the indelible mind's-eye picture he has of Jim's and Ellen's fantastically beautiful road ranch location where the final hours of two innocent homesteaders were played out. My imagination has many times filled in the missing buildings and landmarks so that, in my mind's eye, I can vividly see the whole area as it must have been ten decades ago. It will not disappear from memory, nor do I wish it to.

In the fall and winter the crumbling foundations of the Averell road ranch are still barely visible, but during the lovely summer months, at the highest high-water mark of the Pathfinder Reservoir, its backwaters quietly weep over two lonely graves with gently-rippling shallow water. The water softly laps at the sandy shore with tiny, melancholy waves, only a few feet south of the massive granite toe of beautifully silhouetted Averell Mountain. The evening shadows regularly and gradually throw a heavy, black veil across the now deserted site of Ella's and Jim's eager and desperate hope for the future. That hope was arrogantly and brutally smashed to pieces on the selfish, iron will of one man's insatiable greed. That terrible immolation sadly cannot be undone, but the twisting contortions of a Cheyenne reporter's pen, which has hoodwinked the whole world for a century, is finally exposed for what it was. May that luckless and guiltless couple find an ultimate vindication at last.

Requiescat in pace!

Endnotes

1. The Myth

1. Personal interview with Bernard Sun at Devil's Gate, Wyoming, September 1988. Purportedly said by Albert Bothwell.
2. It is true that one of the only three known photographs of Ellen Watson shows her astride a very old horse in front of her stock shed. The bridle has been hastily placed over the horse's ears, with the throat latch left unbuckled. The horse is bareback, as if no time was taken to saddle-up the mount. Ellen is in a pretty Mother Hubbard dress, she has a matching bonnet upon her head, and she has a soft smile on her face.

   There is little question that this picture was posed, probably to send home to the folks in Kansas. It was possibly taken by a traveling photographer or by Jim Averell himself. Since the horse Ellen sits on is bareback, naturally she is sitting astride. It's quite impossible to ride a bareback horse sidesaddle.

   Many Western women rode astride by 1889. However, Ellen owned only one saddle at the time of her murder—a side saddle. It was sold in the postmortem auction of her things. She was never known to have ridden any way other than sidesaddle. Why riding astride in the wild and woolly West was improper is not clear, but Reporter Ed Towse surely bore down on that fact. One must wonder if somehow he was aware of this posed photograph.
3. Al Bothwell tried on many occasions to buy Ellen out, even offering her the money to prove up early on the homestead, so he could then buy it from her. She told him she didn't need his money and would not sell. This was mentioned in a letter to the editor of the *Casper Weekly Mail* sent from Steamboat Springs, Colorado, from John DeCorey, Ellen's ward and jack-of-all-trades helper. When Ellen refused the offer, the skull and cross-bones began to appear on the doors of Ellen Watson and James Averell.

4. The number of men in the hanging party was only six.
5. Averell was involved in an earlier shooting incident in Buffalo, Wyoming, where he was accused of murder. There is no other such incident.
6. The tree was not a cottonwood tree, but a rather tall pitch pine tree in among the red cedars.
7. The lynching took place at the head of Spring Creek Gulch (or canyon), not on the banks of the Sweetwater River.

2. BACKGROUND

1. For excellent accounts of this era see John Burroughs, *Guardian of the Grasslands* (Cheyenne: Wyoming Stock Growers Association, 1971); Agnes Wright Spring, *Seventy Years Cow Country* (Cheyenne: Wyoming Stock Growers Association, 1942); Agnes Wright Spring, *Cow Country Legacies* (Lowell Press, Kansas City, 1976); and T.A. Larson, *History of Wyoming* (Lincoln: University of Nebraska Press, 1966).
2. *The Magic City of the Plains* (Cheyenne: Cheyenne Centennial Committee, 1967).
3. The author remembers the building well before it was razed in 1961. The references to its earlier social uses are from Agnes' Wright Spring's *Cow Country Legacies*; *The Magic City of the Plains*; and numerous other publications, newspapers and periodicals.
4. The same primary sources listed above were used for these descriptions as well.

3. THE WEATHER

1. John Burroughs, *Guardian of the Grasslands*; T.A. Larson, *History of Wyoming*; Frances Birkhead Beard, *Wyoming from Territorial Days to Present* (Chicago: American History Society, 1933); and I. S. Bartlett, *History of Wyoming* (Chicago: S.J. Clarke, 1918) Robert B. David, *Malcolm Campbell, Sheriff* (Casper: Wyomingana; 1932.)
2. The information about the winter of 1887-1888 has been gleaned from numerous newspapers, books, and periodicals, including those contemporary to the era.

4. ELLEN WATSON

1. "Ellen L. Watson" was the way she signed all official documents before and after her first marriage. During her first marriage she signed her name Ellen Pickell. Her first known signature was at the time of her first wedding. Upon her petition for divorce she signed her name Ellen

Pickell. All other documents were signed Ellen L. Watson, except her wedding certificate which was signed Ellen Liddy Andrews.

2. In all official documents she signed her name as Ellen, but in an informal way, as a nickname, she was addressed as "Ella." During the late 1800s, the name Ella was an extremely popular name, where, by comparison, Ellen, was not.

3. Information from Daniel Brumbaugh, Belpre, Ohio, grand-nephew of Ellen Watson. This can be seen in the family photograph.

4. From Daniel Brumbaugh and verified in the Jewell County, Kansas, records for homestead claims. This was the first claim that Thomas Lewis Watson, Ellen's father, filed upon. He subsequently filed on two other homestead claims which were also sold as was the first one just after the lynching of his oldest daughter, Ellen Watson.

5. Daniel Brumbaugh.

6. Daniel Brumbaugh, and Jewell County, Kansas, marriage licenses, Smith Center, Kansas.

7. Daniel Brumbaugh. Also Pickell's drunkenness, unfaithfulness and horsewhip beatings were well known to the old-time residents of Jewell County. Ellen's father, however, simply referred to the fact that Ellen and Pickell couldn't get along together. That was referred to during the interview in the *Rock Springs (Wyoming) Independent* a few weeks after Ellen's murder.

8. Daniel Brumbaugh.

9. Ibid

10. Ibid

11. Letter from John H. Fales on file in the David Collection, Casper (Wyoming) College Library. Also in *Rock Springs Independent* interview with Thomas Watson. Also see *Wyoming Cowboy Days* by Charles Guernsey.

12. Thomas Watson interview with *Rock Springs Independent*.

13. Letter from John H. Fales. Also *Wyoming Cowboy Days*.

14. According to Daniel Brumbaugh, most of the siblings were tall, many six feet or over. This is also evident in the Watson family photograph in the possession of Daniel Brumbaugh.

15. County Court House records, Red Cloud, Nebraska.

16. The same courthouse divorce records and the *Cheyenne Daily Leader*, July 23, 1889.

17. Daniel Brumbaugh.

18. Thomas Watson interview with *Rock Springs Independent*.

19. Rand McNalley *Pioneer Atlas of the American West.* (San Francisco: Rand McNalley, 1969).

20. *Magic City of the Plains.*

21. Since Ellen's last documented appearance was in Red Cloud, Nebraska, in April 16, 1884, when she filed for divorce, she probably could not have arrived at Fetterman City, if indeed this is the same Ella (Wilson) Watson, before late 1884 or early 1885, several years after the military post was evacuated in 1882.

22. Letter of Harry Ward of Lake Ranch Stage Station. Wyoming State Museum.

23. Anne M. Butler, *Daughters of Joy, Sisters of Misery* (Urbana, Illinois: University of Illinois, 1985).

24. Letter from Abe Abrahams.

25. U.S. Census information for 1880.

26. Letter from Abe Abrahams.

27. All buildings except a sentry overlook, the gazebo, a storage building and one officers' quarters were moved to the new town of Douglas, Wyoming, the townsite the railroad purchased in advance of its arrival. They were moved in the customary way—on skids, pulled by two, four, or eight horses, and often over rolling logs.

28. *Democratic Leader,* (Cheyenne, March 2, 1884).

29. Court records and depositions relative to the altercation in Fetterman City on file in Wyoming State Museum.

30. Letter from Abe Abrahams.

31. John Fenix is buried in the Fetterman City cemetery. All military dead have been moved away to the military cemetery at Fort McPherson, Nebraska, although the headstones are still in place. Several descendants of John Fenix still reside in Douglas, Wyoming. See Sharon Lass Field's *Fort Fetterman Cemetery* (Cheyenne: Author, 1970).

32. Lawrence and Sanders were charged with attempted murder by Wallace and Crosby, but the case was dismissed by Justice of the Peace John O'Brien on the grounds of self defense. Court records, Wyoming State Museum.

33. R. B. David, *Malcolm Campbell, Sheriff.*

34. Lawrence and Sanders charges in the Wallace and Crosby case.

35. Ibid.

36. Ibid. Also Abe Abrahams letter.

37. Doctor J. N. Bradley's report on file with Wyoming State Museum.

38. Court records from Judge John O'Brien. Wyoming State Museum.

39. During the earlier questioning at Judge O'Brien's, this Ella apparently always called herself Ella Wilson. Somehow or another Dr. Bradley inadvertently wrote her name down as Ella Watson on the medical report, an understandable name association confusion. Court records, Wyoming State Museum.

40. Ella Wilson's (Watson's) deposition before Judge O'Brien. Wyoming State Museum.
41. The Fremont, Elkhorn & Missouri Valley Railroad today has been supplanted by the Burlington Northern Railroad. The Chicago & Northwestern Railroad went on to Lander.

5. JAMES AVERELL

1. Ontario, Canada, census of 1851.
2. Lawrence Jaeger, *Jaeger Family History,* (Yuba City, California: privately published).
3. Oshkosh, Wisconsin, Historical Society records; U.S. Census of 1870; and James Averell induction papers of July 1871 from the National Archives.
4. Ralph E. Cole was the son of Able Cole and his wife, James Averell's sister, Sarah. He later came west to Wyoming in April 1889 to live with his uncle several months before the lynching.
5. James Averell induction papers, July 1871.
6. Jaeger family letters and records document Jim's employment at Waukau.
7. James Averell induction papers, July, 1871.
8. Records of Company H, 13th Infantry, National Archives. Also *History of U.S. Army Thirteenth Infantry.*
9. Ibid.
10. Ibid.
11. Ibid.
12. *History of the Thirteenth U.S. Army Infantry.*
13. Both Joe Rankin and Tom Sun were scouts for the Thirteenth U.S. Infantry at Fort Fred Steele. It seems improbable that James Averell would not have known or at least have met them. See also Nute Craig's privately published *Thrills 1861-1887,* (Oakland, est. 1927).
14. *History of the Thirteenth U.S. Army Infantry.*
15. *History of the Thirteenth U.S. Army Infantry* and Army discharge papers, National Archives.
16. He reenlisted in Chicago, Illinois, which is just a short way from Oshkosh, Wisconsin, near Rushford Township, Winnebago, County. Army enlistment records, National Archives.
17. Records from James Averell's second five-year enlistment at Chicago, Illinois, in July 1876, National Archives.
18. Averell's second enlistment was into the Ninth Infantry according to records in the National Archives. The Ninth Infantry was engaged in the Battle of the Rosebud under General George Crook, who was under orders to join forces with Generals Terry and Custer, who were

to seek out the Indian enemy and destroy them. Had the Rosebud battle not occurred, General Crook would certainly have progressed farther into Montana and joined Custer, Benteen and Reno. Unbeknownst to Crook, at the time of that battle he was already within a very few miles of the enormous Little Big Horn Indian encampment that shortly was to defeat Custer.

19. Averell, who had been elevated to Sergeant, was hand-picked by his superior officers and the Indian Scout Frank Grouard, to accompany Grouard on military sorties on horseback into the surrounding territory and into Montana to retrieve stolen property and livestock and return it to the fort or the rightful owners. See Joe DeBarthe's *Life and Adventures of Frank Grouard* (Norman: University of Oklahoma, 1958) and also Robert A. Murray's *Johnson County, 175 Years of History at the Foot of the Big Horn Mountains* (Buffalo, Wyoming: Chamber of Commerce, 1981).

20. Averell learned the trade of surveying well. He helped survey Fort McKinney and its buildings, a job which fine-tuned his surveying talents for later on in the Sweetwater country, where he surveyed at least four homesteads and several irrigation canals.

21. There were non-commissioned officers in the cavalry assigned to Fort McKinney. Why were they not picked instead of Averell who was an infantryman? For information on the era see Robert A. Murray's *Military Posts in the Powder River Country of Wyoming* (Lincoln: University of Nebraska, 1967).

22. It is well documented that General George Crook valued the opinion of the half-breed military scout, Frank Grouard, more than everyone else's when dealing with controversial tactical matters.

23. Military discharge of James Averell in 1881, National Archives.

24. Ibid.

25. U.S. Decennial Census of 1880.

26. Real estate records of Averell home in Buffalo, Wyoming, to Henry Robertson on March 24, 1881. Wyoming State Museum. A photo of that home is in *Buffalo's First Century*, editor, Patty Meyers (Buffalo: Buffalo Centennial Committee, 1984). The building is still standing and is occupied as Parmalee Law Offices.

27. Fort McKinney Courts-Martial records, National Archives.

28. Averell was demoted before leaving Fort McKinney, as he was discharged as a Private. He was demoted for being "Absent Without Leave," a common occurrence in dull isolated posts—just to create something exciting to do.

29. Testimony before Grand Jury in Frances S. Murphy vs. James Averell, May 5, 1880. Wyoming State Museum.

30. Ibid.
31. Ibid.
32. Ibid.
33. Some of the testimony refers to Mrs. O'Dell's place and others refer to Mills Saloon. They must have been adjacent to, or one within the other, or were perhaps even the same place, or the circumstances could not have transpired as described.
34. Medical report following the altercation. Wyoming State Museum.
35. Court records. Wyoming State Museum.
36. August Trabing had an illustrious career in public service to Wyoming beginning with his first store on Crazy Woman Creek in Johnson County about fifteen miles south of Buffalo and continuing through his election to the Wyoming Senate.
37. Court records. Wyoming State Museum.
38. This illustrates that Jim Rankin was well-know in the Rawlins area long before his arrival. Rankin was chosen to be the deputy immediately and later became the sheriff of Carbon County.
39. Homer Merrell was one of the most famous of all attorneys and judges in Wyoming at the time. He was obviously a good choice for Averell's defense in the Buffalo shooting matter. Averell was not able to secure all the witnesses he needed in his defense, so Merrell secured continuance after continuance in the hope they could be located.
40. This curious stroke of fate shows up in the Carbon County records relative to the prosecution of this case. Wyoming State Museum.
41. Apparently the court decided that it was a matter for the U.S. Army to handle through courts-martial, if they should so choose. At least they denied having any jurisdiction in the matter. No record of any subsequent court-martial can be found.
42. Military discharge papers. National Archives.
43. Averell would almost certainly have had to pass through the Sweetwater Country in following the customary military road from Fort McKinney to Rawlins, where he was incarcerated for the shooting in Buffalo. Also supplies and mail to and from the fort followed the same route, and Averell was one of only two infantry sergeants generally on the post who would have been assigned to this detail on the Rawlins-Fort McKinney military road.

6. HOMESTEADING

1. Military discharge record, June 1881. National Archives.
2. Chatterton was the last civilian sutler at Fort Fred Steele before the post was decommissioned in 1881. He then moved to Rawlins where

he was admitted to the Wyoming Bar and engaged in the practice of law. He became a justice of the peace and a probate judge of Carbon County and went into partnership with David Craig, who quickly became assistant prosecuting attorney for Carbon County. Craig later severed his partnership with Chatterton over what he considered the unethical way in which Chatterton handled the legal matters surrounding the Watson-Averell case during Craig's sojourn in Ireland. The author has not discovered exactly what those improper actions were alleged to be, but it is clear that Chatterton favored the wealthy cattle interests. Chatterton later received political support from the Republican Party in his campaign for Secretary of State. He eventually replaced Governor DeForest Richards and became Acting Governor of Wyoming for nearly three years. He was a highly motivated partisan who clearly knew where his bread was buttered. More information on Chatterton can be found in T.A. Larson's *History of Wyoming* (Lincoln: University of Nebraska, 1962) and Chatterton's book, *Yesterday's Wyoming* (Aurora, Colorado: Powder River Publishing, 1957).

3. Lawrence Jaeger.

4. Sophia Averell postscribed her letters home in German. These letters are in family records held by Lawrence Jaeger.

5. Sophia Averell's letters home to her relatives.

6. Interview with Lawrence Jaeger.

7. Another story is that the wedding was held at Sophia's parents' home, but this seems unlikely in view of the father's adamant opposition to the marriage. Lawrence Jaeger interview.

8. Sophia Averell's letters home.

9. Ibid.

10. Ibid.

11. Ruth Beebe, whose residence was at Whiskey Gap about forty miles north of Rawlins, possessed a photograph of Averell's house. Her father, Stewart Joe Sharp, was foreman of the Butler brothers' ranch, and Sharp later purchased Averell's first homestead ranch from the Butler brothers who came from Philadelphia. Averell sold the homestead to the Butlers after the death of his first wife. The homestead land description is on file with Bureau of Land Management, Cheyenne, Wyoming.

12. This clock is about three feet tall and was proudly displayed in Ruth Beebe's home. It chimes on the hour and half hour and is an exquisite piece of period Prussian workmanship. The author and his wife were fortunate to have been a guest in Ruth Beebe's ranch home for a long afternoon interview, and she cooperated with dozens of telephone conversations afterward.

13. This ranch is now the Bar V Ranch and is situated toward the head of Cherry Creek under Ferris Mountain, out of which the creek flows in a northerly direction. The author visited this home and its present owners, Virginia and William McIntosh, in this breathtaking setting one afternoon.

14. Ruth Beebe interview. Many other old timers also know this story. Also James Averell's letters to Sophia's relatives in the possession of Lawrence Jaeger.

15. The sources above plus a letter of Harry Ward, Casper College Library.

16. Letter in possession of Fred Borchardt, Appleton, Wisconsin.

17. Lawrence Jaeger collection.

18. Ibid.

19. Probate records in Carbon County Court House, Rawlins, Wyoming.

20. This sale took place on March 11, 1884. Bureau of Land Management Records, Cheyenne, Wyoming.

21. This new homestead at the base of what was soon called Averell Mountain is where Averell situated his new little general store and home. Land description on file with Bureau of Land Management, Cheyenne, Wyoming.

22. Apparently the name was arbitrarily changed by the BLM to Sanford Mountain on the BLM maps, named after the Sanford family who purchased the ranch from Bothwell. But in the 1800s and early 1900s it was known as Averell Mountain, probably because of Averell's road ranch at its base, and perhaps even because of the lynching.

23. The diagram of the Averell buildings drawn by John Fales is on file in the David Collection, Casper (Wyoming) College Library Archives.

24. Mortgage to Hugus and Company and John Dyer of Rawlins, Wyoming, on file at Wyoming State Museum.

25. The "Sweetwater Rocks" are of the Precambrian geological era and are the oldest known exposed rocks in the world. They appear from a distance to be layered in gigantic, somewhat flattened balls, piled into leviathanic mountains of rock. They are worn smooth by the wind and rain, and have a particularly unique and ominous appearance. On the highway a few miles west from Muddy Gap they are erroneously marked "Rattle Snake Range" which is actually farther north behind the Sweetwater Rocks.

26. This proposed right-of-way was shown on Holt's New 1883 Map of the Territory of Wyoming, reprinted by the Wyoming State Museum.

27. The author had the unusual experience of travelling over this same route on a troop train in 1944 during WWII. It is now the Burlington Route and passes through one of the deepest, narrowest, and most

spectacular canyons in all the world. It is full of springs, tunnels, and waterfalls hundreds of feet in height. It is located about ten miles north of Shoshoni, in central Wyoming. The north end of the Wind River Canyon ends near the largest hot springs in the world at Thermopolis, Wyoming, now a state park, just north of where the Wind River mysteriously becomes the Big Horn River at what is called the Wedding of The Waters.

28. The community of Sand Creek, at the site of the present Buzzard Ranch buildings, was situated on the stream of that name not far from where it runs into the North Platte River. Originally there was a post office located here was called the Ferris Post Office, which was named after George Ferris, the famous miner-explorer who promoted the copper resources of Wyoming and discovered the Ferris Mountain mining district, as well as other deposits through the territory. The post office named Ferris has since been moved to a location on the opposite (south) side of Ferris Mountain.

29. Although the 1880s are a little late for the heavy traffic which once moved along the Oregon Trail, it was nevertheless used by wagons and wagon trains even into the 1900s. The Oregon Trail crosses Wyoming Highway 220 just a few hundred yards north of the point where Ellen Watson built her first cabin and stock shed on her Horse Creek homestead. The Union Pacific Railroad supplanted most of the "westering" traffic after 1869 when the gold spike signaled the completion of the first coast to coast rails.

30. "Waddy" was a common name for a cowboy. Some of the other names were cowhand, cowpuncher, cowpoke, ranch-hand and other equally unglamorous names.

31. This same John Dyer made a fortune discovering and mining the red mineral paint deposits north of Rawlins used as a rust inhibitor in the paint which covered the Brooklyn Bridge, completed in 1883, then the largest suspension bridge in the world.

32. Since payday was quite infrequent on the range, and cattlemen usually obtained income only in the spring and fall when they sold livestock, necessary supplies were purchased during the year with the understanding that upon the sale of the livestock, the debtor would pay back the merchant, often without interest.

33. Wyoming State Museum.

34. Ruth Beebe, Whiskey Gap, Wyoming; Stanford Sanford, grandson of the first purchasers of Bothwell's ranch; and Van Irvine, grandson of one of the most prominent early day ranching families in Wyoming, whose grandfather was one of the early presidents of the Wyoming Stock Growers Association. Van Irvine is himself a past president of

the Association which has evolved into one of the finest trade associations in America. This illegal procedure was immensely widespread during that period.

35. Larson's *History of Wyoming*; Barlett's *History of Wyoming*: and Beard's *Wyoming from Territorial Days to the Present*.

36. A "ditcher" was a triangular device about six feet long, elevated slightly toward the rear, made of wooden two-by-sixes which lay on the ground, and which had a kind of steel plow on the forward point. At that time it was usually pulled along by a team or tandem team of draft horses. It would dig into the soil making a small canal, large enough to carry a substantial amount of irrigation water. The dirt which was gouged up by the plow point was pushed along the wings of the triangle and deposited along the ditch bank, making the ditch even deeper. This device was, however, not always used. Some irrigation ditches were simply dug by hand, a very tedious and back breaking task, but the least expensive way for the homesteader.

37. Bureau of Land Management, Cheyenne, Wyoming.

38. This very ambitious project was to carry water from north of Ellen Watson's newly filed homestead, down to Averell's home and store, requiring about two-and-one-half miles of ditches. The ditch system had to follow the natural contour of the land so required a longer route than a straight line distance. This main ditch ran directly across Bothwell's main hay meadow and must certainly have aggravated him and contributed to the many "straws on the camel's back." The ditches were actually large enough to completely drain all the water out of Horse Creek. Irrigation filings with Wyoming State Museum.

39. The water right subsequently approved by the government was beautifully hand-scribed by Averell. The ditch was in place across Bothwell's hay meadow at the time of Averell's lynching. Wyoming State Museum.

7. THE LYNCHERS

1. Durbin had several other brands, but this is the one he used on his cattle operation in the Sweetwater Valley. His enormous ranch lay on the east side of Split Rock by what is still called Durbin Pocket. A "pocket" is a large cove or recess back in the rocks.

2. Obituaries in the Denver, Colorado, newspapers.

3. Amos Peacock was an early emigrant to the town of Cheyenne. He started a small butcher shop which he later expanded. He then built an additional butcher shop in another section of Cheyenne for the convenience of those across town, which also became popular. Much of the earlier section of Cheyenne was destroyed during the fire of 1870.

John Durbin, who managed Peacock's original store, and his brother, Tom, who managed the other store, took advantage of Peacock's discouragement to offer him a fair price to sell out. Peacock accepted the offer, and the Durbin brothers eliminated the middleman in their marketing of beef.

    This began their enormous empire in the raising and marketing of beef and sheep. Contracts to supply meat to military forts and camps in Wyoming led to one of the greatest fortunes in the whole West. Denver, Colorado, newspaper obituaries.

4. John Durbin decided he wanted to have a repository for the gold, silver and money generated by his precious metal mining in Deadwood, and Lead, South Dakota. Besides it was good business. Later he became disenchanted with the sedentary existence of a banker's life and sold out the successful banking enterprise, together with the mine, to the William Randolph Hearst interests. Hearst subsequently developed the mine into the Homestake Mine of national renown. John Durbin obituaries in the Denver, Colorado, newspapers. The Homestake Mine is the largest gold mine in the northern hemisphere and is still going strong over one hundred years later. It is now down to over eight thousand feet. Durbin sold too soon.

5. Brother Tom Durbin's primary interest was in the political clout accompanying the big livestock businesses in Wyoming. There can be little doubt that he wanted to be Governor, but that ambition was somehow thwarted. He was, however, continuously active in Republican Party politics, and he became an officer in the even more powerful Wyoming Stock Growers Association, which virtually ran Wyoming. Unlike his brother John, he lived out his lifetime in Wyoming.

6. John Burroughs in *Guardians of the Grasslands.*

7. Brother George Durbin also became a multi-millionaire in his own right, but restricted himself to the raising of sheep and horses. He took no apparent interest in his brother's cattle enterprises.

8. John Durbin's foreman in the Sweetwater country was Tom Collins, a notorious cattle rustler. There is nothing unusual in this, however; many of the large cattle ranchers who came up the hard way selected the most efficient cattle thieves for their employees. This supposedly, but not always, kept other employees from rustling their boss's cattle and helped build their employer's herds. Clabe and Nate Young, the first of whom was also employed as foreman by Tom Sun at another time, were infamous rustlers later also employed by John Durbin. See *Guardians of the Grassland.*

9. *Guardians of the Grasslands.*

10. See *Guardians of the Grasslands* for information on the activities of rustlers and cattlemen during this period.
11. Galbraith also had several brands, but the T Bar T was the one primarily used in the Sweetwater country.
12. Galbraith preferred to be addressed as "Captain" according to his wife's obituary in the Pine Bluffs, Arkansas newspaper.
13. From information in a footnote in Bankcroft's *History of Nevada, Colorado and Wyoming,* Vol. XXV.
14. Galbraith's wife's obituary (Pine Bluff, Arkansas, *Pine Bluffs Graphic,* June 1, 1921).
15. Benton is historically considered to have been the most corrupt town ever to grace the Territory of Wyoming. Because of the large deposits of coal for the steam locomotives on the Union Pacific Railroad, it grew very rapidly. It did not last for very long, however, but its reputation for being the wildest and raunchiest "Hell on Wheels" town in Wyoming has never been challenged. The strong criminal element ruled Benton with an iron fist until the town's demise.
16. Galbraith was elected to the Territorial House of Representatives and then to the Wyoming Council and served one two-year term each in 1884 and 1889. He was continually engaged in introducing or supporting special interest legislation pertaining to the livestock business and the enhancement of property values in the Sweetwater Valley such as a proposed tunnel through the Seminoe Mountains.
17. The optimum point from which to view this unusually important eclipse was at Separation, Wyoming, thirteen miles north of Rawlins where the road from the north separated to go either to Rawlins or Fort Fred Steele. The name Separation also reflected the fact that Separation sat in a valley on the Continental Divide with no outlet to either the Atlantic or Pacific oceans.
18. Although this story cannot be authenticated, it has become part of Wyoming's legendary early history. There is a granite stone memorial to this unusual occurrence about two miles uphill from Battle Lake on the only road across this gorgeous, silvan Sierra Madre mountain range, practically unvisited by the travelling public. The highway pass is now almost completely paved west-east from Encampment to Baggs, Wyoming.
19. Bankcroft's *History of Nevada, Colorado and Wyoming,* Vol XXV.
20. According to countless references, this was the generally accepted going rate paid per acre.
21. While Galbraith was in the Wyoming Territorial House of Representatives, he was instrumental in the introduction and passage in 1884 of the most hated and notorious piece of legislation ever passed in the

entire history of Wyoming, the "Maverick" bill. It is discussed in detail later.

22. Bothwell also had several brands in use throughout the Territory, but this is the one he used most frequently in the Sweetwater Valley.

23. Albert J. Bothwell death certificate, Santa Barbara Cottage Hospital, Santa Barbara, California, and records at Inglewood Cemetery, Magnolia Plot, Inglewood, California.

24. According to those who knew him, Bothwell had a splendid education. He believed he had a superior intellectual capacity, and he considered himself an authority on American jurisprudence. He was articulate, handsome and purportedly carried himself well. He also had a strong Roman nose, and he was said to radiate self confidence and authority. Very little has been discovered about his youth, but local residents generally say his father was a wealthy merchant from Iowa. Al sometimes posed as English aristocracy, and he played the part to the hilt. Interview with George Guy, Attorney General, State of Wyoming, March 2, 1976, and the 1988 interview with Ruth Beebe.

25. Bothwell first began running cattle in Wyoming, as many early stockmen did, in the southeastern part of the Territory, south of Cheyenne and on the Laramie Plains. He was not one of the first to discover the Sweetwater Valley, but quickly adopted it as his own. He made his "home ranch" here, making a very assertive and intimidating effort to acquire control over gigantic sections of land over which he could later gain ownership. Averell's and Watson's challenge to Bothwell's authority over the land, legal though it may have been, shook Bothwell's plan to control all that he had illegally put under fence.

26. Bothwell's trick was to frighten all newcomers away from the land over which he exercised control. In the case of James Averell and Ellen Watson, he was unsuccessful, so he resorted to violence. He eventually did gain title to the land after the deaths of Watson and Averell, but not before many bitter legal battles with the State of Wyoming and the Federal Government. From the records of Attorney William R. Kelly, Greeley, Colorado, and U.S. Bureau of Reclamation records in Cheyenne, Wyoming.

27. See Mokler's *History of Natrona County* and the U.S. Bureau of Land Management Records, Cheyenne, Wyoming. Also a letter to Wyoming State Museum by Judge William R. Kelly.

28. See footnote number 23. Also photographs in David Collection, Casper College Library.

29. Interview of March 2, 1976, with George Guy, former Attorney General, State of Wyoming.

30. Ibid.

31. Albert Bothwell may have had more than two brothers, but George and John are the only ones discovered to date.
32. *Casper Weekly Mail,* August 30, 1889.
33. The petroleum geologist from the neighboring towns of Oil City and Ervay, where there really was oil, were convinced that there was no oil within twenty miles of the Bothwell property. *Casper Weekly Mail,* February 8, 1889.
34. John quickly disappeared from Wyoming records, and it was not long before the name of George also disappeared.
35. The local newspapers, particularly the *Casper Weekly Mail,* loudly pooh-poohed the Bothwell town scheme. *Casper Weekly Mail,* February 6, 1889.
36. See the sources above plus the *Carbon County Journal,* August 10, 1889, on the Bear Lake project and the *Casper Weekly Mail,* August 16, 1889 for the Sweetwater, Wyoming, project.
37. It would seem that Bothwell perhaps underwrote the newspaper and Fetz and Speer's move to the town of Bothwell in order to create the image that things were beginning to prosper there. *Casper Weekly Mail,* February 6, 1889.
38. The newspaper is referred to in print as both the *Sweetwater Chief* and the *Sweetwater Chieftain.* Since none of the limited number of issues of the newspaper are known to have survived, the official name cannot be determined. The name *Chief* is used most often in other newspapers when referring to the Fetz/Speer newspaper.
39. Only a few references appear concerning the newspaper. Only one mentions the setting up of the presses.
40. After dismantling the presses at Bothwell, Fetz moved his machinery to Rawlins where he started a primarily Republican paper in opposition to the Democratic slanted *Carbon County Journal.* The *Carbon County Journal* was under the editorship of John Friend, a former military volunteer and a soldier who was at Camp Reno during the famous massacre of nearly one hundred men near Fort Philip Kearny, Wyoming. That battle and the Custer defeat about ten years later are the two greatest military losses in the opening of the West.
41. Hiram M. Chittenden, *A Western Epic, 1897,* (Tacoma: Washington State Historical Society, 1961).
42. Photos from the David Collection, Casper College Library.
43. The local old timers all agree that she apparently was too citified to have fit into a very primitive rural setting. Ruth Beebe interview. Also photographs in the David collection Casper College Library, which show her in her attire.
44. This cannot be documented, but old-timers agree that Bothwell's first

wife came from and returned to southern California. A picture of her is in the Casper College Library, David Collection. Also Ruth Beebe interview.

45. Where Bothwell's second wife was from is a mystery, nor has this writer been able to discover her first name. She is not buried in the Bothwell family plot in Ingelwood, California. However, her sister, Alice E. Wadsworth, was born in Connecticut and died at the age of 62 in an automobile accident caused by a blowout on the Old Trails Highway (a year later to become the famous transcontinental highway Route 66) near the Berry railroad station a few miles west of Kingman, Arizona. Bothwell's older son, M. B. Bothwell, believed to be of the first marriage, was driving, but survived with minor injuries. Bothwell's youngest (and allegedly favorite) son, John Randolph Bothwell, age twenty-nine, also born in Connecticut, was also travelling with his aunt and died of injuries sustained in the same accident. Both boys had recently returned from London where John Randolph "held the highest obtainable awards for bravery from the English Army" according to the paper. Both bodies were shipped to the Los Angeles area and interred in the Bothwell family plot in the Magnolia section of the Inglewood Cemetery. How Bothwell's second wife ever secured employment with Bothwell and his first wife as a domestic in the Sweetwater country is also still a mystery. See *Mohave (Arizona) Miner*, January 1, 1926, also the funeral records for 1926 of the Van Marter Mortuary, Kingman, Arizona, numbers 1276, 1277, and the Inglewood, California, Cemetery genealogical records.

46. See footnotes 41 and 44. Also a photograph of Bothwell's second wife with their son, Jack, is in the collection of Bernard Sun at the Hub and Spoke Ranch just above Devil's Gate but was not made available for publication. Also Ruth Beebe interviews.

47. Ruth Beebe interview.

48. It is significant that Bothwell's second wife is not buried in the Bothwell Magnolia cemetery plot with their children and no trace of her can be found. Also there are two mysteriously unoccupied cemetery lots in the Bothwell family plot. They were probably purchased for the twins. No reason can be discovered for their vacancy.

49. It was generally agreed that both his first and second wives were very cultured and artistic. See H. M. Chittenden, *A Western Epic*.

50. John Clay, *My Life on the Range*. Ruth Beebe, *Reminiscing Along the Sweetwater*.

51. Coutant's *History of Wyoming*.

52. Marc Countryman article in *Wyoming State Journal* (Lander, Wyoming: January 10, 1935).

53. Beebe's *Reminiscing Along the Sweetwater.* To bring cattle from Oregon was unusual at this time, although it later became common. Most of the early Wyoming cattle came from Texas.
54. The poison weed referred to is almost certainly larkspur which, in large quantities, results in enormous amounts of abdominal gases and the animal dies from bloating. It was sometimes alleviated by jamming a sharp object into the abdominal wall allowing the gases to escape through the resulting hole. Often, however, this resulted in infection and the animal died anyway. A two hundred head loss out of two thousand is a rather heavy ten percent loss.
55. Granger was another name for a homesteader, especially if he were engaged in farming rather than ranching.
56. Government homesteading requirements for title to the land included raising irrigation water high enough so that the water could be released at this high point and run down the ditch slowly. The ditch was dammed up with canvas dams at whatever part of the land was particularly dry and the water flowed over the sides of the ditch, resulting in an inundation of the grasses or crops in that area with sufficient water to supplement inadequate amounts of rainfall.
57. Obituaries in the Mauch Chunk, Pennsylvania, newspapers, on September 14, 1921.
58. So many of the neighboring ranchers made complaints to the Wyoming Stock Growers Association that they were compelled to blackball Tom Collins. Burroughs, *Guardians of the Grasslands.*
59. Searight's main original stone Goose Egg ranch building just a few miles south of Casper, Wyoming, on Wyoming Highway 220 was torn down in the 1950s, but its clone, on the east side of the highway, built at the same time, has been restored and is now a splendid and charming restaurant with the same delightful ranch atmosphere. It is still called the "Goose Egg Inn." Succulent steaks and prime rib are the "piece de resistance," of course. Not to be missed!
60. *Guardian of the Grasslands.*
61. Ibid. This is, of course, in reference to Conner's and Durbin's urging to steal the Goose Egg Ranch blind.
62. Mokler's *History of Natrona County.*
63. Ruth Beebe interview.
64. Ibid.
65. Ibid

8. BEGINNING OF THE END

1. The original can be found in Fremont County Courthouse, Lander, Wyoming, where historian "Pat" Hall of Cheyenne discovered it.

2. There was no stage service through the Sweetwater country north of Sand Creek or east of Rongis. See *Bessemer Journal*, August 1, 1889; *Carbon County Journal*, August 3, 1889; and *Carbon County Journal*, August 10, 1889.

3. When Fort McKinney was decommissioned in the mid-1880s many of the troops from the Ninth U. S. Infantry were reassigned to Fort Washakie, headquarters of the Wind River Indian Reservation.

4. *Cheyenne Daily Sun*, August 3, 1889.

5. Ellen's kindness and thoughtfulness seems to have been generally well recognized around the Sweetwater country. Ruth Beebe learned these stories from Emma Claytor, the daughter of Dan Fitger who was a Bothwell employee.

6. Ferris Post Office was in the tiny community of Sand Creek on the north side of Ferris Mountain. Ferris has been relocated, and on contemporary maps, it is now found on the south side of Ferris Mountain.

7. Lake Ranch Stage Station was located about halfway between Rawlins and the tiny community of Sand Creek (Ferris Post Office), twenty-five miles south of Bothwell.

8. Not much can be found out about Fales. As a young man in the Sweetwater country, he apparently did odd jobs, including building Ellen Watson's cabin. He later lived in Casper, and as an old-timer he was interviewed by the historical society and has left us some very important information relative to this story. See the David Collection, Casper College Library.

9. It is evident, by the gift of a bonnet to Ellen, that Fales' mother (who probably lived on Fales Creek in the vicinity) had considerable friendship for Ellen. But it is the first time that we have heard that Ellen was purportedly wearing a bonnet when she was hanged. But it is not surprising. When women were in the sun, they often wore bonnets to keep the sun from wrinkling their faces prematurely; more often than not the bonnet was made to match the dress. Bonnets were regularly worn with a Mother Hubbard dress. That kind of dress also was the customary dress for women in the early West even when dressed for a fancy affair. So it might be logical to surmise that on her way to the Indian encampment, Ellen wore a Mother Hubbard, with a matching bonnet, and that she wore a pair of Indian moccasins on her feet on the way back to her house, when she was dragged off to be lynched. She must have looked much as she did in the photograph which shows her bareback on a horse.

10. Bothwell's hayfield was a part of Bothwell's "north ranch" on Horse Creek, which he was in the process of irrigating extensively. The terrible winter of 1886-87 taught stockmen to store hay as supplemental

feed for unexpectedly severe winters. Not more than a few weeks prior to the lynching, Bothwell purchased a right-of-way across Averell's road ranch property for a huge irrigation project to irrigate this pasture land out of the Sweetwater River. Bothwell had to purchase the right of way from Averell because without going across Averell's road ranch land Bothwell could not have irrigated his main meadow adequately. This is the same property that Averell crossed with a large irrigation ditch out of Horse Creek, to irrigate his own road ranch property.

11. Marc Countryman, in an article in Lander's *Wyoming State Journal,* January 10, 1935.

12. Sam Johnson was foreman of the Bar Eleven Ranch which was on Pete Creek, just two-and-one-half miles east of Averell's first homestead on Cherry Creek, at the base of Ferris Mountain.

13. Reverend Frank Moore in his book *Souls and Saddlebags.* (Denver: Souls and Saddlebags, 1962).

9. BUSINESS OF RUSTLING

1. Holt's New Map of Wyoming, 1883, shows virtually all the Sweetwater area ranches. The map has been been reprinted and is available from the Wyoming State Museum.

2. Good horsemen never abuse an animal. Stockmen generally agree that one hundred miles in a day is the outer limit of what a good horse can sensibly handle without harming the animal.

3. In the early West, a cutting horse was any horse that was taught to cut out particular calves and cows from the herd and keep them separated from that herd. It is a very specialized job. With a well-trained cutting horse, it is possible to show the animal that needs to be cut out of the herd to the horse, and the horse will do the job alone. A good rider is sometimes hard pressed to stay aboard these quick and explosive animals unless he is quite experienced and alert. Today some horses are bred specifically to be cutting horses.

4. "Post hay" is a Wyoming stockman's expression for the feed a horse gets while tied up to a hitching post. That is obviously nothing at all!

5. Carbon County Courthouse, Rawlins, Wyoming.

6. Probate Judge's Office, Carbon County Court House, Rawlins.

7. BLM Records, Cheyenne, Wyoming.

8. Ibid.

9. During the spring and summer snow runoff, a little creek ran parallel and a little north of Horse Creek, which apparently had no name. It may not even exist anymore except rarely, with heavy irrigation upstream today.

10. Quitclaim deed from Averell to Bothwell. Wyoming State Museum.

10. MAVERICK LAWS

1. Wyoming Session Laws of 1884.
2. In response to local territorial voter pressure, the Wyoming Territorial Legislature repealed the Maverick Law. Since the cattle industry was so heavily represented in that body, the majority decided to accomplish the same thing under a new and different guise. This gave the stockmen another two years in which to solidify their ultimate control over what had been the open range.
3. *Wyoming Blue Book*, Election of 1886, Constable for Ferris Post Office (community of Sand Creek). Averell received 2 votes—as a Democrat, and even more surprising—as a newcomer.

11. MORE DIFICULTIES

1. This is mentioned in several references to the affair. Whether it is true or not cannot be documented. It is included for completeness.
2. This was the pasture, where she had kept her livestock since late in 1888 or early in 1889, that Thomas Watson, Ellen's father, speaks of in his interview with the *Rock Springs Independent.*
3. It is logical to conclude that the footsore stock that Ellen purchased were in extremely poor shape, otherwise the emigrants would never have parted with the livestock. She purportedly paid only a dollar apiece for them. Typical of the stock accompanying the overland covered wagon traveller was a mixed herd with some older stock and younger steers and heifers.

12. THE FINAL HOURS

1. A Chicago newspaper, the *Inter Ocean,* on Tuesday, July 23, 1889, printed this information which was credited to a telegram from Cheyenne on the previous day. Because of the unusual terminology, "Cattle Queen" and "Range Queen" and other similarities, plus other information, it is logical to conclude that it originated with reporter Ed Towse of the *Cheyenne Daily Leader.* Towse used the word "queen" in his vituperous editorial and sprayed the information out to hundreds of other papers across the country by telegraph for maximum effect.
2. Most other accounts of this event seem to include this information. It was also confirmed in the Ruth Beebe interview; the *Cheyenne Daily Leader,* July 22, 1889; in a 1976 interview with nonagenarian Charles Lee Vivion of Rawlins, Wyoming, whose father was employed by Bothwell at the time; in a letter from Marie Danks, daughter of Dan Fitger, found at Wyoming State Museum; and by Rob and Will Hays in letter from Jean Lambertson of Rawlins, Wyoming.

3. This information is from Jean Lambertson's letter of January 31, 1989, to the author from Rawlins, Wyoming, which states, "Mrs. Irving Hays told me Will and Rob Hays (her sons) were riding for Bothwell at the time. They heard the cattlemen discussing the plans and knew that Tom Sun and one other man opposed the plans with vigor." The same information was given the author by Ruth Beebe, in the Whiskey Gap interview, and by Charles Lee Vivion in a 1976 interview in Rawlins, Wyoming.

4. Ruth Beebe interview.

5. The moccasins were recovered at the site of the lynching by Mr. and Mrs. Frank Jameson and are now in possession of the Wyoming State Historical Museum, Cheyenne, Wyoming. Jameson became the justice of the peace from Ervay, Wyoming, shortly after the lynching.

6. The following events are taken from the sworn testimony of Frank Buchanan, Eugene Crowder, Ralph Cole and Charles Buck, the latter from a ranch on Poison Spring Creek, as well as the published letter of John DeCorey who the *Carbon County Journal* reported on August 20, 1889, had escaped to Steamboat Springs, Colorado, for safety and protection. The subsequent letter from John DeCorey was written to Editor Casebeer of the *Casper Weekly Mail* and was printed in an edition of August 31, 1889. The author physically followed the route taken by the lynching party.

7. Ibid. John DeCorey said that Bothwell often came to Ellen's place to try and buy her out and even offered to loan Ellen the money to prove up earlier on her claim. After a certain period, a homesteader could pay $1.25 an acre and secure early title. Bothwell had the opportunity to see Ellen's little herd of cattle in her pasture by her house on his several trips to try to buy Ellen's homestead.

8. Ruth Beebe interview.

9. Stanford Sanford interview, Casper, 1988, and Haney Stevenson interview, Pathfinder Ranch, 1987. Mr. Stevenson said that the bottles were scattered all about in that general area for many years but that he thought souvenir hunters had taken them all. The author himself found the upper half of one of the bottles north and near the site of the Averell road ranch.

10. Marc Countryman article in *Wyoming State Journal,* January 10, 1935; and in articles in the *Cheyenne Daily Sun,* July 27, 1889, and *Bill Barlow's Budget,* July 31, 1889.

11. Thomas Watson interview in the *Rock Springs Independent.*

12. Bairoil, Wyoming, topographical map of U. S. Bureau of Land Management, Cheyenne, Wyoming, Section 14, Township 29N clearly shows Spring Creek Gulch as an intermittent "Spring."

13. *Cheyenne Daily Leader*, August 27, 1889.
14. Galbraith and his wife were in the forefront of many important functions in the Rawlins Methodist church during the 1880s.
15. Galbraith was elected to the Territorial Legislature twice. The first time was as a Representative to the House, the second time in 1890 to the Territorial Council (Senate). He was also on several municipal committees in Rawlins. It is evident he was a real political animal.
16. John Burroughs documents many cases of John Durbin's and Robert Conner's complicity with rustlers and thieves in his fine history of the Wyoming Stock Growers Association entitled *Guardian of the Grasslands*. Their money brought them political power, not their deeds.
17. Bob Conner never married according to Mauch Chunk, Pennsylvania, obituaries.
18. The almost certain point at which the lynchers and their hostages left the Sweetwater River is a point at which the river comes closest to the Spring Creek Gulch (or Canyon) in the Sentinel Rocks. The river is about 300 yards from the rocks at this point.
19. On-site exploration clearly shows the trees to be varieties of pitch pine and red cedar or juniper.
20. The actual location is determined by the photographs taken on the site by Mr. and Mrs. Frank C. Jameson and published in the *History of Natrona County* by Alfred Mokler. The spot was also clearly described by Thomas Watson (father of Ellen Watson) in his interview with the *Rock Springs Independent* . On-site exploration verifies the location by reference to the easily recognized geological formations in the photo.
21. Letter of August 11, 1958, from Marie Danks of Lander, Wyoming, who heard the story from her father, Dan Fitger, who was a Bothwell cowboy during parts of the roundup, Wyoming State Museum.
22. Mokler's *History of Natrona County, Wyoming, 1883-1922.*
23. Several days after the lynching, Mr. and Mrs. Frank C. Jameson from the Ervay/Oil City area in the Rattlesnake Range country a few miles away, came over and took photos of the hanging tree as well as the rest of the canyon around it. They verified the spot because of evidence on the ground of heavy struggling and scuffing and Ellen's moccasins on the ground under the tree. The moccasins are at the Wyoming State Historical Museum in Cheyenne, Wyoming.

13. THE AFTERMATH

1. Seminoe does not come from the word Seminole as some have thought. It is named after an early French-Canadian fur trapper in the area. His name was Basil Cimineau Lajeunesse, and his middle name has been corrupted and misspelled through the passage of time.

2. Ruth Beebe and many others remembered that the Sand Creek community was a thriving little settlement at one time. Many of the buildings are still standing there and are now used as ranch buildings and bunk houses on the Buzzard Ranch.

3. It is through Ruth Beebe that we have learned these three intriguing stories. There may be others, but the author has not been able to root out any more, except for the matter of Bothwell's wolves which he brought to his ranch for his protection. Residents of the area kept their mouths pretty tightly shut after the lynching in fear of their lives. It was a very nervous time for everyone. Certainly the lynchers themselves did not talk about it openly at all. The relatives of the lynchers probably have learned less about the matter than most because it wasn't discussed in their presence. It is still a somewhat tender and sensitive subject even today.

4. The rancher's name was Irving Hays, who lived just south of Whiskey Gap, and whose cowboy sons, Rob and Will, overheard the fateful neighbors' meeting in Bothwell's main pasture and hay meadow.

5. Ruth Beebe remembered her father, Stewart Joe Sharp, recounting this story to his family. Sharp was the Butler brother's foreman and worked the same general roundup with the other ranchers and cowboys.

14. Coroner's Posse

1. Articles vary as to the exact time, but it was certainly close to midday.

2. Those deputized by Justice of the Peace Emery were Arthur Post, Frank and Tom Denson, Jess Lockwood, Ed Jim "Tex" Healy, and Jud Brazil. See Mokler's *History of Natrona County*. Also *Bill Barlow's Budget,* September 24, 1889. Much of the information about the activities of Tex Healy are from articles in *Bill Barlow's Budget* on September 24, 1889, and the *Cheyenne Daily Sun,* August 25, 1889.

3. It has been said that, as an experienced carpenter, John Fales, who built Ellen's first cabin, was also called upon to help in the construction of the caskets, but that cannot be verified. It makes sense, however, because the young men (Cole, Crowder and DeCorey) may not have been very handy with such a task. It has also been put forth that Ellen and Jim were buried in a single casket, though that seems improbable in view of the strong affection everyone had for the murdered couple. Almost all the stories refer to two caskets in a single grave.

4. *Bill Barlow's Budget,* July 24, 1889.

5. From depositions taken at Coroner's Inquest #1, Wyoming State Museum and from Mokler's *History of Natrona County.*

6. From depositions, Coroner's Inquest #2, Wyoming State Museum.

7. Haney Stevenson, who now manages the original Bothwell ranch, and

Stanford Sanford, who lived on the ranch from boyhood and whose grandfather purchased the ranch from Bothwell, both report that they have known of these markers for as long as they can remember. The writer himself rediscovered the location through finding the old road ranch foundations and then a wheel hub and parts of the iron tires which were still in place exactly where the graves were reported to be in the *History of Natrona County* by Alfred Mokler and in the first and second Coroner's inquests.

8. The Sun Ranch (Hub and Spoke) is about eight miles distant in a southwesterly direction. It was the first stop before travelling to arrest the other lynchers, going next to the Bothwell Ranch.

15. THE LIE

1. *Cheyenne Daily Leader,* July 23, 1889. Wyoming State Museum.
2. This is the first time that Ellen Watson was purposefully confused with much earlier "Cattle Kate Maxwell" of Bessemer, Wyoming. But the image and confused identity stuck hard and fast!
3. Helen Huntington Smith in her fine book, *The War on Powder River,* explodes this contrived myth completely through exploration of the court records of the time. In the incident where Tom Sun protected Ben Carter, Ben was legally hanged in Rawlins for his crimes.
4. Not one shred of substantive evidence existed in advance of Towse's original editorial to show that Jim Averell was anything but a desperately hard-working farmer and storekeeper. Of course, Ed Towse, seemingly intentionally, confused Jim Averell with Kate Maxwell's husband, whoever he was, over on the North Platte River at Bessemer Bend, a little southwest of Casper.
5. The business of a fine educational background is sheer fabrication. Nobody apparently knew where or how much he was educated. It was, however, generally believed that he had received a better-than-average education. He wrote with intelligence and sensitivity, his hand script was beautiful indeed, and it was said he spoke not as a cowboy, but as a well-educated man.
6. This is the first mention of Ellen's being "queen" of anything. Later authors picked up this little innuendo and tagged her "Queen of the Sweetwater." It is absurd fabrication.
7. *Bill Barlow's Budget,* July 24, 1889.
8. At the time of the appraisal of Averell's possessions, a cartridge belt is listed. There is however, not even a tiny thread of evidence to show that Ellen ever employed, or even owned, any firearm at all while in the Sweetwater Valley. Ralph Cole owned a shotgun at the time of his death. It is abundantly documented that both Watson and Averell were

gentle, courteous, big-hearted people. How these two homesteaders could have met all those ranchers with "threats and depredations" is difficult to imagine.

9. It is quite the other way around. Ellen and Jim received skulls and crossbones and were constantly under intimidation by Bothwell who had reason to want them to quit the country.

10. Coroner Bennett from Rawlins was very much on the side of the settlers and homesteaders, and even wrote an accusing letter to Governor Francis E. Warren charging him, the state, and county officials with complicity in the subsequent farce of the prosecution of the lynchers. Governor Warren wrote a letter of reply denying all the accusations. History has subsequently shown, however, that Governor Warren was not above such goings-on. See Larson's *History of Wyoming*. Also the *Carbon County Journal* of November 30, 1889, excoriates the state and county government for not providing the witnesses with protection and monitoring them to assure their appearance as witnesses at the Grand Jury hearing in Rawlins in October. It will also be remembered that Coroner Bennett prepared Averell's first wife Sophia and the baby for burial and had great sympathy for Averell.

11. *Cheyenne Daily Leader,* August 30, 1889. No other notice of their arrival has been found, nor does there seem to be any official or unofficial attempt to use these cattle as incriminating evidence to support the lynchers' outcry of rustling. Such evidence was obviously not found or virtually everyone would have heard about it.

12. Two hundred head in her pasture is pure fabrication.

13. *Carbon County Journal,* August 27, 1889.

14. That is exactly what Jim Averell did. He filed on a homestead that was smack dab in the middle of what Bothwell claimed as his hay meadow which he had illegally fenced in. Also Averell filed right on top of Horse Creek where Bothwell thought he had everybody scared off.

15. The local residents believed Bothwell was an English lord. Bothwell did nothing, of course, to correct this subterfuge.

16. Editor Merris Barrow (*Bill Barlow's Budget*) was very discerning in his observations. He hit the nail right on the head this time, too.

17. The reader will recall that Editor Slack of the *Cheyenne Sun* realized how hoodwinked he had been by Towse's first editorial after the lynching and retracted his original editorial which confused Kate Maxwell with Ellen Watson. He referred to Towse's editorial as "the veriest bosh!"

18. Although it cannot be documented, since we have none of the issues of the *Sweetwater Chief,* it appears that the *Dublin Times* picked up Towse's editorial and pretty much copied it. It was therefore safe

enough for Fetz and Speer to write their editorials relative to the lynching based on *Dublin's* article. None of the cattlemen in the Sweetwater area could possibly be offended, and Fetz and Speer would not have to confront the business end of a Colt .44.

19. The editor of the *Carbon County Journal,* John Friend, was a Democrat and former soldier at Fort Reno at the time of the famous Fetterman Massacre in 1866. Camp Reno was located near Averell's Fort McKinney (Number One) country, although Reno predated McKinney. Editor Friend and Averell therefore had a great deal in common and were apparently close friends. As a result Editor Friend would also have been aware of Ellen's activities in the Sweetwater country. He was obviously aware of the improvements she made to her homestead (buildings, ditches, fences, etc.) with Jim's help. Since the cattlemen were on the Republican side of the issue, and since Democrat John Friend was very well acquainted with Averell, he could be perfectly honest about the whole affair without suffering any political consequences. The town of Rawlins is today still highly Democratic, perhaps partly because of the initial Democratic Party emphasis cultivated by editor John Friend.

20. Wyoming State Museum.

21. Wyoming State Museum.

22. Since Jim already had filed on all the claims he legally could, this could indicate that Jim had filed a homestead claim in someone else's name. He may have planned to see that the property was proven up on earlier with the $300 sent by his brother-in-law, Asa Cole. It is possible that Bothwell discovered this intention, and it might very well have been the "straw that broke the camel's back." Or the $300 could have been used for Ralph Cole to file on his own claim when he reached the age of twenty one—another reason for Bothwell wanting both Averell and Cole out of the way.

23. Sam Johnson was the foreman for the Bar Eleven ranch on Pete Creek quite close to Averell's first homestead claim. If nothing else, he might have had a friendly personal interest in Averell's nephew. In any event he came quite a long way to see Ralph Cole, from down near Sand Creek.

24. Wyoming State Museum.

16. A FATHER'S AGONY

1. We have been unable to discover why or how George Durant was chosen as administrator for both Jim's and Ellen's estates. Was he perhaps a personal friend? He certainly acted like it.

2. It is curious that we find eight head of cattle still around to be sold at

auction. Why didn't Bothwell and Durbin take them, too? Perhaps they were out of the pasture at the time of Bothwell's and Durbin's illegal cattle acquisition after the lynching. Did Ellen own a total of forty-nine head and Bothwell and Durbin overlooked these, or did they actually ship only thirty-three head to Cheyenne? Curious.

3. With Bothwell looking for any excuse to invalidate Ellen's homestead claim, she must have worked at Averell's road ranch during the day, returning to her cabin each evening to validate her residency requirement. The two boys who resided with her must have been taking care of the premises, the livestock, chickens, garden, fencing repairs, and such during the daylight hours.

4. Regarding the number of livestock, Watson must have been repeating what someone had told him, since most of the animals had been removed by the time he arrived.

5. Legally all unbranded cattle were the property of the Territory of Wyoming, to be sold under the auspices of the Wyoming Stock Growers Association to the highest bidder. In this case they were sold to Durbin and Bothwell probably for next to nothing, since that was the customary way to liquidate mavericks or allegedly misappropriated livestock.

6. Ruth Beebe interview.

7. Everyone immediately began to pack firearms around. No one knew exactly whom they could trust. Certainly the six perpetrators couldn't trust anybody. The valley was in a constant state of alert according to Ruth Beebe, in the Whiskey Gap interview.

8. In his letter to the Lebanon, Kansas, newspaper, Thomas Watson said: "During the afternoon I happened to meet several citizens of the city [Rawlins] and was informed that they would like to see me in the evening at the city hall. I promised to meet them in the evening. I went and heard what they had to say. The chairman of the meeting, after calling it to order, said that the hanging of Ella Watson and James Averell was one of the most cold-blooded murders on record, and that something must be done to prevent such crimes. A fund was started to bring these criminals to justice and there was $75 raised and $100 subscribed that evening."

9. The half brother of Jim Averell, R. W. "Will" Cahill, came through the Sweetwater country on the lookout for witnesses he could depend upon to testify before the grand jury to be held in Rawlins.

10. The witnesses may have been Buchanan, Crowder, DeCorey, Fetz, and Speer. The latter two must have decided later to remain perfectly tacit. There were several others who, we discover later, saw the two homesteaders carted off in the buggy, some of whom were: Dan Fitger,

according to his daughter Mrs. Clayton (Marie) Danks, Lander; Stewart Joe Sharp, according to his daughter Ruth Beebe; and Will and Rob Hays, according to Jean Lambertson, intimate friend of the Hays family, Rawlins. All of them were employed in the roundup.

11. Winchester did not necessarily refer to the rifle manufacturer. It was the common term for a long rifle of any manufacturer.

12. Ruth Beebe interview.

13. The officers were U.S. Marshal Hadsell and Deputy Sheriff Lineburger. (This is the correct spelling. The name was often misspelled as Lineberger.)

14. Judge B. F. Emery was from Casper. He was deputized by Phil Watson as the presiding judge and accompanied the arresting party. He was the justice of the peace used in adjudicating this preliminary matter the morning of the arrival. He was a practicing attorney but we do not know how capable or schooled he was. He may have been duped to pass down a poor decision. Deputy County Attorney H. H. Howard and U.S. Marshal Frank Hadsell may have advised him to pass down a judgment of suspected manslaughter, or it is possible that influential politics and money may have carried the day. Since Judge Emery actually saw and helped cut down the bodies, it is difficult to believe that politics or money would have swayed him.

15. They must have been Deputy Sheriff Jim Rankin, Assistant County Attorney H. H. Howard, U.S. Marshal Frank Hadsell and Justice Emery. No others are known.

16. This would indicate that Jim Averell came from a staunch non-drinking, Protestant family if his nephew is any criterion. Jim was never accused by anyone, except Ed Towse, of imbibing, or even smoking.

17. THE LOST CAUSE

1. Judge Samuel T. Corn, a Democrat, was a splendid, impartial judge in this matter. He was later rewarded by appointment to the Supreme Court of the new State of Wyoming. His eloquent charge to the grand jury was as follows:

"It is not ordinarily necessary to charge the Grand Jury with reference to special crimes. The prosecuting attorney is authorized to be present during your sessions (except during the expression of your views, or when a vote is being taken) and will advise you. But it has come to my ears and is the object of much conversation in this community, and has been widely published in the newspapers, that certain persons are charged with the hanging of a certain man and woman by lynch law in this country, and it is evident there is a great feeling and excitement in the community in regards to it.

"In such matters you are preeminently the guardians of the safety of the people and the good order of society. You have sworn to present none through malice or ill, and to leave none unpresented through fear, favor or affection. It becomes you in connection with this matter to be especially regardful of this oath.

"Some of the ancients portrayed justice as a goddess blindfolded. Her eyes were hoodwinked that she might not know even the persons upon whom she was called to pass judgement. In one hand she held the balances to weight the evidence with impartiality, and in the other a sword with which to execute her decrees. This idea of 'justice blind' should be your guide in this matter. Weigh the evidence with absolute impartiality and without regard to persons, and then strike no matter where the blow may fall." *Casper Weekly Mail,* October 25, 1889.

2. Prosecutor David Preston seems to have done very little, if anything, for the prosecution and was perhaps poorly prepared for the trial. Apparently Craig did the lion's share, with Howard reluctantly dragging his feet along. Howard seems to have been easily swayed by party politics.

3. David A. Preston went on to become one of the most revered defense attorneys in Wyoming. He finally settled in Rock Springs, Wyoming, where he tragically died prematurely from the effects of exposure following an automobile accident.

4. *Carbon County Journal,* November 23, 1889. Craig strongly suspected Chatterton of having accepted a bribe, but fell short of accusing his partner publicly insofar as he had no definite proof.

5. Jungquist was very angry about the challenge to fitness as a grand juror when he was unseated. He wrote a scathing letter to the editor in the October 26, 1889, *Carbon County Journal* excoriating his challenger and attempting to exonerate his own bruised integrity. It was evident, however, that he sympathized with Averell and Watson.

6. Buchanan, the real key to the prosecution of the lynchers, was placed under a bond of only $5000. Supporters of the homesteaders quickly raised the $500 bail to get Buchanan released. This is, of course, the worst possible thing they could have done in view of his subsequent disappearance. It allowed him to run for his life, to be bought off, or to be dry gulched, and thus destroyed the prosecution's hopes of ever securing the conviction against the lynchers. It is clear that such a small bond did infinitely more harm than good.

7. Buchanan should have already learned not to get in any buggy, especially with the opposition! How he was allowed to be in the custody of the inimical friends of the lynchers, in the middle of that hotbed of cattle baron influence in the first place, is mind boggling!

8. The letter to Governor Francis E. Warren of July 28, 1889, has disappeared, but the letter denying all charges leveled against him has survived. It was published in the *Carbon County Journal* August 2, 1889. Editor and Democrat John Friend was delighted to publish it in his paper.

9. Crowder was something of a footloose cowboy. The wagon and team he left abandoned by the roadside were not even his. They were borrowed from Irving Hays, a local rancher, whose two sons, Rob and Will, were Bothwell cowboys. It is strange that the wagon was not retrieved for two whole years, except, perhaps, for the fact that it was left on Bothwell's ranch. From the interview with Ruth Beebe.

10. Court records in the Carbon County Court House show he showed up to testify. It would have been a futile gesture without Buchanan's testimony, anyway, because his testimony would have been judged hearsay in any event. It could have served no other purpose than to excite and infuriate the local citizens further, something the stock interests would have avoided like the Black Plague.

11. If John DeCorey returned to Steamboat Springs, it cannot be verified. He seems simply to have disappeared.

18. POSTLUDE

1. Durbin's obituary was in the Denver papers and his story is also in nearly every complete history of Wyoming.

2. Conner, with an "e", is the correct spelling according to his last will and testament, and obituaries in the Mauch Chunk, Pennsylvania obituaries.

3. From Reverend Moore's book *Souls and Saddlebags*.

4. This can easily be seen in the curious collection of period photographs and Bothwell's accompanying original poetry in the family archives of Bernard Sun at the Hub and Spoke Ranch at Devil's Gate, Wyoming. The photos and poetry in a black folder were a gift from Bothwell to Tom Sun on some now-forgotten occasion. Most of the fifteen or so photographs are devoted to the wolves. Perhaps only a half dozen photographs are those of his wife and young son Jack.

   Two of the photos showed Bothwell's son, Jack, playing inside the pen with the four wolves, apparently at feeding time. The wolves were originally taken as pups from a den at the base of Ferris Mountain according to Stanford Sanford, Casper, Wyoming; Bernard Sun, Devil's Gate, Wyoming; and Ruth Beebe. Unfortunately, this collection of photographs was not made available for publication.

5. Judge William R. Kelly practiced law in Greeley, Colorado. Since the Sanfords were also originally from that part of Colorado they were

well acquainted with Kelly and trusted his ability and integrity. Therefore, rather than choose a local Wyoming attorney, they engaged Kelly as their defense attorney. The letter is on file with the Wyoming State Museum.

6. It seems as though Bothwell was continuously in controversy or litigation in one matter or another. It is said that he considered himself quite capable of defending himself legally, and would apparently have done so, had the law allowed him to.

7. William Riner was one of the attorneys who defended the cattlemen after the lynching. He was also Mayor of Cheyenne at the time. Notice also at this time that his son District Judge Riner had been appointed a Federal Judge. Judge Riner could have sworn himself off the bench in this matter because of his father's very close legal relationship with Bothwell, but he apparently chose not to.

BIBLIOGRAPHY

Adams, Ramon F. *Burrs Under the Saddle*. Norman, OK: University of Oklahoma, 1964.

—. *More Burrs Under the Saddle*. Norman, OK: University of Oklahoma, 1979.

Anderson, Maybelle Harmon. *Appelton Milo Harmon Goes West*. Glendale, CA: Arthur H. Clarke, 1946.

Baber, D. F. *The Longest Rope*. Caldwell, ID: Caxton Printers, 1940.

Bancroft, Hubert Howe. *History of Nevada, Colorado & Wyoming Vol. XX*. San Francisco: Bancroft History Pub., 1890.

Bard, Floyd C. *Horse Wrangler*. Norman, OK: University of Oklahoma, 1962.

Bartlett, I. S. *History of Wyoming*. Chicago: S. J. Clarke, 1918.

Beard, Frances Birkhead. *Wyoming from Territorial Days to the Present*. Chicago: American History Society, 1933.

Beebe, Lucius, and Charles Clegg. *The American West*. New York: E. P. Dutton, 1955.

Beebe, Ruth C. *Reminiscing on the Sweetwater*. Boulder: Johnson Publishing, 1973.

Boots, John Mercer. *Powder River Invasion, War on the Rustlers in 1892*. Evanston, WY: Author, 1923.

Bourke, John G. *On the Border with Crook*. New York: Charles Scribner's Sons, 1892.

Bronson, Edgar Beecher. *Reminiscences of a Ranchman.* Chicago: A. C. McClurg, 1910.

Brooks, Brant B. *Memoirs of Bryant B. Brooks.* Glendale, CA: Arthur H. Clarke, 1939.

Brown, Dee, and Martin F. Schmitt. *Trail Driving Days.* New York: Charles Scribner's Sons, 1952.

Brown, Mark H., and W. R. Felton. *Before Barbed Wire.* New York: Branhall House, 1955.

—. *The Frontier Years.* New York: Branhall House, 1955.

Buffalo Centennial Committee. *Buffalo's First Century.* Buffalo, WY: Buffalo Centennial Committee, 1984.

Burns, Robert, Andrew Gillespie, and Willing Richardson. *Wyoming's Pioneer Ranches.* Laramie: Top of the World Press, 1955.

Burroughs, John Rolfe. *Guardians of the Grasslands.* Cheyenne: Wyoming Stock Growers Association, 1971.

Burt, Struthers. *Powder River Let 'Er Buck.* New York: Rinehart, 1938.

Butler, Anne M. *Daughters of Joy, Sisters of Misery.* Urbana, IL: University of Illinois, 1985.

Canton, Frank M. *Frontier Trails.* Boston: Houghton Mifflin, 1930.

Casper Story Zonta Committee. *Casper Chronicles, Casper's Diamond Jubilee.* Casper: Casper Zonta Club, 1964.

Chaffin, Lorah B. *Sons of the West.* Caldwell, ID: Caxton Printers, 1941.

Chatterton, Fenimore. *Yesterday's Wyoming, The Intimate Memoirs of Fenimore C. Chatterton, Territorial Citizen, Governor, Builder.* Aurora, CO: Powder River Pub., 1957.

Cheyenne Historical Committee. *The Magic City of the Plains.* Cheyenne: Cheyenne Centennial Committee, 1967.

Clay, John. *My Life on the Range.* Norman, OK: University of Oklahoma, 1962.

Clover, Samuel Travers. *On Special Assignment.* New York: Argonaut Press, 1965.

Coutant, C. G. *History of Wyoming.* Laramie: Author, 1899.

Craig, Nute. *Thrills 1861-1887.* Oakland, CA: Author, n.d.

David, Robert B. *Malcolm Campbell Sheriff.* Casper: Wyomingana, Inc. 1932.

Deal, Scott. *A Place To Raise Hell.* Boulder: Johnson Pub., 1977.

DeBarthe, Joe. *Life and Adventures of Frank Grouard.* Norman, OK: University of Oklahoma, 1958.

Drago, Harry Sinclair. *The Great Range Wars.* New York: Dodd, Mead & Co., 1970.

Driggs, Howard R. *The Old West Speaks.* Englewood Cliffs, NJ: Prentice Hall, 1956.

Eaton, Herbert. *The Overland Trail.* New York: G. P. Putnam's Sons, 1974.

Eggenhofer, Nick. *Wagon, Mules & Men.* New York: Hastings House, 1961.

Ellison, Robert Spurrier. *Independence Rock.* Fairfield, WA: Ye Galleon Press, 1975.

Erwin, Marie. *Wyoming Historical Blue Book.* Cheyenne: State of Wyoming, 1943.

Federal Writers' Project of Wyoming WPA Program. *The Oregon Trail, U. S. 30, The Missouri River.* New York: Hastings House, 1939.

Field, Sharon Lass. *Fort Fetterman's Cemetery.* Cheyenne: Author, 1970.

Forbis, William H. *The Cowboys.* New York: Time-Life Books, 1973.

Frazer, Robert W. *Forts of the West.* Norman, OK: University of Oklahoma, 1965.

Frink, Maurice. *Cow Country Cavalcade.* Boulder: Johnson Pub., 1954.

Frison, Paul. *Grass Was Gold*. Worland, WY: Worland Press, 1970.

Gage, Jack R. *Wyoming Afoot and Horseback*. Cheyenne: Flintlock Pub., 1966.

Gallagher, John S., and Alan H. Patera. *Wyoming Post Offices 1850-1980*. Burtonsville, MD: The Depot, 1980.

Gould, Lewis L. *Wyoming A Political History 1868-1896*. New Haven: Yale University Press, 1968.

Greenburg, Dan W. *Sixty Years, A Brief Review of Wyoming Cattle*. Cheyenne: Wyoming Stock Growers Association, 1932.

Gress, Katherine. *90 Years Cow Country*. Cheyenne: Wyoming Stock Growers Association, 1963.

Gressley, Gene M. *Bankers and Cattlemen*. New York: Alfred A, Knopf, 1966.

Guernsey, Charles A. *Wyoming Cowboy Days*. New York: J. P. Putnam's Sons, 1936.

Hafen, Leroy, and Ann W. Hafen. *Powder River Campaigns and Sawyer's Expedition*. Glendale, CA: Arthur H. Clarke, 1961.

Haines, Aubrey L. *Historic Sites Along the Oregon Trail*. Gerald, MO: The Patrice Press, 1983.

Hall, Charles "Pat." *Documents of Wyoming History*. Cheyenne: Wyoming Bicentennial Committee, 1976.

Hanway, Edwin. *Memoirs of Edwin Hanway*. Casper: Author, 1942.

Hart, Herbert M. *Old Forts of the Northwest*. Seattle: Superior Publishing, 1963.

Hebard, Grace Raymond, and E. A. Brininstool. *Bozeman Trail*. Cleveland: Arthur H. Clarke, 1922.

Homsher, Lola M. *Guide to Wyoming's Newspapers 1868-1967*. Cheyenne: Wyoming State Library, 1971.

Horan, James D., and Paul Sans. *Desperate Women*. New York: Bonanza Books, 1952.

—. *Pictorial History of the Wild West*. New York: Crown Publishers, 1954.

—. *The Great American West.* New York: Crown Publishers, 1954.

Hunt, Lester C. *Wyoming, A Guide to Its History, Highways and People.* New York: Oxford University Press, 1956.

Jackson, W. Turrentine. *Wagons Roads West.* New Haven: Yale University Press, 1965.

Jones, Ralph F. *Longhorns of North of the Arkansas.* San Antonio: Naylor, 1969.

Karolevitz, Robert F. *Newspapering in the Old West.* New York: Bonanza Books, 1965.

Knight, Oliver. *Life and Manners of the Frontier Army,* Norman, OK: University of Oklahoma, 1978.

Kukura, Edna G., and Susan N. True. *Casper, A Pictorial History.* Norfolk: Donning Co., 1986.

Larson, T. A. *History of Wyoming.* Lincoln, NE: University of Nebraska Press, 1966.

LeRoy, Bruce. *H. M. Chittenden, A Western Epic.* Tacoma: Washington State Historical Society, 1961.

Linford, Dee. *Wyoming Stream Names.* Cheyenne: Wyoming Game and Fish Department, 1975.

Linford, Velma. *Wyoming Frontier State.* Denver: Fred A. Rosenstock, 1958.

Marcy, Randolph B. *The Prairie Traveler.* New York: Harper & Bros., 1968.

Mead, Jean. *Casper Country.* Boulder: Pruett Publishing Co., 1987.

Mercer, Asa S. *Banditti of the Plains, Cattlemen's Invasion.* Norman, OK: University of Oklahoma, 1954.

Miller, Donald C. *Ghost Towns of Wyoming.* Boulder: Pruett Publishing, 1977.

Mokler, Alfred James. *History of Natrona County 1888-1920.* Chicago: R. R. Donnelley & Sons, 1923.

Monaghan, Hay. *The Book of the American West.* New York: Bonanza Books, 1963.

Moody, Dan W. *The Life of a Rover 1865-1926.* Chicago: Author, 1926.

Moody, Ralph. *Stagecoach West.* New York: Thomas Crowell, 1967.

Moore, Austin L. *Souls and Saddlebags, Diaries and Correspondence.* Denver: Big Mountain Press, 1962.

Moore, Vandi. *Brands on the Boswell.* Glendo, WY: High Plains Press, 1986.

Morgan, Dale L. *Rand McNalley's Pioneer Atlas of the American West.* Chicago: Rand McNalley, 1969.

Morris, Robert C. *Collections of the Wyoming Historical Society.* Cheyenne: Wyoming Historical Society, 1897.

Mothershead, Harmon Ross. *The Swan Land and Cattle Company.* Norman, OK: University of Oklahoma, 1979.

Munkres, Robert L. *Saleratus & Sagebrush.* Cheyenne: State of Wyoming, 1980.

Murray, Robert A. *Johnson County, 175 Years of History at the Foot of the Big Horn Mountains,* Buffalo, WY: Buffalo Chamber of Commerce, 1981.

—. *Military Posts of Wyoming.* Ft. Collins: Old Army Press, 1974.

—. *Military Posts of Wyoming.* Lincoln, NE: University of Nebraska, 1967.

Ostrander, Alson. *After Sixty Years.* Seattle: Gateway Printing, 1925.

—. *Army Boy of the Sixties.* Yonkers on Hudson, NY: World Book Co., 1924.

Patterson, Richard. *Wyoming Outlaw Days.* Boulder: Johnson Pub. 1982.

—. *The Laramie Story.* Laramie: Author, 1968.

Pence, Mary Lou. *The Laramie Story.* Laramie: Author, 1968.

— *Boswell, The Story of a Frontier Lawman.* Cheyenne: Author, Pioneer Printing, 1978.

Pence, Mary Lou, and Lola M. Homsher. *The Ghost Towns of Wyoming.* New York: Hastings House, 1977.

Radcliffe, Mabel. *From Cattle to Cadillacs*. Buffalo, WY: Author, 1978.

Rawlins Centennial Committee. *100 Years in the Wild West, Pictorial History*. Rawlins, WY: Rawlins Centennial Committee, 1968.

Reinhart, Harman Francis. *The Golden Frontier*. Austin: University of Texas, 1962.

Reiter, Joan Swallow. *The Women*. Alexandria, VA: Time-Life Books, 1978.

Ricketts, W. P. *Fifty Years in the Saddle*. Sheridan: Star Publishing Co., 1942.

Rollins, Philip Ashton. *Jinglebob, A True Story of a Real Cowboy*. New York: Grosset & Dunlap, 1927.

Rollinson, John K. *Pony Trails in Wyoming*. Caldwell: Caxton Printers, 1945.

—. *Wyoming Cattle Trails*. Caldwell: Caxton Printers, 1948.

Sandoz, Mari. *The Cattlemen*. New York: Hastings House, 1958.

Sanford, Ethel. *As I Remember*. Casper: Author, n.d.

Schmitt, Martin F. *The Settlers West*. New York: Bonanza Books, 1955.

—. *General George Crook*. Norman, OK: University of Oklahoma, 1960.

Scott, Mary Hurlburt. *The Oregon Trail Through Wyoming*. Aurora, CO: Powder River Publishing, 1952.

Settle, Raymond W., and Mary Lund. *Overland Days to Montana*. Glendale, CA: Arthur H. Clarke, 1971.

Sheridan, Philip H. *Outline Descriptions of the Posts in the Military*. Chicago: U. S. Government, 1876.

Smith, Helen Huntington. *The War on Powder River*. New York: McGraw-Hill, 1966.

Spring, Agnes Wright. *70 Years Cow Country*. Cheyenne: Wyoming Stock Growers Association, 1942.

—. *William Chapin Deming*. Glendale, CA: Arthur H. Clarke, 1944.

—. *Cheyenne and Black Hills Stage Route*. Glendale, CA: Arthur H. Clarke, 1949.

—. *The Cheyenne Club, Mecca of the Aristocrats of the Old-Time Cattle Range*. Kansas City: Don Ordnuff, 1961.

Stewart, Edgar I. *Penny an Acre Empire*. Norman, OK: University of Oklahoma, 1968.

Tanner, Ogden. *The Ranchers*. New York: Time-Life Books, 1977.

Thompson, Martha. *Pioneer Parade*. Cheyenne: Logan Printing, 1967.

Trachsel, Herman H., and Ralph M. Wade. *The Government and Administration of Wyoming*. New York: Thomas Y. Crowell, 1960.

Trachtman, Paul. *The Gunfighters*. New York: Time-Life Books 1974.

Trenholm, Virginia Cole, and Maurine Carley. *Wyoming Pageant*. Casper: Prairie Publishing, 1946.

Unrau, William. *Tending the Talking Wire*. Salt Lake City: University of Utah, 1979.

Urbanek, Mae. *Ghost Trails of Wyoming*. Boulder: Johnson Publishing, 1978.

—. *Wyoming Place Names*. Boulder: Johnson Publishing, 1967.

—. *Wyoming Wonderland*. Boulder: Johnson Publishing, 1964.

Vaughn, J. W. *The Battle of Platte Bridge*. Norman, OK: University of Oklahoma, 1964.

—. *With Crook at the Rosebud*. Harrisburg, PA: The Stackpole Co., 1956.

Vorpahl, Ben Merchant. *My Dear Mr. Wister*. Palo Alto: American West Publishing Co., 1972.

Wells, Charles. *Apache Slave*. Worland, WY: Worland Press, 1969.

Wheeler, Homer. *Buffalo Days*. New York: A. L. Burt, 1925.

Wister, Fanny Kemble. *Owen Wister Out West*. Chicago: University of Chicago, 1968.

Wyoming Recreation Commission. *Wyoming, A Guide to Historic Sites*. Basin, WY: Big Horn Publishing Co. 1971.

Wyoming State Archives and Historical Society. *Annals of Wyoming*. Cheyenne: Wyoming State Archives and Historical Society, 1923 to present.

Yost, Nellie Snyder. *Boss Cowman, The Recollection of Ed Lemmon 1857-1946*. Lincoln, NE: University of Nebraska, 1969.

Acknowledgments

I am indebted to:

Ruth Beebe, sunny, lovely and delightful lady and nonagenarian who was born and raised in the Sweetwater country before the turn of the century. Ruth was an author, former school teacher and acknowledged historian of the Sweetwater country, whose father was a witness to many of the events of that awful July day. Ruth graciously spent many delightful hours and days with my wife and me at her Whiskey Gap ranch helping to answer questions in my eager search for information. She was well-acquainted with many of the principals in this story and helped us to see them through her lovely soft eyes and glowing personality. She has most sadly parted from us now, and we miss her very much indeed.

Virginia MacIntosh, wife of one of the largest ranchers in the Sweetwater country and daughter of Ruth Beebe. She and her husband Bill, still reside in Averell's original homestead cabin, expanded now into a lovely and much larger ranch home. She has been most kind in showing me around the house and premises and has informed me about people and events of days gone by.

Jean Brainerd, wonderful director of the Wyoming State Archives and Historical Department in Cheyenne, for her knowledgeable, tireless, exhaustive and constant research in my behalf, affording tons of information, photos, maps, facts, newspaper articles and every imaginable kind of information surrounding this tragic incident. Her ever-charming and delightful energy and her dedication seem utterly inexhaustible. I should also like to thank

Ann Nelson, Paula Chavoya, Cindy Brown, and Ida Wozny and the whole wonderful department without whose uncomplaining help I would have been at sea without a sail to catch the wind.

Dan Brumbaugh, grand-nephew of Ellen Watson who before I discovered him, had already done a splendid job of researching his family's roots and has thereby been able to dig up much material surrounding the event of his great-aunt's life and violent death. He was most gracious in supplying photos, names and family documents and in sharing his knowledge of events surrounding this sad history. He even finally succeeded in accomplishing the monumental task of rounding up a very widely scattered and far-flung family of Watsons for the first time in a century for a glorious first family reunion which was held in Wyoming's still wild Sweetwater country at the scene of, and on the one hundredth anniversary to the day and hour of Ellen Watson's destruction.

Lawrence Jaeger, grand-nephew of Averell's first wife Sophia, who has supplied me with historical facts surrounding his aunt's delightful but short life with her husband, James Averell. Larry has been thorough and unstinting in supplying photos, letters, and family history gathered over many long, interesting years of research.

Art Randall, until recently of Casper, Wyoming, whose exciting on-site investigations with his amazing metal detector were shared with the author. We happily found many otherwise forever hidden artifacts at the site of Jim Averell's homestead and road ranch situated at the side of the Fort McKinney-Rawlins/Fort Fred Steele Military Road. Art's invaluable professional geological expertise in matching timeless boulders with ancient photographs led to his discovery of the unmistakable, still-standing hanging tree, now dead, upon which young Ellen Watson and her new husband met their indescribably terrible eventuality.

Bernard Sun, grandson of Tom Sun who was intimately connected with the tragic events of 1889. Although I often felt uneasy about my probing questions about his grandfather, Bernard was always philosophical about the matter and put me at ease with his pleasant, easy and gracious hospitality. I learned much about his family and much about his grandfather's close friend, Albert

Bothwell. I also learned much about human nature from this splendid man.

Patty Meyers, cheerful Librarian at the Johnson County Library in Buffalo, Wyoming, for the help she supplied on several occasions in my quest for information on James Averell while he was stationed at Fort McKinney and on his regular visits to Buffalo where he eventually became a landowner.

Jamie Ring, winsome historian, former librarian and custodian of the David Collection at Casper College, for her help in finding photos of Albert Bothwell from that collection and for her discovery of manuscripts expanding my knowledge of the participants involved in this immolation. I'm also grateful to her successor, the capable Kevin Anderson.

William Harschmann, Carbon County Clerk in Rawlins, historian and early researcher of this sad story who was always most pleasant and helpful in securing any and all information I asked for from his files. He has also been able, often off the top of his head, to answer many of my questions from his many ardent years of research into the "Cattle Kate" incident.

Ann Masson, most pleasant clerk of Carbon County District Court in Rawlins, who furnished me with copies of petitions of George W. Durant, Jim Averell's court appointed administrator, to dispose of his property after his murder.

Haney Stevenson, manager of the Pathfinder Ranch, who was most gracious on many occasions in letting us scrounge and scratch about on the ranch all by ourselves where all the events of that dreadful day in 1889 took place. We were warned that we had free access to everything, "just as long as we kept the wire gates closed," something very important indeed to every rancher, but unfortunately not always respected by the careless. Haney was also most helpful in pointing out important sites and locations and filling me in with details about which I would otherwise have been uninformed.

Maribelle Lambertson, genial curator of the Carbon County Historical Museum who was most attentive to every and all questions I had and who cheerfully supplied the photos I asked for. I'm also indebted to her mother-in-law Jean Lambertson who, as a past long-time resident of the area, supplied me with much interesting information I had not earlier known.

Charles "Pat" Hall, Cheyenne resident, Western historian, author, rare Western Americana book dealer and devoted friend, who has been an afficionado of the historic legend of "Our Kate" for at least as long as I—and that's a long time! We first met when he was Executive Director of Wyoming's 1976 Bicentennial Commission when Wyoming's and my first grand opera was performed for four glorious performances at the then-new University of Wyoming Fine Arts Center in Laramie before it toured to five other Wyoming communities. Pat's lovely and talented daughter played a "cool" bassoon in the opera orchestra. He has also trekked all over the location of the story of this book and has been helpful in so very many countless other ways. It is to him that I am indebted for his discovery of the actual wedding license of Ellen Liddy (Andrews) Watson and James Averell in the Fremont county courthouse in Lander—a most exciting serendipity!

Lola Marie Van Wey, of Cawker, Kansas, niece of Ellen Watson, whom I had the great pleasure of meeting at the centennial family reunion in Wyoming and who graciously supplied me with an otherwise utterly unknown photograph of her aunt in Red Cloud, Nebraska. Also for a photo of Ellen Watson's cruet set brought home from Wyoming to the family in Kansas by her father after her aunt's cruel demise.

Emmett Chisum of the Historical Research Division at the Coe Library of the University of Wyoming in Laramie. Gentleman and tireless archivist, he graciously catered to my every whim as I groped back a hundred years into the history of this terrifying and sad event.

Dorothy Kangas, of Rawlins, who graciously allowed the publication of part of the manuscript of her grandfather, John Burke. Her conversations with me about him were all the more fascinating since it turns out that he was personally involved in the story when he became one of those who contributed to the $500 bail each for Frank Buchanan and "Tex" Healy, witnesses for the prosecution after the lynching.

Ruth Nelson, of Hastings, Nebraska, who kindly supplied me with a photo of what is probably a wedding picture of Ellen Watson, her great aunt, in a beautiful formal dress. Ruth still lovingly preserves her aunt's pedal sewing machine which is still in working condition and which she brought all the way out to Wyoming on the occasion of the hundredth anniversary reunion of her great aunt's death in July of 1889 here in central Wyoming.

Sharon Lass Field, delightful and charming author and versatile historian, who was raised on a ranch near Douglas, Wyoming, only a few miles from the site of Fort Fetterman and the subsequent, notorious, wild-and-wooly town of the same name. She is always happy to share her broad historical knowledge about that exciting part of Wyoming and its history where part of our story unfolds. She has also graciously helped and directed me in my ongoing search for information on the Hufsmith family which settled in the then fledgling western town of Cheyenne in 1874. Sharon is also the author and compiler of the marvelously comprehensive new history of Wyoming's capitol city, Cheyenne, where my lovely and wonderful middle daughter Emily Ward Hufsmith resides with her family.

Dave Love, of Laramie, geologist of world renown, athletic septagarian and longtime friend who, in the delightful company of his vivacious wife, interesting in her own right, trudged and roved, bumping and bouncing all over the scene of the lynching with my wife and I as though we were all teenagers. As a native of the Sweetwater country, Dave afforded me much insight into the region and its people and he has supplied me with otherwise obscure and unobtainable information about some of the principals about which I would never have known and will never tell.

Vernon Vivion, lifetime Carbon County resident, longtime friend and fellow legislative colleague, whose gracious hospitality my wife and I have enjoyed in Rawlins. I'm especially indebted to his nonagenarian father, who in 1976, still in high button shoes, shared with us early recollections from his days as a young working man in the Sweetwater Valley and many unique and interesting facts surrounding the lynching.

Ken Raymond, Carbon County historian and tireless advocate of its rich heritage, who has been helpful in my search for the location of the site of the then-well-known Lake Ranch Stage Station whose buildings and memory seem now almost to have evaporated away into the pure, cool mountain air of Wyoming.

George Guy, now sadly departed from out midst, former Attorney General of Wyoming, relative and friend, who in 1976 shared with me his vivid recollections about a very strange man, whom he had known well, Albert Bothwell, who is so important to this story.

James Scarlett, now of Jackson, Wyoming, with whom I had my first wonderful encounter with the upper Sweetwater Valley on his former "O-H-O" ranch. I gorged myself on his mother's wonderful cooking and shared an evening with his hospitable family while visiting there in pursuit of the furtive deer on Tin Cup Mountain. Although I was unsuccessful in my quest for game, I still had as delightful a time as I could have had anywhere else in the whole world. Jim and I have since shared many more stories, and I still often call upon him for additional information about that spectacular country and its wonderful breed of rugged Western individuals, some of whom still live and love in much the same uncomplicated way they did on the Sweetwater River a hundred years ago. Many of them are still without telephones, for which they must be eternally grateful!

Helen Mathew, pleasant and animated historian and museum curator in Red Cloud, Nebraska who furnished me with photo copies of the information I needed on the Ellen Pickell (Watson) divorce records, material about Ellen's attorney G. R. Chaney, and pertinent newspaper articles.

Brenda L. Tatum, Genealogist of the Jefferson County, Arkansas, Library, who supplied me with photostats of the obituaries of Robert Galbraith and wife.

Frank L. Green, Librarian of the Washington State Historical Society, who supplied me with information on James Averell's half brother Robert Cahill.

Ruth M. Allen, who obtained the Death Records and Last Will and Testament of Robert Conner in Jim Thorpe, Pennsylvania (formerly Mauch Chunk), from the files of the Mauch Chunk Trust Company.

T. A. Hutchinson, of Evanston, Wyoming, who dug out genealogical information on Dan Fitger who was present at the coroner's inquest after the terrible lynching.

Gaylene McDowell, resident of Lebanon, Kansas, who managed to dig up some interesting material and documents about Ellen Watson's early farm-girl life and about her first unfortunate marriage to a problem homesteader in that area.

Margaret Wilson, of Glendo, Wyoming, daughter of George Mitchell, the first mayor of Casper and a member of the grand jury in the Cattle Kate affair, for her delightful story of her father's encounter with Judge Corn.

Tracy Eller, Patsy Parkin, Judy McElwain, and Edwina Johnson for patient editorial assistance.

In this author's attempt to express his grateful appreciation to everyone who has been helpful in assembling this historical research, I will undoubtedly have left out some who have helped materially to make this book a reality. Although it is indeed a bitter pill for them to swallow, I extend by sincerest apologies to those I may have thoughtlessly overlooked, but they should know that they can wreak their wildest revenge upon me by telling me about it. May God deliver me!

Index

*This book was printed on
55-pound Huron Natural
acid-free, recycled paper.*

Author George Hufsmith and granddaughter Brooke Eleanor Schupman, 1987.

George Hufsmith's roots go deep into Wyoming's past. His great-grandparents came from Prussia to settle in Cheyenne two years before Custer's Last Stand. His keen interest in Wyoming history began upon hearing his grandfather, Will, spin fascinating stories about his early days around the forgotten ghost town of Parkerton on the lonely prairies of central Wyoming.

Hufsmith has a master's degree in musical composition and has studied with Heitor Villa-Lobos in Rio de Janeiro and at Yale University with Paul Hindemith and Normand Lockwood. On a commission from the Wyoming Bicentennial Commission, he composed a tragic opera based upon the lynching of Ellen Watson and Jim Averell, which had nine touring performances to rave reviews. He lived for several years in Brazil, has travelled extensively and is fluent in six European languages. He resides in Jackson Hole, Wyoming, with his delightful wife, Eleanor.